The Extraordinary World Of YES

The Extraordinary World Of YES

Alan Farley

iUniverse, Inc.
New York Lincoln Shanghai

The Extraordinary World Of YES

iUniverse, Inc.

For information address:
iUniverse, Inc.
2021 Pine Lake Road, Suite 100
Lincoln, NE 68512
www.iuniverse.com

ISBN: 0-595-33133-5

Printed in the United States of America

For my Parents

Contents

Acknowledgements

In many ways my research for *The Extraordinary World Of Yes* has been ongoing since I first began listening to Yes in the early seventies. Over that time I've collected an enormous amount of information about Yes and it is tremendously satisfying to finally be able to utilize it in a form that can be shared with many others. The longevity of Yes means it is possible in 2004 to bring a great sense of perspective to the monumental musical achievements of the band. It remains of prime significance that Yes dared to transgress the traditional boundaries of rock and break out of the syndrome that arbitrarily confined music to the standard three minute pop single.

I'm indebted to several people in the professional media and elsewhere who have kindly given permission for the use of material in *The Extraordinary World Of Yes*. I've otherwise adopted the principle of fair use. I'd particularly like to thank: Nicola Parker of IPC regarding *Melody Maker, NME, Music Scene, Vox* and *The Guitar Magazine*; Robert Garofalo of Classic Pictures; Christie Eliezer of the Australasian bureau of *Billboard;* Angela Catterns of ABC Radio 702 Sydney; Alex Lepelaar of Radio 2SM Sydney; Alison Ninio of John Fairfax Holdings regarding *Juke* and *The Sun*; Alan Paul of *Guitar World*; Sophie Balbo of the Montreux Jazz Festival Foundation; Valerie Pippin of the Music Player Network and *Keyboard*; Vicki Hartung of the Music Player Network; Emily Fasten of *Guitar Player*; Greg Olwell of *Bass Player*; Dave Henderson of EMAP regarding *Sounds*; Dave Adams of BeyondSound regarding the *Steve Howe Interactive CD-ROM*; Andy Sutcliffe of Future Publishing regarding *Classic Rock* magazine; and David Frith regarding *Soundblast.*

I'd also like to thank my Yes friends, especially Rene Lester, Mike Nanasy and all at YesFANZ. Last but certainly not least, a special thanks to Gail Hosford for encouragement and assistance with editing.

Alan Farley
August 2004

Introduction—The Firebird

"Yes" is the most positive word and it is the name of the legendary rock band whose amazing music has the magical power to transport the listener to a higher plane and into a different extraordinary world. The multitudes of Yes fans around the globe are abundant testimony to how very successfully this unique band has followed its own special musical path—a path sometimes so exceptional that it hasn't always been fully understood. *The Extraordinary World Of Yes* celebrates the stunning achievements of Yes as one of the greatest bands in the history of rock and places some important sign posts along the road towards a better understanding of the mastery behind its complex music.

The central theme in *The Extraordinary World Of Yes* is to address the implicit question: What makes Yes so outstanding and what is it that is truly significant about the band and its music? The relevant issues are brought into focus in a four part, unfolding sequence—the exceptionally talented people associated with Yes in Chapter 1, the fascinating history of Yes in Chapter 2, the remarkable music of Yes in Chapter 3 and the brilliant concerts of Yes in Chapter 4, backed up by relevant quotes from the members of Yes themselves.

One of the aims along the way is to highlight the positive and often profound messages to be found in the substantial musical output of Yes over a career that has lasted more than thirty-five years and is still flourishing. Above all, the goal of *The Extraordinary World Of Yes* is to enhance your enjoyment of Yes music whether you are an already dedicated fan or an uninitiated new listener. A different and fun way of exploring Yes is provided by the Yes 35th Anniversary Quiz in the Appendix. Additionally, you'll find exclusive photographs of Yes by visiting my web site at www.farley.ozefamily.com.

Yes has had its ups and downs over the years along with an inevitable "rock'n'roll moment" from time to time. However, Yes deserves the greatest of respect because since it's beginnings in 1968, the band has kept adventurously pursuing its very ambitious musical goals and continues to do so to this day. The body of work by Yes, both collectively and individually, has no parallels in rock music and its depth and breadth is truly remarkable with everything from number one hit singles through to complex epics contained on number one platinum albums. The most famous Yes lineup—the classic Yes lineup of Jon Anderson,

Steve Howe, Chris Squire, Rick Wakeman and Alan White—came together again in 2002 and it speaks volumes for these hard working, exceptional musicians that at such an advanced stage in their careers they spoke of a five year plan aimed at exploring still more new musical horizons in the twenty-first century.

The voice of Yes, Jon Anderson, was able to wonderfully put his own career and that of the band in perspective during an interview with Angela Catterns on ABC 702 Australian radio in late 2002 to promote Yes's *Full Circle* tour: "We just love what we do…We just believe in our music. We have a very positive attitude towards our work…I was twenty-seven years old at the start of the band, twenty-eight actually. Pop stars were in their early twenties, so you always felt…well, I just wanted to make good music. And then you find the right kind of musicians and by the time I was thirty years old, Yes became successful. I never thought of Yes as a commercial pop singles type of band. I was more interested in adventure in music you know…When you come and see the show (in 2003), I hope you come and see the show, you'll be happily surprised at how powerful the band is. We still put on a good show…You go through periods of time for maybe two or three years, have a break and do other things and then get together for three or four more years, have a break and then get together again. So it's been ongoing over the whole thirty-three years we've been going together as a band. And it's just the way we are. The band has changed over, musicians in and out of the band but the feeling of the band and the positiveness of our work is still there…I live in central California, Chris (Squire) lives about 100 miles away, Alan (White) lives in Seattle, Steve (Howe) lives in Devon in England and Rick (Wakeman) lives in Milano! (laughs) It's like any family, we always have group therapy every month. We sit down and make sure we still believe in each other. But on stage we just come alive. No matter what we have to go through in our lives together, just getting on stage is an incredible feeling playing the way we do—it's just a very magical experience in this life. I feel very blessed, (my voice) is more powerful than ever. I just feel happy to still be making music and still believe in the work we started thirty years ago. To have a band called 'Yes' is kind of very daunting. People say you've got to live up to a positive message in your life and I've done nothing but work on my spiritual awareness, my positiveness about life in general and I've been very fortunate to grow into what I believe Yes music is all about which is a positive statement about life and what surrounds us."[1]

References

1 Radio interview by Angela Catterns, ABC Radio 702 Sydney, December 2002
(N.B. Jon Anderson was actually 23 years old when Yes started in 1968 but his comments in this interview about his age could be interpreted as referring to when the core of the classic Yes lineup first came together in the early seventies.)

1

I've Seen All Good People

THE MEETING

When a diminutive, determined man met a tall, thoughtful man in a bar in London, England in May 1968, no one could have predicted that it would put in motion a creative musical powerhouse called Yes that would excite and entertain audiences for so many years into the future and leave an indelible stamp on the annals of rock music.

The men concerned were respectively Jon Anderson and Chris Squire and they met in a small, dark, upstairs, "Members Only" bar called La Chasse in Wardour Street, Soho in the West End of London. The bar was owned by Jack Barrie and was a popular meeting place for people from the very buoyant rock music scene of the late sixties. Jon was broke at the time and temporarily shared Jack's flat, working at La Chasse helping to clean up in order to pay his rent. Jon didn't mind working there because he felt that the right break would come along sooner or later. And so at about six o'clock one evening it came to pass that Jack introduced Jon to Chris who was said to be a very good bass player with a band known by the very unusual name of Mabel Greer's Toyshop.

Jon said: "I met Chris in this bar that he frequented and I frequented. I was working there. And we got together and after a couple of days we were writing songs which was really nice to get together so quickly…Then we started working and doing gigs and things. Things started developing musically very well. At that stage it was more or less Mabel Greer's Toyshop. Most of the people who were in the band had been in this band called Mabel Greer's Toyshop. We got Bill Bruford in, then Tony Kaye and eventually Peter Banks."[1]

Chris said of that fateful first meeting: "We were still pretty young at the time, and I think we talked about songs and vocal harmonies and discovered we both liked Simon and Garfunkel. He seemed like a nice enough geezer and we suggested putting something together. That was the first concept of the band: great vocals and exciting, adventurous playing."[2] Jon hailed from the north of England while Chris was a public school boy from the south and they felt that combining those contrasting backgrounds would work in their favor. The partnership immediately bore fruit when the first writing session yielded the song "Sweetness" that appeared on the first Yes album.

The music scene in England at this time was a creative hothouse with a host of famous bands either in the ascendant or soon to come to prominence. The Beatles were still flying high and the array of other now legendary names included The Who, Pink Floyd, Cream, the Rolling Stones, Jethro Tull, Deep Purple, The Nice and the Moody Blues. The bands about to form that would prove to have a major impact on the music world included Yes, Led Zeppelin, King Crimson, Genesis and Emerson Lake & Palmer. The Beatles in the late sixties were breaking new musical ground with every album and their influence on the entire music scene was enormous. Socially and culturally barriers were being broken down in the era of flower power and the environment was consequently becoming very fertile for the adventurous and ground-breaking progressive rock music for which Yes and others would soon become famous.

Venues such as the famous Marquee Club, coincidentally also in Wardour Street downstairs from La Chasse, played host to a procession of famous bands as well as some not so famous names. Influential figures in the music scene were frequently in the audience and the acts included Jimi Hendrix, Jethro Tull, John Mayall's Blues Breakers, Fleetwood Mac, Manfred Mann, Traffic, Ten Years After, Spooky Tooth, The Nice and that band called Mabel Greer's Toyshop. The Marquee would also eventually play host to a new group called Yes.

Mabel Greer's Toyshop soon evolved to become Yes and in regard to the change of name, Jon Anderson said: "We all decided to bring in some names for the band. I was thinking of 'Life', Chris thought of 'World' and Peter Banks said we should call the band 'Yes'. We said 'The Yes'? He said, no no—'Yes'. We said, 'No, it's not going to work'. After about an hour or so we started rehearsing and I turned around to Chris and said, 'Yes, it sounds pretty cool!' So that's how we got the name."

The Yes Sound

The essence of the Yes sound is the combination of the musical contributions of the individual members of the band. Where many top bands might feature one or two exceptional performers, the best Yes lineups have contained nothing but outstanding musicians. It is also true to say that the musicians in Yes have always been of high calibre and it is a characteristic of the band that the combination has typically been so compelling that the overall sound has substantially exceeded the sum of the high quality individual components.

To focus on the elements of the classic Yes lineup, it is primarily Jon Anderson's high, clear, beautiful voice; Steve Howe's mercurial, eclectic finesse on electric and acoustic guitar; Chris Squire's characteristically prominent, agile bass guitar and strong backing vocals; Rick Wakeman's spectacular multi-keyboard wizardry and Alan White's soulful power on his drum kit. Collectively the sound is unique, innovative, melodic, powerful, symphonic, dramatic, precise, dynamic, exciting, beautiful, intricate, colorful, warm and always capable of surprise. Sometimes it becomes quiet and delicate, or wild and atonal, or classical and graceful, or modern and futuristic. It is most certainly not ordinary or average. Perhaps with almost any other band it would be a pretentious over-statement but with Yes it is a true indication of what a tuned-in, open-minded listener will hear. It was music that received the label of "progressive" and it came out of a great deal of forward and creative thinking.

Chris Squire in early 2004 saw the longevity of Yes as stemming from the eclecticism of the different band members with everyone having "a slightly different angle coming in and so what you get is not by any means a format sound".[3] Rick Wakeman expressed a similar view: "I think the fact that the five of us are so completely different is why it works...For whatever reason, you put this five together (the classic Yes lineup) and it adds up to ten. There's a certain telepathy that goes on, there's a certain understanding that goes on musically and I think there's a certain genuine respect that goes on both on stage and off stage."[4]

No two Yes albums have ever sounded quite the same, nor have any two Yes songs for that matter. The musicians in Yes have changed from time to time and the creative winds have blown from different directions. Yes has always looked for a different path forward, sometimes becoming more complex or making it simpler, sometimes employing a harder feel or being less intense and more accessible, always experimenting and never sounding exactly the same as the album before. However, there has been a consistent two-stranded golden thread running through the work of Yes and that is the pursuit of musical adventure and the communication of a positive message. The official Yes internet site is called YesWorld and it is almost as though the band has continued to explore that extraordinary world by travelling through the cities, valleys, mountains, forests, deserts, rivers and oceans in it's ongoing exploration of all that comprises Yes music. And now so many years into the journey, the band and the music seem to be well up to meeting that crucial challenge of the test of time.

THE YES MUSICIANS

Here in profile are the exceptionally talented musicians who comprise the current Yes lineup in 2004—the classic Yes lineup. Yes has a history of relatively frequent changes in personnel but it is notable that these five musicians have always been irresistibly drawn to return to the band as demonstrated by the reunion of this lineup in 2002.

Jon Anderson

BORN: John Roy Anderson, 25 October 1944, Accrington, Lancashire, England.
TALENT: Lead vocalist, composer, lyricist, harpist, keyboardist, percussionist, guitarist.
YES STATUS: Member 1968–80, 1983–88, 1991–present (2004).

KEY CONTRIBUTIONS TO YES: Jon's outstanding voice and his creativity and drive have been enormously influential factors in the career of Yes. While on the one hand he is a gentle smiling man with a deep spirituality, Jon also has great personal strength and determination. He appears to put his soul into Yes and all that the band represents.

BEFORE YES: Jon grew up as part of a working class family of four children in Accrington in northern England and the ill health of his father led him to work on a farm from an early age. He began singing with brother Tony while delivering milk for a local farmer and artists such as The Everly Brothers, Dionne Warwick, Nina Simone and Frank Sinatra were early influences. Jon eventually joined Tony as a vocalist in The Warriors and they had reasonable success in the mid 1960s performing songs by people such as The Hollies, the Beatles, Lou Rawls, Aretha Franklin, Lena Simon and the Beach Boys. After five years with the Warriors, Jon tried his hand in the London music scene in 1968 with two singles recorded under the unlikely pseudonym of Hans Christian but neither made an impact on the charts. After a brief unproductive association with a band called the Gun, Jon was soon to be introduced to Chris Squire at La Chasse and the Yes story began.

BEYOND YES: Jon has a very wide experience in different types of music and has worked extensively outside of Yes in both a solo context and in various collaborations. His definitive solo album arguably remains *Olias Of Sunhillow* (1976) and he enjoyed considerable commercial success with the series of albums he recorded with Vangelis, particularly *The Friends Of Mr Cairo* (1981). Jon has worked with a number of other famous musical names such as Mike Oldfield, King Crimson, Kitaro and Tangerine Dream. Jon currently lives near San Luis Obispo in California with wife Jane. He has three children from a previous marriage and his solo tour of South America in 1993 interestingly included his daughter Deborah as a backing vocalist.

Chris Squire

BORN: Christopher Russell Edward Squire, 4 March 1948, Kingsbury, North London, England
TALENTS: Bass guitarist, vocalist, composer.
YES STATUS: Member 1968–present (2004).

KEY CONTRIBUTIONS TO YES: Chris is one of the prime creative and steadying forces behind Yes and he brings a highly skilled and distinctive approach to bass guitar that takes it from the traditional supporting role to that of a vital lead instrument. Chris is the only original member of Yes to never leave the band and he was once dubbed "the keeper of the flame". He is extroverted on stage but also seems to have a much deeper side to his personality.

BEFORE YES: Chris grew up in the Wembley/Kingsbury area of North London. Through his friend Andrew Jackman who would later work with Yes on the *Tormato* album, he became involved in music via the choir at St Andrews Church in Kingsbury under the guidance of Barry Rose who was reputed to be one of the best choirmasters in England. The fact that Chris was tall with quite large hands encouraged him to gravitate towards the bass guitar as an instrument and an important early influence was John Entwistle of The Who. Chris's first band was The Selfs that around 1965 evolved into The Syn, a group that started out playing Tamla Motown music before becoming more psychedelic with original compositions. The Syn lineup eventually included guitarist Peter Banks who Chris would later join up with again in Mabel Greer's Toyshop in the evolution towards forming Yes.

BEYOND YES: Chris has released one solo album *Fish Out Of Water* (1975) and has recorded two albums in collaboration with Billy Sherwood (in 2000 and 2003). He has also made occasional guest appearances such as recently with Gov't Mule in *The Deep End* project, with Eddie Harris on the album *E.H. In The UK* in the early 1970s and as part of *An All Star Lineup Performing The Songs Of Pink Floyd* DVD (2004) project with Alan White and Billy Sherwood. Chris currently lives in Los Angeles with wife Melissa and young daughter. He has three other children from a previous marriage.

Steve Howe

BORN: Stephen James Howe, 8 April 1947, Holloway, North London, England
TALENT: Guitarist, vocalist, composer.
YES STATUS: Member 1970–80, 1991–92, 1995–present (2004).

KEY CONTRIBUTIONS TO YES: Together with Jon Anderson and Chris Squire, Steve is one of the main creative forces in Yes. His supreme mastery of a wide range of guitars in many musical styles has become an integral feature of Yes music. He appears to be a quiet but intense man who has a warm sense of humor when not immersed in the great depths of his music.

BEFORE YES: Steve grew up as the youngest in a family of four children in London and he received his first guitar as a Christmas present at the age of twelve. Completely self taught as a musician, Steve's early musical influences included rock'n'roll artists such as Bill Haley and the Comets, The Shadows and Chuck Berry as well as musicians such as Chet Atkins, Tal Farlow and Les Paul. He made his first record with The Syndicats in 1964, a band that played a mixture of songs ranging from those by the Beatles and Chuck Berry through to more unusual pieces such as Django Rheinhardt's "The Continental". Steve moved on to work with the In Crowd followed by the psychedelic Tomorrow and then Bodast in 1968. He rejected an offer to join The Nice and after playing with PP Arnold on the Delaney & Bonnie European tour, took up the opportunity to play with Yes in 1970.

BEYOND YES: Steve has recorded many solo albums in various musical styles and continues to do so today. During a period away from Yes in the 1980s, he enjoyed a very high level of success with Asia and went on to collaborate with Steve Hackett in GTR. He has also worked with several other musicians including Lou Reed, Paul Sutin, Martin Taylor, Oliver Wakeman (Rick's son), Billy

Currie and Queen (on "Innuendo" in 1991). In 1993 he teamed with Bill Bruford to record the orchestral *Symphonic Music Of Yes* album, with a guest vocal appearance from Jon Anderson and most recently formed his own band Remedy that includes his sons Dylan on drums and Virgil playing keyboards. Steve lives in Devon, England with wife Jan and they have four children.

Rick Wakeman

BORN: Richard Christopher Wakeman, 18 May 1949, Perivale, Middlesex, England
TALENT: Keyboardist, composer.
YES STATUS: Member 1971–74, 1976–80, 1991–92, 1995–97, 2002–present (2004).

KEY CONTRIBUTIONS TO YES: Rick's exciting multi-keyboard wizardry has consistently been a highlight of Yes's music. His tenure in the band is notable in that he has left and rejoined the band more times than any other member. Rick is an extrovert with a famous sense of humor that seems to help bind the band together. The other side of his character is that he is a committed Christian who has done a great deal of work for charity.

BEFORE YES: Rick was inspired to try his hand at music after watching his father play the piano. At the age of seven he started receiving piano lessons from a Mrs Symes in Harrow and over the next thirteen years it helped Rick to win countless musical competitions and pass the Associated Board of Royal Schools of Music exams with distinction. His early bands included the Atlantic Blues and the Concord Quartet, the latter playing a mixture of dance and pop music in the period around 1966. Rick began to attend the Royal College of Music with the intention of being a concert pianist but didn't finish his studies after becoming one of the most in demand session musicians in London. He played on a host of recordings by famous names including David Bowie, Cat Stevens, T-Rex, Black Sabbath and Elton John. After a stint with folk rock band the Strawbs, Rick received the call to join Yes in 1971.

BEYOND YES: Rick is a prolific solo artist and has recorded a long list of albums in various musical styles including his famous first solo album *The Six Wives Of Henry VIII* (1973). He is perhaps best known for his epic work in combining orchestras with rock bands as exemplified by *Journey To The Center Of The Earth* (1974). He released the sequel *Return To The Center Of The Earth* in 1999 with narration by Patrick Stewart of Star Trek fame and continues to pursue his solo career when not working with Yes. Rick has been married and divorced three times and has children. Rick's own band, the English Rock Ensemble, has in recent years included his son Adam on keyboards as documented by the *Live in Buenos Aires* DVD (2001).

Alan White

BORN: Alan White, 14 June 1949, Pelton County, Durham, England.
TALENT: Drummer, percussionist, vocalist, pianist, composer.
YES STATUS: Member 1972–present (2004).

KEY CONTRIBUTIONS TO YES: Alan displays an ability to play both the complex and rock facets of Yes music with an apparently inexhaustible supply of energy and enthusiasm teamed with considerable skill. His quiet good humor seems to lend stability to Yes and he has made significant contributions to the writing of the band's music.

BEFORE YES: Alan was an only child and grew up in northern England where he started taking piano lessons from the age of six. His uncle noticed how he had a percussive approach to the piano and it led to Alan receiving his first drum kit. At only thirteen years of age he was playing semi-professionally in a band called the Downbeats at night doing cover versions of songs by the Beatles, Searchers and Gerry and the Pacemakers while still going to school during the day. As he became older, Alan played in a succession of bands including The Gamblers, Alan Price Big Band, Happy Magazine (later called Griffin) and Ginger Baker's Airforce. A major break came when John Lennon invited Alan to join the Plastic Ono Band for the famous *Live Peace In Toronto* gig in 1969. It ultimately led to Alan playing with John on the legendary *Imagine* album and to performing with George Harrison on the landmark *All Things Must Pass* album. A period touring with Joe Cocker came to an end with a call from Yes in 1972.

BEYOND YES: Alan has so far recorded one solo album *Ramshackled* (1976). He formed Crash and Bang with Reek Havoc in a partnership aimed at providing music to the entertainment industry including video games and television shows. Alan has also collaborated with Seattle band MerKaBa and has performed with artists such as Spencer Davis, The Ventures and Charlie Daniels. Additionally, he conducts drum clinics at various locations around the world and has worked on the joint projects of Chris Squire and Billy Sherwood. Alan currently lives in Seattle, Washington with wife Gigi and they have two children.

THE FORMER YES MEMBERS

Yes has had many fine musicians over the years and the people who have graced the band's ranks in earlier eras are briefly profiled here.

Peter Banks

BORN: 15 June 1947, Barnet, North London, England.
YES STATUS: Member 1968–70.
TALENT: Guitarist, vocalist.
WITH YES AND BEYOND: Peter made an important contribution in helping to initially establish the early Yes sound with a distinctive guitar style that was later built upon and expanded by Steve Howe. He is presently pursuing a solo career and session work as well as participating in a planned reunion of The Syn (sans Chris Squire).

Tony Kaye

BORN: 11 January 1946, Leicester, England
YES STATUS: Member 1968–71, 1983–88, 1991–95.
TALENT: Keyboardist.
WITH YES AND BEYOND: Tony helped to establish the early Yes sound with his swirling Hammond organ and made a return to the band in the 1980s when he primarily played keyboards in live performances. After departing Yes, Tony went on to work as a touring and session musician.

Bill Bruford

BORN: 17 May 1950, Sevenoaks, Kent, England.
YES STATUS: Member 1968–72, 1991–92.
TALENT: Drummer, percussionist, composer.
WITH YES AND BEYOND: Bill was a very talented and major contributor to the creation of the Yes sound with an innovative, sophisticated and highly distinctive approach to the drums. He has gone on to have a successful solo career with his own jazz band Earthworks and has played with such famous rock groups as King Crimson, Genesis and UK.

Patrick Moraz

BORN: 24 June 1948, Morges, Switzerland.
YES STATUS: Member 1974–76.
TALENT: Keyboardist, composer.
WITH YES AND BEYOND: Patrick was a very skilled and flamboyant multi-keyboardist with Yes who capably took over from Rick Wakeman in the mid 1970s. He spent a period with the Moody Blues after departing Yes and now continues to pursue a solo career and session work.

Trevor Horn

BORN: 15 July 1949, Pelton County, Durham, England.
YES STATUS: Member 1980.
TALENT: Lead vocalist, producer, composer.
WITH YES AND BEYOND: Trevor had the virtually impossible task of filling the shoes of Jon Anderson for the *Drama* album with Yes and the ensuing tour. His effort was commendable under the difficult circumstances. He went on to produce the *90125* album for Yes and became a very successful producer of other high profile artists.

Geoff Downes

BORN: 25 July 1952, Stockport, Manchester, England.
YES STATUS: Member 1980.
TALENT: Keyboardist, composer.
WITH YES AND BEYOND: Geoff was given the onerous task of taking over from Rick Wakeman for the Yes *Drama* album and the following tour. His performances with Yes were very capable and he went on to have a long and successful career with the band Asia where he still plays a leading role.

Trevor Rabin

BORN: 13 January 1955, Johannesburg, South Africa.
YES STATUS: Member 1983–95
TALENT: Guitarist, vocalist, keyboardist, composer, producer, engineer.
WITH YES AND BEYOND: Trevor played a major and dominant role in Yes during his time with the band and was pivotal in taking Yes towards a more commercial and more orthodox rock sound in the 1980s. He has gone on to have a very successful solo career, particularly in creating music for films.

Billy Sherwood

BORN: 14 March 1965, Las Vegas, Nevada, USA.
YES STATUS: Member 1997–2000
TALENT: Guitarist, vocalist, keyboardist, composer, producer.
WITH YES AND BEYOND: Billy was a multi-talented member of Yes who made a significant contribution to the Yes sound of the late nineties. Prior to actually joining the band, he toured with Yes as an additional backing musician during the *Talk* tour in 1994 and was involved in the production of later albums. Billy now pursues a solo career and an ongoing collaboration with Chris Squire.

Igor Khoroshev

BORN: 14 July 1965, Moscow, Russia.
YES STATUS: Temporary member 1997–2000.
TALENT: Keyboardist, vocalist, composer.
WITH YES AND BEYOND: Igor demonstrated that he was a highly talented keyboardist with Yes and performed the band's most demanding music with great style. He has gone on to pursue a solo career with an emphasis to date on film soundtrack work.

Tom Brislin

BORN: 6 October, USA (year of birth unpublished).
YES STATUS: Temporary member 2001–02.
TALENT: Keyboardist, vocalist.
WITH YES AND BEYOND: Tom did an impressive job in playing keyboards for Yes during the *Yessymphonic* tour when the band performed every show with an orchestra. He continues to be a member of the band Spiraling and has also toured with Camel.

THE YES ARTIST—ROGER DEAN

Go into any good record store and the first thing that will strike you after finding the "Yes" section will be the vivid, imaginative, artwork adorning the albums. The man responsible for most of that art is Roger Dean and his brilliant work uncannily mirrors the unique music that Yes creates. The experience of listening to Yes music is enhanced by the combination of the visual art with the sound.

BORN: Roger Dean, 31 August 1944, Ashford, Kent, England.
TALENT: Artist and designer.
WEB SITE: www.rogerdean.com
WITH YES AND BEYOND: Roger is a warm and very intelligent man who has created the artwork for the most popular Yes album covers. He studied design at Canterbury School of Art from 1961 to 1965 before going on to the Royal College of Art in London to graduate in 1968 with MDesRCA. Roger has worked with Yes on a regular basis since 1971 and his creative efforts for the band have extended to memorabilia, T shirts and stage set designs, assisted by his brother Martyn. Roger has also created artwork for many other musicians such as Osibisa, Uriah Heep, John Lodge (of the Moody Blues), Greenslade and Asia. Additionally, he has at various times been involved in publishing, furniture design, architecture and artwork for computer software. Roger's excellent books *Views* and *Magnetic Storm* provide substantial details of his work for Yes and he has a new book *Dragon's Garden* due to be published in 2004. There is also a Roger Dean DVD titled *Views: The Official Authorised Biography* that is presented by Rick Wakeman and gives some worthwhile insights.

THE YES FANS

The other vitally important people that can be thought of as being associated with Yes are the fans of the band. Yes fans must be some of the most enthusiastic, demanding and discerning fans in the world and while there is much diversity of opinion amongst them as to the particular strengths of different Yes albums and songs, they are united by an undying passion for Yes music. Yes and their fans can effectively be viewed as forming an interdependent relationship that revolves around the music and there are legions of long term, loyal, knowledgeable fans as well as keen newer followers. The longevity and classic appeal of Yes has seen fans who are parents often bringing their children to concerts.

The results of surveys at the YesFans web site in 2004 are of assistance in learning something about the people who enjoy Yes music. According to the figures, sixty-three percent of the Yes fan base is between thirty-four and fifty-four years of age while there is a significant youthful fan segment of seventeen percent between the ages of thirteen and twenty-three. The most common occupations for Yes fans are in the fields of Arts/Design/Entertainment/Sports, Management, Education/Training, Healthcare, Architecture/Engineering and Business/Financial. Sixty percent of the fan base became interested in Yes during the seventies while a quite healthy portion of nine percent have come on board in the last five years. Fifty-six percent of the fans have attended somewhere between six and twenty-five Yes concerts while thirty percent have been present at up to five concerts. Only a few exceptionally keen fans have attended more than seventy Yes shows. These figures can only be regarded as somewhat indicative but the results have reasonable significance given that between 175 and 420 people responded to the particular survey questions.

There has been a growing trend for Yes fans to gather together before or after Yes concerts to celebrate their mutual interest in Yes music. Sometimes these are highly organized events but more often they are quite informal gatherings in places like bars and restaurants. Tailgate parties in the car parks of some Yes concert venues in America are also popular. It is not unusual to find people from many regions and indeed from many parts of the world at these various Yes fan gatherings. The consistent feedback is that the atmosphere is always warm and friendly and it enhances the overall experience of attending a Yes show.

In some instances fan gatherings have been organized months in advance and the members of Yes have even put in an appearance. Major fan events in recent years include Yestival in America in 1994 and 1998, Yescapade in America in 2001 and 2002, the YesFocus gatherings in Holland in 2001 and 2003, and the YesFANZ parties in Australia in 2003. It underlines the tremendous interest in Yes across the world and the exceptional dedication and enthusiasm of the Yes fans.

The Yes tour of Australia in September 2003 was a very special event for fans in that country because it marked the return visit of the band after a thirty-year hiatus. The activities organized by the YesFANZ group brought fans together from all over Australia as well as from New Zealand. Given the usual demands of a hectic touring schedule, it is fair to say that Yes went beyond the normal call of duty to satisfy its Australian supporters and the band generously made itself available for public appearances in a manner that undoubtedly exceeded all reasonable expectations. In the course of a single weekend it included Yes not only performing two concerts but also attending the YesFANZ functions in Sydney and Melbourne, an album signing session at Borders Books in Sydney and the opening of the Roger Dean art exhibition in nearby Glebe. Further details about the development and activities of the YesFANZ group are included in the Appendix.

References

1 Radio interview by David Watts, 2SM Sydney, March 1973
2 Interview by Dave Ling, *Classic Rock*, December 2001
3 Radio interview by Joe Benson, *Off The Record*, January 2004
4 *Yesspeak* DVD, Classic Pictures, 2003

2

Wonderous Stories

The Yes Story

The Yes story is a fascinating one that has seen the band evolve through many changes of lineup from Yes "mark 1" in 1968 to Yes "mark 15" in 2002, with the addition of one further lineup that was Yes in all but name that came together in 1988 under the label of Anderson Bruford Wakeman Howe (ABWH). It is important to have an understanding of the history of Yes before moving onto a detailed review of the music because the evolution of the band has had a fundamental effect on the music being created at any given point in time. Let's now go on the journey to follow the development of Yes from the beginning to the present day.

Yes mark 1 (June 1968 to January 1970)

Lineup: Jon Anderson—lead vocals/Chris Squire—bass, vocals/Peter Banks—guitar, vocals/Tony Kaye—organ, piano/Bill Bruford—drums, percussion.

Jon Anderson and Chris Squire set about putting the first Yes lineup together and asked Peter Banks to join after he had previously worked with them for a time when the band was still known as Mabel Greer's Toyshop. It was Peter in fact who first thought of the name "Yes". Chris had met Tony Kaye at La Chasse and was sufficiently impressed to invite him to also join the band. Bill Bruford had placed a work wanted advertisement in *Melody Maker* and he too received the call from Jon and Chris. Yes were partly sold on Bill because of his Ludwig drum kit but it amusingly turned out to be a budget Olympic kit painted black to disguise its origins. Similarly, Tony Kaye had indicated to Peter that he owned a Hammond organ but it was in reality a mere Vox Continental.

At La Chasse, Jon had met a man by the name of John Roberts who was a factory owner from the north of England and his generosity resulted in the sum of 300 pounds to get the band started. A basement below The Lucky Horseshoe Café in Shaftesbury Avenue, Soho was subsequently rented as a rehearsal room and the group spent hours perfecting their sound. The first gig officially as Yes was at the East Mersea Youth Camp, Essex on 4 August, 1968 and it was followed the next night by the first of many shows at the Marquee Club. Jon at around this time received the nickname of "Napoleon" because of his aggressive commitment to the Yes cause. After playing a number of minor gigs organized by small time promoters at twenty pounds a time, a vital break came when Yes filled in at short notice for Sly And The Family Stone who had cancelled a show at a London club known as Blaise's. At the suggestion of Tony Stratton-Smith who managed The Nice, the owner of the club Roy Flynn visited Yes at their flat and convinced them to do the show that same night on 16 September, 1968. It gave Yes a needed lift and Roy Flynn was impressed enough to become the manager of the band.

Roy had an immediate effect and within twenty-four hours had bought Yes a van and other new equipment including a Hammond organ and a drum kit. He also brought in Mike Tait as the driver of the van and Mike would subsequently make a major contribution as Yes's lighting engineer. Additionally, Roy found living accommodation for the band at a flat in Munster Road, Fulham including space for wives and girlfriends. Bill Bruford commented that the Yes communal flat was like a fire station because no one could leave in case a gig was organized at short notice. Chris Squire started earning his nickname "Fish" after he spent so much time soaking in the bath and kept other band members waiting to use the shared facilities.

Bill quit the band for a short time in favor of studying economics at Leeds University but he was coaxed back in time to play with Yes in their first major appearance at the prestigious Royal Albert Hall as a support act at Cream's farewell concert on 26 November, 1968. Roy helped the band obtain their first record deal with Atlantic Records and this lineup recorded two albums *Yes* (released U.K. July1969, U.S. October 1969) and *Time And A Word* (released U.K. July 1970, U.S. November 1970). Neither album made any real impact on the charts although the band's potential was becoming increasingly apparent. Yes continued to work hard at building a following with live performances that included a sought after residency at the Marquee club.

Yes had used an orchestra on the *Time And A Word* album and it was an innovative but somewhat controversial concept that had displeased Peter Banks and it ultimately led to him leaving the band. The morale of Yes was rapidly dropping and financial pressures were mounting with the lack of a break through album.

Yes mark 2 (March 1970 to August 1971)

Lineup: Jon Anderson—lead vocals/Chris Squire—bass guitars, vocals/Steve Howe—guitars, vocals/Tony Kaye—piano, organ, moog/Bill Bruford—drums, percussion.

Steve Howe had made a lasting impression on Jon and Chris as a very talented guitarist when they'd seen him play with Tomorrow and Bodast. After some discussion, Steve came on board with Yes and rehearsed with the band in Roy Flynn's basement in Putney. The band then decided to retreat to the countryside of Devon late in the English spring of 1970 to write and rehearse new material. They stayed at a cottage called Church Hill before moving on to Langley Farm.

It was during this time that Roy Flynn parted company with Yes when it became obvious that he couldn't provide the guidance needed to take the band to the next level. In came new manager Brian Lane via the unlikely source of Chris Squire's hairdresser who provided the introduction. It appears that Roy was a nice guy but the situation demanded someone like Brian who was more of a pro-active go-getter.

Things started to come together and this lineup went on to record *The Yes Album* (released U.K. January 1971, U.S. March 1971) but only after Atlantic Records had been persuaded not to drop the band in the wake of the low sales of the first two albums. It turned out to be an excellent decision by Atlantic when *The Yes Album* went to number one in the U.K. charts and the single "Your Move" did well in the top forty. An appearance on BBC TV's *Top Of The Pops* kept the momentum going and the band toured extensively throughout Britain and Europe.

In January 1971 Yes did a short tour of Europe and the U.K. as a support for the popular Iron Butterfly and were so impressed by the sophisticated sound system owned by that group that they bought it after the tour had ended. It was a crucial acquisition to enable Yes to properly reproduce their complex sound on stage at a time when concert sound systems were still very much in the early stages of development.

The next critical break through was the first Yes tour of America that started on 24 June 1971. It saw Yes play as the support act to the extremely popular Jethro Tull and in doing so was able to reach a very large audience. *The Yes*

Album was promoted at every opportunity and the hard work started to pay off with it becoming regarded as Yes's first great album, notably the first album to contain all original material.

Nevertheless, a problem developed with Tony Kaye and it led to another change of personnel. Tony had been reluctant to experiment with keyboard instruments such as the mellotron and moog synthesizer and the band consequently felt that it was being held back. Additionally, Yes at this stage were still sharing rooms while on tour and Tony's room mates seemed to be having some difficulty in coping with his single and social lifestyle.

Yes mark 3 (August 1971 to July 1972)

Lineup: Jon Anderson—lead vocals/Chris Squire—bass guitars, vocals/Steve Howe—guitars, vocals/Rick Wakeman—keyboards/Bill Bruford—drums, percussion.

Rick Wakeman made the same kind of positive impression on Yes that Steve Howe did a year earlier. Rick brought with him a prodigious multi-keyboard talent that made the band's sound more colorful and his arrival completed what many fans consider as being the most gifted Yes lineup ever. It was obvious at the first rehearsal with Rick that the new combination would work and Jon and Chris subsequently went to give Tony Kaye the bad news.

Yes immediately began work on the album that would be titled *Fragile* (released U.K. November 1971, U.S. January 1972). It was the first Yes album with a cover by the artist Roger Dean and it was the start of his long association with the band. Roger's work uncannily suited the band's music and he would prove to have a major influence in guiding the visual perception of Yes with designs for stage sets, T shirts, tour programs and other memorabilia in addition to the album covers.

The band prepared for the tour promoting *Fragile* by rehearsing for a week at South Molton, Devon before performing a series of gigs in the U.K. in October 1971. Yes then did its second tour of America starting in November 1971 and was the opening act for bands such as Procol Harum, King Crimson and Ten Years After. It proved to be a test of endurance but very effective in spreading the word about Yes. *The Yes Album* was still doing well in the American charts but *Fragile* sprinted past it into the top five and a single edit of "Roundabout" went into the top twenty. *Fragile* would come to be accepted as a classic album and Yes was on the way to becoming a star attraction in both America and the U.K. with a reputation for hot live performances. Unfortunately, the desire to maintain high standards of performance sometimes led to blazing backstage post-gig arguments amongst the members of Yes over any alleged mistakes as the band's fortunes continued to rise.

Yes at this point started examining areas of personal self-improvement. The band's producer and sound engineer Eddie Offord was a vegetarian and he encouraged Yes and especially Steve Howe to look into the benefits of good food. Most of the band subsequently became vegetarian except for Rick who maintained his fondness for meat and alcohol. Bill was encouraged to develop his composing talents and Jon delved into books and classical music by composers such as Stravinsky and Sibelius. In February 1972 Rick began recording an album titled *The Six Wives Of Henry VIII* that would become the first solo record by any Yes member. Most of the members of Yes in later years would follow that trend and pursue their own specialized musical interests outside of the band.

In May 1972 Yes started rehearsals for their next album at Una Billings School Of Dance in Shepherd's Bush, London and the recording sessions took place in June 1972 at Advision Studios. The album was called *Close To the Edge* (released September 1972) and it would prove to be arguably the finest record ever made by Yes. The recording process had been very demanding with a painstaking level of perfectionism and Chris in particular spent many hours in fine-tuning his bass work. The whole process frustrated Bill to the point where he left immediately after the album was completed to join King Crimson in a move that also suited his love of jazz and it sent shock waves through Yes given that success was at hand.

Yes mark 4 (August 1972 to May 1974)

Lineup: Jon Anderson: lead vocals/Chris Squire—bass guitars, vocals/Steve Howe—guitars, vocals/Rick Wakeman—keyboards/Alan White—drums, percussion.

Alan White was a friend of producer Eddie Offord and he entered Yes with a reputation as a powerful drummer with an enviable career history of having played with such luminaries as John Lennon and George Harrison. When Bill had momentarily walked out during one of the sessions for *Close To The Edge*, Alan stepped in and took the opportunity to play with the band and it had obviously made an impression on all concerned. His arrival completed the most famous configuration of the band and what ultimately became known as the legendary "classic Yes" lineup.

Alan joined Yes only three days before the start of the *Close To The Edge* tour and he had to rehearse virtually non-stop to be ready for his debut with the band on 30 July 1972 in Dallas, Texas. It was a remarkable effort considering the complexity of Yes's music. The extensive tour took the band to America, England, Japan, Australia, New Zealand and finally finished back in America at the end of April 1973. *Close To The Edge* made the top five in the American and U.K. album charts and Yes were enjoying heady success as demonstrated by their impressive showing in the 1973 *Melody Maker* Readers Poll awards that saw them voted Best Band in the international category. To top it off, Rick's instrumental *Six Wives* album showcasing his multi-keyboard talents had made the top ten in the U.K. album charts and the top thirty in America.

The growing wealth of Yes was becoming conspicuous and Rick was at the forefront when he assembled a fleet of Rolls Royces and other classic cars. It was another indication of Yes's rapid climb to the top of the rock music world after the lean early years. Yes had recorded several shows during 1972 and it resulted in the very popular live triple album *Yessongs* (released May 1973) which reached number twelve in the American album charts and number seven in the U.K. A show was also filmed at the Rainbow Theatre in London in December 1972 and was released for viewing in cinemas in 1975 under the title of *Yessongs* with subsequent release years later on video and DVD.

During the *Close To The Edge* tour, the band started writing material for their next album with Jon and Steve working closely together on the concept. Roger Dean travelled with Yes on the tour leg to Japan and he began formulating ideas for the cover art. It gradually turned into a massively ambitious, highly experimental double album called *Tales From Topographic Oceans*. It was an album that polarized the fans, critics and even the band members with Rick being especially dubious about the merits of the music. Some people believed that it was Yes's greatest moment while others lashed it with stinging criticism. Nevertheless, the album went to number one in the U.K charts and it made the top ten in America. *The Topographic Oceans* world tour was a state of the art affair featuring a spectacular stage set designed by Roger and Martyn Dean and it reflected the growing sophistication of the band.

Just prior to the second leg of the *Topographic* tour, Rick staged his solo extravaganza *Journey To The Center Of The Earth* at the Festival Hall in London on 18 January 1974 complete with the London Symphony Orchestra. The show was recorded and the resulting album was later released to widespread acclaim around the world. Rick made the decision to quit Yes with his solo career beckoning, his considerable disenchantment with *Topographic Oceans* and with emerging differences in lifestyle as exemplified by Yes's vegetarianism. He resigned from Yes on his twenty-fifth birthday, 18 May 1974, and on the same day learned that *Journey* had made the number one spot in the album charts. However, exhaustion and stress ultimately contributed to the very serious situation of Rick having a heart attack and being admitted to hospital in August 1974.

Yes mark 5 (August 1974 to November 1976)

Lineup: Jon Anderson—lead vocals/Chris Squire—bass guitars, vocals/Steve Howe—guitars, vocals/Patrick Moraz—keyboards/Alan White—drums

Yes considered many possible new keyboard players including Vangelis before choosing the flamboyant Swiss born Patrick Moraz from Refugee, a band that was effectively The Nice without the formidable Keith Emerson. Preparations had already commenced for the next Yes album titled *Relayer* (released U.K. November 1974, U.S. December 1974) that was one of the most adventurous records ever made by the band. It made the top five of the album charts on both sides of the Atlantic and the subsequent large scale tour of America and the U.K. was a vividly memorable event with new stage sets created by the Dean brothers.

In 1975 Yes decided to take a slightly different musical route and all five members of the band recorded solo albums to highlight their particular talents. The albums were Jon's *Olias Of Sunhillow*, Chris's *Fish Out Of Water*, Steve's *Beginnings*, Patrick's *i* and Alan's *Ramshackled* and all achieved respectable results around the middle regions of the charts when they were gradually released during 1975 and 1976. In this period the *Yessongs* movie finally made it into the cinemas and it managed to climb into the top fifty highest grossing films. The compilation *Yesterdays* was released in early 1975 and it contained material taken mainly from the first two Yes albums together with an extended arrangement of Paul Simon's "America".

The American tour that started in May1976 saw the biggest and most spectacular shows ever staged by Yes. It featured the stunning new "Crab Nebula" stage set created by Roger and Martyn Dean and the band performed to massive numbers of people. The crowd at one show in Philadelphia at JFK Stadium on 12 June 1976 was estimated to be as large as 150,000 people and the tour represented the pinnacle of success in rock music. The band had interestingly started out playing selections from their solo albums as part of the set list but gradually dropped most of that material as the tour progressed. A film crew had covered part of the tour with the aim of producing a *Yessongs 2* movie but the footage has never been released.

Yes mark 6 (November 1976 to February 1980)

Lineup: Jon Anderson—lead vocals/Chris Squire—bass guitars, vocals/Steve Howe—guitars, vocals/Rick Wakeman—keyboards/Alan White—drums, percussion.

In late 1976 Yes re-convened in Switzerland to record the album *Going For The One* (released July 1977). It was soon apparent in rehearsals that Patrick Moraz was on a different musical wavelength to the rest of Yes and he departed the band. Rick Wakeman happily rejoined Yes in November 1976 after realizing that the band had returned to a music format that he liked with a style comparable to *Fragile. Going For The One* with Rick back on keyboards made number one in the U.K. album charts and the top ten in America while the single "Wonderous Stories" became a top ten hit in the U.K. The accompanying tour commenced in America in July 1977 followed by dates in Britain and Europe. There were no Dean stage sets this time around but Mike Tait's dramatic lighting contributed substantially to another successful Yes tour.

The musical landscape had begun to change with the New Wave of Punk music but Yes continued on. Yes were far removed from the sentiments of Punk having acquired opulent homes and adopted a tour lifestyle characterized by classy hotels and private jets. Although Yes are reputed to have sometimes "let their hair down" after a gig, the reports suggest that it fell well short of the infamous, very extreme excesses of some other high profile rock bands. But by 1978 Yes were well and truly being labelled as "dinosaurs" by the Punk fraternity and hostile critics. However, it is more than likely that none of these people had any appreciation of the struggles that Yes had endured in their early days with constant financial hurdles and the far from luxurious lifestyle in the communal flat in Munster Road.

The next Yes album *Tormato* (released September 1978) was disappointing and of uneven quality, receiving a predictably mixed reaction. However, the underlying strength of Yes amongst the fans still saw it make the top ten in the U.S. and the U.K. album charts and the single "Don't Kill the Whale" inched into the lower reaches of the top forty. Whatever the album might have lacked, the *Tormatour* celebrating Yes's tenth anniversary abundantly compensated with the band performing from an incredible, innovative revolving stage designed by Mike Tait. The revolving stage was located in the centre of the arena rather than at one end and the excited audience was consequently much closer to the band. The tour started in America in August 1978 and audience reactions were stupendous as Yes made its way to England in October 1978. A second leg of equally successful touring comprising three months of concerts took place in America starting in April 1979.

Rick had continued his solo career with his album *Rhapsodies* while Steve recorded his second solo effort *The Steve Howe Album*. However, the wheels began to fall off the Yes machine in an alarming fashion when the band gathered in Paris at the end of 1979 to record a new album. Nothing could seemingly be agreed and the sessions came to an abrupt end after Alan White slipped and broke his leg while ice skating with Virgin boss Richard Branson. By March 1980, Jon and Rick had quit with musical differences, financial disagreements and ebbing energy all playing a part. The years of pressure had taken their toll and the growing discontent became much too personal.

Yes mark 7 (March 1980 to December 1980)

Lineup: Chris Squire—bass guitars, vocals/Steve Howe—guitars, vocals/Alan White—drums, percussion/Trevor Horn—lead vocals/Geoff Downes—keyboards

Over the years Yes had gained a reputation for frequent changes of personnel but the most bizarre move was the arrival of Trevor Horn and Geoff Downes in May 1980, better known as the pop duo The Buggles. Yes had originally considered continuing as a trio but instead recorded the appropriately titled album *Drama* (released U.K. August 1980, U.S. September 1980) with the new five man lineup. It contained some surprisingly strong music and went to number two in the U.K. album charts and made the top twenty in America. The ensuing tour started promisingly in America in August 1980 highlighted by three consecutive nights at Madison Square Garden in New York. However, by the time Yes performed in England in November 1980, the fans had made it clear that they were not prepared to accept another vocalist in place of Jon Anderson.

Yes were chastened and the band came to a quiet and complete halt. It ended in confusion with manager Brian Lane being fired and Steve and Geoff moving on to form the supergroup Asia. The *Yesshows* live album featuring earlier performances from the 1970s was released at the end of November 1980 in the U.K. and shortly after in America.

Yes mark 8 (June 1983 to September 1988)

Lineup: Jon Anderson—lead vocals/Chris Squire—bass guitars, vocals/Trevor Rabin—guitars, keyboards, vocals/Tony Kaye—keyboards/Alan White—drums, percussion.

In 1981 Chris and Alan attempted to form a band with ex-Led Zeppelin guitarist Jimmy Page to be called XYZ (ex-Yes and Zeppelin) but it never got off the ground despite a few songs being recorded. Chris and Alan then moved on and released the Christmas single "Run With The Fox" at the end of 1981 before meeting the multi-talented ex-Rabbitt guitarist Trevor Rabin in 1982. With the addition of former Yes member Tony Kaye, the new combination tentatively called themselves Cinema and proceeded to record an album. It was decided that another vocalist was needed to maximize the potential of the music and Jon Anderson was convinced to return on the basis that the band would be called Yes.

Atlantic Records became involved and Tony Dimitriades was appointed as the band's manager. The album was eventually released under the title of *90125* and it proceeded to become the biggest selling Yes album with sales of some nine million copies. The music was quite different in style and far more commercial than previous Yes albums with the single "Owner Of A Lonely Heart" making the number one spot in charts around the world. Yes even managed to a win a Grammy award for the instrumental track "Cinema", the origins of the title being self-explanatory given the original band name that this lineup had chosen. While *90125* won Yes plenty of new admirers, it alienated some fans who preferred the more adventurous music that the band had become famous for in the seventies.

Yes set out on an extensive and hugely successful world tour, commencing in America in January 1984 and continuing through to South America in February 1985 where a highlight was performing at Rock In Rio which attracted 250,000 people. The tour was well captured by the camera in the *9012 Live* video which was filmed in Vancouver and released in 1985, complete with visual effects by Charlex. At one point talented ex-U.K. keyboardist Eddie Jobson had intriguingly joined the band before the tour but quickly departed as soon as he discovered that he would have to share the stage with Tony Kaye.

In September 1985 Yes commenced recording *Big Generator* but technical problems and disagreements precluded the troubled album from being released until September 1987. Although it sold in excess of one million copies, it received a mixed reaction from fans who felt that it had strayed too far from the classic Yes sound. The *Big Generator* tour went on the road in November 1987 and concluded in April 1988 in New York at the 40th anniversary celebrations for Atlantic Records. Jon had felt unhappy about his creative input into Yes becoming marginalized with Trevor Rabin now handling most of the song writing and he disliked the heavy guitar sound that dominated *Big Generator.* The result was that Jon again departed Yes to seek a different musical direction.

Anderson Bruford Wakeman Howe (September 1988 to March 1991)

Lineup: Jon Anderson—lead vocals/Steve Howe—guitars, vocals/Rick Wakeman—keyboards/Bill Bruford—acoustic and electronic drums/augmented by other musicians including Tony Levin on bass guitar.

Jon had the idea of taking the Yes sound from the 1970s and updating it for the 1990s and he sought the help of Steve, Bill and Rick. Brian Lane returned as manager and obtained a deal with Arista Records while Bill's former King Crimson colleague Tony Levin was invited to play bass. Rehearsals took place in Paris before the band moved on to Air Studios in Montserrat in February 1989 to commence four months of recording sessions. The album titled *Anderson Bruford Wakeman Howe* (released June 1989) sold 750,000 copies and convinced most fans that this lineup was in fact Yes under a different name. The so-called "Yes West" band (Chris Squire, Trevor Rabin, Alan White, Tony Kaye) were concerned enough about ABWH to initiate legal action to prevent them using the Yes name.

The ABWH world tour that started in July 1989 was shrewdly promoted as *An Evening Of Yes Music Plus* and audiences unambiguously loudly acclaimed the band as being the "real Yes". Everything about the shows was very much in the classic Yes style including the elaborate Roger Dean stage set. A double live album and video recorded during the tour was eventually released in late 1993 under the title of *An Evening Of Yes Music Plus.* After the tour ended in March 1990, ABWH set to work on their second album but it surprisingly became the basis for the next Yes album.

Yes mark 9 (March 1991 to March 1992)

Lineup: Jon Anderson—lead vocals/Chris Squire—bass guitars, vocals/Steve Howe—guitars, vocals/Trevor Rabin—guitars, vocals/Rick Wakeman—keyboards/Tony Kaye—keyboards/Bill Bruford—drums, percussion/Alan White—drums, percussion.

With encouragement from Arista Records who were exerting considerable influence over musical direction, Jon and Chris agreed on a somewhat fragile alliance to combine Yes West and ABWH under the banner of Yes. The resulting album *Union* (released April 1991) was openly disliked by all eight members of the band but even so, it still managed to sell 750,000 copies. The main producer was Jonathan Elias and the project seemed to go terribly awry in the production phase. In a baffling move, the ABWH tracks were significantly changed without the knowledge of the musicians and vital parts of the music were edited out or otherwise altered. The album had been extremely expensive to make and yet Steve's guitar solo track "Masquerade" was ironically nominated for a Grammy award, a piece that he'd recorded in his home studio at virtually no cost.

The bright spot for audiences was the *Union* world tour that ran from April to August in 1991, capped off by a handful of shows in Japan in February and March 1992. The novelty of an eight piece Yes made for a powerful and interesting spectacle performed mostly in the round on a revolving stage but the tensions between the members ensured that the lineup would not continue. Nevertheless, Rick declared it to be the most enjoyable tour he'd had with Yes up to that point although he disparagingly called the album *Onion* because it made him want to cry. The relationship between Arista and Yes proved to be short lived and there was a parting of ways without agreement being reached for another album.

Yes mark 10 (1992 to May 1995)

Lineup: Jon Anderson—lead vocals/Chris Squire—bass guitars, vocals/Trevor Rabin—guitars, keyboards, vocals/Tony Kaye—keyboards/Alan White—drums.

A period of confusion reigned after the *Union* tour before it was announced that Steve Howe, Rick Wakeman and Bill Bruford were no longer part of Yes. Long time Yes associate Phil Carson had formed a new record label Victory Music and he signed the *90125* lineup. A new album *Talk* was released in March 1994 and it made the top twenty in the English album charts and the top thirty in America with a musical style that was strongly influenced by Trevor Rabin in creation, production and execution with a copious heavy guitar presence.

The *Talk* tour spanned a period of five months starting in June 1994 with Billy Sherwood from the band World Trade providing additional guitar and vocals. But many fans made their feelings clear that they resented what had now become the musical direction of Yes. It was clear that Yes had made too many changes of direction and had alienated too many fans. The influential fanzine Yes Magazine wrote an editorial proclaiming "Change They Must" imploring Yes to bring Steve and Rick back into the band and to return to the classic Yes principle of collectively creating the music rather than allowing any one member to dominate. Strangely enough, Yes agreed.

Yes mark 11 (July 1995 to April 1997)

Lineup: Jon Anderson—lead vocals/Chris Squire—bass guitars, vocals/Steve Howe—guitars, vocals/Rick Wakeman—keyboards/Alan White—drums, percussion.

To the great excitement of fans around the world, the classic Yes lineup assembled in the Californian town of San Luis Obispo (SLO) in late 1995 and began rehearsals. New material was recorded and three concerts took place in SLO at the small, art deco Freemont Theatre in March 1996. The results surfaced as two double albums titled *Keys To Ascension* (released October 1996) and *Keys To Ascension 2* (released October 1997) with each containing new live and studio recordings. Unfortunately the record company Castle Communications didn't appear to have the resources to widely promote the albums. Yes undertook some promotional activity including a couple of live performances in unusual and unlikely locations such as the Tower Records store in Hollywood and a street corner in New York for the Fox After Breakfast TV program.

What at face value seemed to be a promising new start for Yes began to fall into ruins when the band was unable to agree on the next step and the management situation was also unsettled. Rick then decided to leave the band once more and went on to record *Return To The Center Of The Earth*. It should be noted that the various members of Yes by this stage in their careers were all pursuing independent musical ventures of one description or another with Jon and Steve being the most prolific on the solo front. Perhaps this period is best summed up by the release of the *Keys to Ascension* video that had to be recalled within days of its release in February 1997 due to a sound reproduction problem. It was frustrating for all concerned.

Yes mark 12 (August 1997 to June 2000)

Lineup: Jon Anderson—lead vocals/Chris Squire—bass guitars, vocals/Steve Howe—guitars, vocals/Billy Sherwood—guitars, keyboards, vocals/Alan White—drums, percussion, vocals/Igor Khoroshev—keyboards.

After a period of uncertainty, the first half of 1997 saw Yes regroup with new management Left Bank in place and a new lineup including Billy Sherwood and the talented but unknown Russian keyboardist Igor Khoroshev. However, the new album *Open Your Eyes* (released November 1997) was somewhat confusing being mainly the creation of Chris and Billy and quite commercial in character while *Keys to Ascension 2* hit the stores at almost the same time with overtly progressive music in the classic Yes style. *Open Your Eyes* received a lukewarm reception selling about 200,000 copies and Steve in particular was reluctant to play much of the material on stage having been brought into the project late in the creative process. Yes had successfully confused the audience yet again.

Yes finally got back on the right course with the subsequent world tour that started in America in June 1997 and extended until October 1998 with shows along the way in South America, Britain, Europe and Japan. The band undertook a second leg of concerts in America in June 1998 under the banner of the *30th Anniversary Tour* and Yes emphatically demonstrated to audiences that it was back in business and firing on all cylinders after the false starts of recent years.

Yes gathered in Vancouver in April 1999 to record *The Ladder* (released October 1999) with impressively credentialed producer Bruce Fairburn. However, Bruce tragically died from natural causes before the album was completed. Jon was nevertheless very pleased with the album with its mixture of progressive and commercial music and the very collective approach taken by the band to its creation. The problem was that changing radio formats and narrow perceptions of what music was suitable for radio airplay unfortunately made it difficult for Yes to receive exposure for the album.

In spite of the disappointing lack of radio support, *The Ladder* world tour that commenced in South America in September 1999 and ran for six months continued to enhance Yes's reputation for excellence on stage. The tour took the band to venues as diverse as the venerable Royal Albert Hall in London where they'd supported Cream thirty years earlier, to the fashionable House Of Blues venues in America where in Las Vegas they recorded the very strong *House Of Yes* live DVD and CD (released September 2000).

Yes mark 13 (June 2000 to August 2000)

Lineup: Jon Anderson—lead vocals/Chris Squire—bass guitars, vocals/Steve Howe—guitars, vocals/Alan White—drums, percussion/Igor Khoroshev—keyboards.

With it dawning on Yes that the way forward was to again pursue a progressive and adventurous musical style, Billy Sherwood announced his departure from the band. Yes reverted to its traditional five piece grouping and embarked on the *Masterworks* tour that saw two months of shows in America starting on 20 June 2000 with Kansas supporting as special guests.

Audiences were stunned and delighted when Yes concentrated on its legendary epic works, some of which hadn't been heard live since the seventies. Many fans felt that Yes on this tour had extraordinarily equalled or even surpassed its previous brilliant best with a series of unforgettable shows performed with a highly distinctive sail-like stage setting. The only negative was the subsequent departure of Igor who had not been a full member of Yes and he left under somewhat of a cloud to pursue solo projects.

Yes mark 14 (August 2000 to April 2002)

Lineup: Jon Anderson—lead vocals, guitar/Chris Squire—bass guitars, vocals/ Steve Howe—guitars, vocals/Alan White—drums, percussion, piano, vocals.

Yes elected this time to remain as a four piece unit and carried on undaunted to record the highly ambitious *Magnification* album which included the San Diego Symphony Orchestra with orchestrations by Larry Groupe. Yes has always had a strong orchestral element in its music and the album gave the opportunity for that characteristic to be fully expressed in the absence the traditional keyboard role. Regarded by many fans as the best Yes album since the seventies and despite several good reviews, *Magnification* received shamefully little exposure. The fact that it was released on the fateful day of 11 September 2001 obviously did not bode well.

The *Yessymphonic* world tour that commenced in July 2001 was a brave move by Yes to say the least and it featured an orchestra consisting of approximately fifty pieces at every show, augmented by the versatile Tom Brislin on keyboards from the band Spiraling. The tour was a magnificent triumph heavily featuring the classic Yes epics together with new material and it was brilliantly captured on the *Yessymphonic Live* DVD released in 2002. The tour included Yes's return engagement at the famous Hollywood Bowl in Los Angeles where they'd played once before in 1975.

Yes mark 15 (April 2002 to the present 2004)

Lineup: Jon Anderson—lead vocals, percussion, guitar/Chris Squire—bass guitar, vocals/Steve Howe—guitars, vocals/Rick Wakeman—keyboards/Alan White—drums, percussion.

The rumors were circulating but no one would dare believe it until the band walked out on stage together. And then it actually happened that Rick Wakeman returned to the classic Yes lineup for the 2002 tour of America that kicked off on 17 July 2002 in Seattle. After brushing off some initial cobwebs, the classic lineup of Yes was back performing at the highest level in the best traditions of the band by the end of the tour. It was obvious from the broad smiles on the faces of the musicians that they were very happy to be together again and the band appeared to be looking optimistically to the future. The *In A Word: Yes* 5 CD compilation was released during 2002 and it extensively covered highlights of the band's career from 1969 to 2001.

The appropriately named *Full Circle* tour in 2003 took Yes to Europe, Britain, Australia, Asia and America and it was an extremely successful tour with most of the shows being sold out. Yes followed up in 2004 with a spectacular *35th Anniversary* tour featuring a stage set designed by Roger Dean that saw the band once again grace the stages of the major arenas of the world. *The Ultimate Yes* thirty-fifth anniversary 2 CD compilation released in mid 2003 made the top 10 in the UK album charts. It was released in America in early 2004 featuring a different track list and a bonus third disc of new recordings including a new acoustic arrangement of "Roundabout".

The name of Yes's management team changed in 2003 to 10th Street Entertainment although the same people from the now defunct Left Bank headed by Allen Kovac, Jordan Berliant and Jeff Varner remained involved under the new banner. November 2003 saw the UK release of the new Yes DVD documentary *Yesspeak* with subsequent release in the rest of the world. A special live acoustic performance by Yes to support the cinematic release of *Yesspeak* in America was itself released on DVD in June 2004 as *Yes Acoustic* which promptly went to number one in the UK DVD charts. A live DVD filmed at Tsongas Arena in Lowell, Massachusetts during the 2004 tour titled *Songs From Tsongas* is in production and there is a possibility that Yes will record new music in the studio in 2005. The Yes Story is a long and amazing one that has turned through the full circle as Yes continues to explore even more new musical horizons in the year of its thirty-fifth anniversary.

YES—BUT HOW HIGH?

Yes has received a great deal of publicity at different times in its long career, particularly during the seventies and eighties. However, the band has never purported to be fashionable and its music has never conformed to the normal formats of rock with the consequential result that Yes has had to sometimes struggle to obtain the media exposure that it rightfully deserved. The music industry over the years has become increasingly corporate and unfortunately narrower in outlook. Unlike the early seventies, intrinsically talented musicians with a unique sound presently do not seem to receive a great deal of encouragement. The main focus more than ever tends to be on the latest musical fashion to sell the maximum amount of product as quickly as possible. Unfortunately such an outlook isn't conducive to creative music and ultimately it is unlikely to be in the long term, best interests of the music industry.

Rick Wakeman gave some insights into the music industry in 2002 when speaking of what he'd learned about the business from David Bowie: "He said if you really believe in something when you do it, then the people you've got to convince are the audience—not the heads of record companies. He always considered them to be complete and utter idiots. I think to a lot of extent, sometimes he's right. They don't know a hatchet from a crotchet. And the danger is, sometimes people in record companies, because they have no talent themselves, try to get the bands and musicians they've got to play what they would like. And that's absolutely crazy, because they don't have the imagination to do that…There's so much music, so many bands sounding the same these days."[1]

The music industry, print media, radio and television have appeared to be somewhat unsure of how to deal with a band like Yes that has lasted for years, continues to perform with distinction, still attracts significant audiences around the world and yet doesn't produce mere "standard" pop and rock music. Nevertheless, it is a fact that millions of people have heard and enjoyed Yes songs such as "I've Seen All Good People", "Owner Of A Lonely Heart" and "Roundabout". It is intriguing to speculate that other more recently recorded Yes songs could find a similarly wide audience if they were given the necessary exposure.

I submit that the classic yet adventurous rock music of Yes would find that wide audience if only people were given the opportunity to hear it and become accustomed to it. One only needs to have attended a Yes concert in recent years to appreciate that the band continues to have the abundant talent to justify the exposure. My contention is supported by the fact that *The Ultimate Yes* compilation immediately soared into the top 10 of the U.K. album charts in mid 2003 when promoted by a comprehensive marketing campaign on radio and television. The 1 November 2003 issue of *Billboard* magazine in America featured a special tribute to Yes and it not only became *Billboard's* best selling issue of the year but also broke some sales records and the Yes content had to be re-printed to satisfy demand. These examples suggest that the music industry and the media at large have at last started to re-discover Yes and it is not before time.

In some ways the absence of a constant high profile in the media has been a blessing for Yes fans because it has contributed to requiring the band to continue working hard on a regular basis to keep the finances ticking over. Steve Howe said: "We used to joke about Pink Floyd that while we'd been arguing for the last three hours they'd sold another million records. But although we've sold zillions of records, we've never had that absolute monster like *Dark Side Of The Moon*. But at least we're still respected as a pretty good band."[2]

It was demonstrated in the seventies how high Yes could rise given the right exposure. For instance, the previously mentioned massive crowd of 150,000 at the Yes concert at JFK Stadium, Philadelphia in 1976 was claimed to be a world record attendance. By 1980, Yes held the record for the most sold out shows at Madison Square Garden in New York, eclipsing even Led Zeppelin. To demonstrate that Yes still has what it takes, the band pulled a near capacity crowd of 15,000 to Madison Square Garden in May 2004 to rank in the top ten highest grossing concerts for that week in America.

Perhaps one of the best indications of the success of Yes comes from the readers polls in the respected English music newspaper *Melody Maker*. Yes achieved astounding success in the *Melody Maker* polls with votes that came solely and directly from the fans—the very same people who listened to the music, bought the albums and attended the concerts. The results for the polls were tellingly not dependent on radio, the print media, television, marketing managers or music industry executives who have too often appeared to have had little idea of what Yes music is all about—the people who today are so influential in determining what music receives widespread public exposure. The following is a selection of the results from the *Melody Maker* polls for 1976/77/78.

Melody Maker Readers Poll 1976:
Best Band—Yes
Best Male Singer—Jon Anderson (Yes)
Best Guitarist—Steve Howe (Yes)
Best Bass Guitarist—Chris Squire (Yes)
Best Composer—Jon Anderson (Yes)
Best Keyboards—Rick Wakeman (prior to re-joining Yes)

Melody Maker Readers Poll 1977:
Best Band—Yes
Best Male Singer—Jon Anderson (Yes)
Best Bass Guitarist—Chris Squire (Yes)

Melody Maker Readers Poll 1978:
Best Singer—Jon Anderson (Yes)
Best Guitarist—Steve Howe (Yes)
Best Bass Guitarist—Chris Squire (Yes)
Best Keyboards—Rick Wakeman (Yes)

It should be clarified that these results are only those where Yes or its members achieved first place. There were other categories where Yes was highly ranked but didn't quite make the top spot. For example, *Going for The One* was voted into second place in the Best Album category in 1977 and Yes was third in the Best Band vote in 1978. It should also be pointed out that all of the results are for the international category in the polls except the Male Singer award for 1976 which was in the British category.

It is particularly fascinating to note the host of very famous names that Yes soared above to secure first place in the various rankings in the *Melody Maker* polls and the list includes Paul McCartney, Elton John, Led Zeppelin, the Rolling Stones, The Who, Genesis, Queen, the Eagles, Emerson Lake & Palmer, Pink Floyd and Fleetwood Mac. It is a veritable who's who of classic rock and emphasizes that Yes had achieved success at the very highest level.

References

1 Interview by Tom Brislin, *Keyboard*, November 2002
2 Interview by Dave Ling, *Classic Rock*, December 2001

3

Close To The Edge

THE MUSIC OF YES

The extraordinary music of Yes is unparalleled and not easily categorized. It is an incomparable catalog of music that has sold in excess of forty million albums and has also yielded the occasional hit single along the way. Yes music has a distinctive timeless quality combining the adventurous excitement of rock with a virtuoso complexity befitting the great classics while communicating a vividly poetic, positive view of life. Here the focus is on the music of Yes and all of the band's studio albums are reviewed in chronological order together with some live recordings and solo material from the members of the classic Yes lineup.

The obvious disadvantage of writing about music is that music is an entity that by its very nature needs to be heard. To counteract that problem, I'd encourage you to actually listen to the music after reading about it in order to fully appreciate and experience the creativity of Yes, even if you have heard the music many times before. Towards that end, I've selected certain key tracks from each Yes album to showcase the musical achievements of the band and many of the most important works of Yes are included. With a view to making that music easily obtainable for anyone who doesn't have access to the original albums, those selections have been mainly derived from the *In A Word: Yes* 5 CD set—the single most comprehensive compilation of Yes music from the beginning of Yes's recording history in 1969 up to and including the *Magnification* album in 2001. The studio tracks have been supplemented with live recordings from the albums *Yessongs* and *House Of Yes* to represent Yes on stage while the *Affirmative: Yes Family Solos Album* compilation provides a taste of the best solo work of the members of Yes.

It is certainly possible that a newcomer might feel somewhat daunted about approaching the entire catalog of Yes music for the first time but an economic way for the novice to sample a wide cross section of Yes music is the budget priced but well packaged *The Ultimate Yes* compilation album. However, the ideal way to listen to Yes music is to own all of the original albums and it should be noted that Rhino Entertainment in 2003 began to progressively re-release a large proportion of the Yes back catalog with the bonus inclusion of some previously unreleased outtakes and other material.

Let's now explore the unique music of Yes, both in the studio and live in concert.

YES

YES:
Jon Anderson—lead vocals, incidental percussion/Chris Squire—bass, vocals/ Peter Banks—guitar, vocals/Tony Kaye—organ, piano/Bill Bruford—drums, vibes
PRODUCED BY:
Paul Clay & Yes
ENGINEERED BY:
Gerald Chevin
RECORDED AT:
Advision Studios, London and Trident Studios, London during the English Spring in 1969
RELEASED:
July 1969 (UK), October 1969 (US)
TRACKS:
Beyond And Before/I See You/Yesterday And Today/Looking Around/Harold Land/Every Little Thing/Sweetness/Survival

The career of Yes started with the group doing cover versions on stage of songs written by other artists and it quickly saw them make a reputation for themselves as a band to be watched. In fact, when the first line up of Yes was being recruited and drummer Bill Bruford played his first ever gig with Jon Anderson and Chris Squire, the band was still called Mabel Greer's Toyshop and they played Wilson Pickett's "Midnight Hour"—twice or three times during the same gig according to Bill! When the name of the band changed to Yes they became known for their unique renditions of songs by other performers such as the Byrds, the Fifth Dimension and the Beatles.

The musical influences of Yes are many and varied but there is no doubt that the Beatles were a very important influence on Yes. If one listens to Beatles albums such as *Revolver, Sgt Pepper* and *Abbey Road* and songs such as "All You Need Is Love", "Strawberry Fields Forever" and "I Am The Walrus", the musical progression from the Beatles to Yes is very logical. The Beatles were very creative and innovative and often accompanied their music with messages of love and peace—similar characteristics can be found in abundance in the music of Yes.

Jon Anderson once commented: "I think any band goes through a kind of corridor. You know, it sticks to a certain route for a long period of time and then maybe it'll open up and try and be adventurous. With the Beatles it started with *Revolver* and then it sped to *Pepper*...I can't think of any band who have been able to keep up a better progression of LPs (albums)."[1] The Yes link with the

Beatles was amusingly underlined when Jon said: "I used to copy other people's voices. I used to do a great Paul McCartney. My best copy was 'I'm Down' but I was a bit shattered when somebody said that I sounded like Cilla Black."[2] In retrospect it is obvious that Jon needn't have been concerned and it should be noted that a remarkable live version of "I'm Down" performed by Yes in 1976 appears on the "Yesyears" 4CD compilation.

Two of the other strong musical influences on the early Yes sound were The Nice and the Fifth Dimension. Jon said: "At the time of getting Yes together, The Nice were my favorite band with Keith Emerson and Blinky and Lee Jackson. I also liked the Fifth Dimension around the time of the *Magic Garden* album...with the Jim Webb songs. We used to do most of that album, we just fused the two ideas together of the heavy type arrangements with strong vocals as well. At that time most bands had heavy arrangements with not very strong vocal ideas. And you also had the Beach Boys (and) Association type thing. The Fifth Dimension was strong on vocals but didn't have the very strong backing as well, it just didn't complement each other. It was just one or the other, so we tried to fuse them together to create an energizing sphere of sound."[3]

The unique musical style being developed by Yes allowed space for its individual musicians to bring many different influences into the music and there is no better example than Bill Bruford who was passionate about jazz. Bill has commented in his highly intelligent and droll manner that nobody ever told him that "Yes wasn't going to be a jazz group", so he felt free to bring a definite jazz influence to the progressive rock of Yes.[4] It was hardly surprising coming from someone who had grown up more enthused by the jazz of people like Art Blakey, Max Roach and Joe Morello than by the pop stars of the day.

Manager Roy Flynn signed Yes to the Atlantic label in the English spring of 1969 but the much anticipated first recording session unfortunately didn't get off to good start. An eight hour recording session had been booked and Yes had specially ordered a Hammond organ to be delivered to the studio to help them achieve the right sound. As it transpired, Atlantic boss Ahmet Ertegun was there to watch his new band in action but after waiting for six hours he was forced to give up without a note being recorded when the elusive Hammond failed to materialize. Eventually recording went ahead without the organ and it had to be added later.

The first album simply titled *Yes* was co-produced by Paul Clay and the band. It featured six original songs plus two other tracks in the form of imaginatively arranged, energetic cover versions of "Every Little Thing" by the Beatles and "I See You" by the Byrds. The songs were drawn from Yes's stage act along with other new material. The opening song was appropriately titled "Beyond And Before", a stirring effort written by Chris Squire and Clive Bailey who had been the original guitarist in Mabel Greer's Toyshop. The first song written by the soon to be famous Anderson/Squire combination, "Sweetness", appeared on the album and it was also released as the band's first single backed with a cover version of "Something's Coming" from *West Side Story*.

The album cover as originally released in England was of gatefold design with a large, bold, red "Yes" on the front in a format that became the band's first logo. However, some editions of the album released elsewhere had a front cover featuring a photograph of the band taken at an architectural centre in Fulham, London. One thing that all editions had in common was a dissertation from Tony Wilson of *Melody Maker* that sang the praises and potential of Yes.

It might be a strange experience for some people to hear Yes for the first time because the band has such an individual sound but it is perhaps slightly less so with this early and relatively conventional music. It is advisable to keep in mind that it is necessary for even the most devout Yes fans to hear a new Yes song several times before being able to fully appreciate it. What might at first sound unexpected or slightly odd tends to eventually become accepted by the listener as the being the optimum treatment for any particular Yes song. This is a typical characteristic of Yes music—it takes some time to initially digest because it is usually more complex than most rock music but once taken on board, it will reward the listener for literally years to come.

I'd generally recommend that any new Yes song be listened to at least six times before drawing any conclusions. The effort will definitely be worthwhile and you will often be surprised at how your own appreciation of the music develops. It might be helpful to realize that there is frequently the basis of a melodic "Beatlesque" song enveloped within even the most ambitious Yes epic and it can serve as a useful point of reference to mentally grab hold of in coming to terms with the more complex aspects of the music which surrounds it.

Although the album *Yes* showed definite promise and received some positive press, the band was disappointed with the results. Jon Anderson said: "We were very enthusiastic about doing this music we were doing. We didn't get the right people around us. We didn't know you had to have the right people around to make a good record. We just thought an engineer's an engineer—he knows his job and you expect him to do a good job. And by the time we finished the album we were a bit demoralized by the lack of attention the sound we thought deserved. There's so much enthusiasm on the album, I think it comes through anyway. 'Survival' I like. I like a lot of the songs thinking back on it. 'I See You' is a great song anyway and we just rummaged around with a basic Beatlely feel about it—it's really a beautiful song to play with. At that time we weren't very strong in writing a lot of material. We were writing some but we needed other people's material to create more of a show."[5]

Chris Squire also felt let down because the band had set out to create "something monumental" and he had expected the album to sound "grander and much more together."[6] The views of Jon and Chris are indicative of the high musical standards that Yes aspired to but ultimately it was a mixture of inexperience and a lack of the right technical support that were the main factors working against Yes on this first album.

Yes supported the album with a string of performances in Britain and Europe at venues ranging from clubs and universities through to festivals. It wasn't all easy going by any means but the band gradually won admirers along the way. The situation was made more challenging by the fact that there was little promotion of the album in both England and America and the "Sweetness" single only sold about 500 copies.

The *Something's Coming* 2 CD set released in 1997 featured rawer versions of some songs from the album *Yes* as recorded by the BBC in 1969 and early 1970. It should be noted that the same recordings have subsequently been released under a variety of different album titles including *Beyond and Before*. Although the sound quality of these old recordings is variable to say the least, they give an indication of the impressive musical energy that this incarnation of Yes was capable of. The performances were recorded very quickly in the BBC studios and have a very "live" feel, some having been staged in front of a small audience.

The comments of Peter Banks in the CD booklet of *Something's Coming* defined some important facets of the Yes sound: "We wanted the tightness and controlled power of a jazz big band, lots of light and shade, all with great three-part harmony vocals…(we) began to develop a style, that for its time, was astoundingly diverse and eclectic…arrangements were fast, tight and controlled but still allowed room for the band to swing in a natural way…the complex chord changes, the dynamics of light and shade, the dramatic mood swings reflected as much of the musicians personality as it did their playing ability…should have sounded like musical anarchy, but it worked…mostly."[7]

"Every Little Thing" (Lennon/McCartney)

It is immediately apparent how different the Yes version of the Lennon/McCartney song "Every Little Thing" sounds from the original Beatles version. Yes starts with a strong instrumental introduction with plenty of dynamics—Yes is never afraid of variation and to turn the volume up and down for added interest. A few notes of another Beatles song "Day Tripper" are tastefully allowed to slip through just before the vocals commence to underline the flair of Yes for arrangement.

The bass guitar is clearly of driving importance to this music and it takes a lead role with a typically treble edge to the sound while still supplying a warm bottom end. The guitar is nothing like the abrasive playing typically found in rock music—it often has a jazz-like tone and is fluent and alive. The lead vocals are utterly distinctive—they are high, clear and soar gracefully over the instrumentation while meshing seamlessly with the strong harmony vocals. The drums are crisply energetic and distinctively played—like the bass, they seem to have more to say than is usual in rock music and the rhythmic possibilities extend beyond the norm. This music has energy, power and precision without metallic heaviness. It has a unique personality and a sense of adventure with a discernible warmth and an emphasis on melody.

If "Every Little Thing" is your first experience of Yes music then listen to it several times and take special note of the components. While the melody and words are drawn from the Beatles, the vocals, arrangements and instrumentation are pure Yes and represent the foundation building blocks that the band would use in the future to develop its highly original and imaginative music. The excellent musicians in Yes may have come and gone over the years and each has undoubtedly brought his own very special talents to the band but somehow the same original and strong musical principles have endured. However, it is certain that no one at the start could possibly have foretold how exciting the future would be for Yes and how far the music would progress. It was most appropriate in 2004 that Yes included "Every Little Thing" in the set list for the American leg of the *35th Anniversary* tour as a poignant reminder of the origins and influences of the band.

◆ ◆ ◆

It didn't set the world on fire when first released but the music on the album *Yes* still sounds very fresh today. This is especially so when listening to the recently remastered CD editions of the album that make it sound as though it is newly recorded and the rich potential of the band is allowed to shine through. In fact, most of the Yes catalog has now been re-released in Japan in remastered high definition CD (HDCD) format with superbly reproduced miniature replica cardboard sleeves and the early albums in particular have benefited substantially from this process. HDCDs are heard to best advantage on HDCD players but they are also compatible with standard CD players and I've observed that the high definition discs still produce substantially improved sound when played on standard equipment. Reports have also been very positive about the quality of the remastered and expanded editions on the Rhino label that include bonus tracks.

From this first album, I recommend "Looking Around" and "I See You" as further prime examples of early Yes recordings.

Time And A Word

YES:
Jon Anderson/Chris Squire/Peter Banks/Tony Kaye/Bill Bruford
PRODUCED BY:
Tony Colton
ENGINEERED BY:
Eddie Offord
ORCHESTRAL ARRANGEMENTS:
Tony Cox
RECORDED AT:
Advision Studios, London in late 1969 and early 1970
RELEASED:
July 1970 (UK), November 1970 (US)
TRACKS:
No Opportunity Necessary, No Experience Needed/Then/Everydays/Sweet Dreams/The Prophet/Clear Days/Astral Traveller/Time And A Word

The second Yes album *Time And A Word* saw the band taking an adventurous step forward when Jon Anderson had the somewhat controversial idea of creating a more expansive sound by using an orchestra to supplement the instrumentation of the group. At this time bands such as The Nice and Deep Purple had pointed the way in experimenting with orchestras. Jon held the view that Yes hadn't yet achieved a distinctive "sound aura" and that the music needed to have a "bigger feel", no doubt at least partially influenced by the fact that he'd been listening to a lot of classical music for inspiration. He also perceived Tony Kaye and Peter Banks as inhibiting the realization of an exciting, cohesive sound by not "interweaving" and sparking off each other.[8] Yes gave some consideration to using keyboard instruments such as mellotrons in a bid to simulate a symphonic effect but ultimately decided to use a small orchestra that turned out to be a disparate collection of session brass players and student string musicians from the Royal College Of Music.

The band started work on the album at Advision Studios in London with Tony Colton in the producer's chair and Eddie Offord handling the engineering role. Jon Anderson observed that Yes needed some "egging on" and that Tony Colton gave them the kind of encouragement they needed. However, not all members of the band were enamored with the idea of using an orchestra and it ultimately led to problems, particularly with Peter Banks. More drama came when the use of the orchestra led to a blow out in costs to the extent of double the budget allowed by Atlantic Records and company head Ahmet Ertegun consequently moved to end the project—until he heard the music on a visit to the studio and gave it his blessing to continue.

Even at this early stage in the career of Yes, there is clear evidence that Jon Anderson had a vision to create music that mattered. In late 1969 he said: "What we (Yes) do, we like and people enjoy. We give them music that can create different moods and feelings. I write meaningful lyrics, not just pop songs. When you think of the life span we have given to us, if everybody made an effort, we really could get rid of war and starvation and make peace and better living a reality. Each individual knows the difference between the good and bad in life. I wrote a song called 'The Prophet' about a man everybody follows like people follow Dylan and the Beatles. But he tells them they should find and believe in themselves and be their own prophets and not just follow like sheep."[9]

The writing of the original songs that appeared on *Time And A Word* began while Yes were touring to promote their first album. Bill Bruford said at the time: "Jon is pouring out new numbers for us to play but we don't have time to rehearse. Usually he writes a tune and we listen to the tape and take it from there. We use complicated arrangements that can be great, or they can baffle an audience. 'The Prophet' has about five changes of tempo and key changes before the singing comes in."[10]

One of the most profound statements about *Time And A Word* comes from Steve Howe who didn't play on the album but nevertheless acknowledges its legacy. In 1999 Steve said: "The design of Yes was there before I joined (in mid 1970). I think it was in *Time And A Word* when that second great album had so much style in it and it was almost as though you could take yards of it and keep working it, reworking it, and in a way that's kind of what we've been doing. There's some magic moments in *Time and A Word*. I think there was a great deal of ground laying, foundation laying, in that time."[11]

While *Time And A Word* certainly had its strengths as an album, the high standards of Jon Anderson and Chris Squire were such that they were still disappointed with the result. They realized that Yes had the potential to go much further. The band also still didn't have full confidence in it's own developing song writing talents as shown by the inclusion of dynamic cover versions of "Everydays" by Stephen Stills and "No Opportunity Necessary, No Experience Needed" by Richie Havens with a snatch of the "Big Country" theme flamboyantly thrown into the middle for good measure. Nevertheless, the original Yes material was really the centre of attention and songs such as "Then", "Sweet Dreams", "The Prophet", "Astral Traveller" and the title track were full of musical interest. The original song "Dear Father" was also recorded during the same sessions but didn't appear on the album. It was instead released as the 'B' side of the single "Sweet Dreams" and was ultimately included on the compilation *Yesterdays* that was released in 1975.

One important facet of the Yes sound that became firmly established on *Time And A Word* was the prominent bass of Chris Squire and it came about more by accident than design. Tony Colton mixed the album using headphones and it didn't permit him to properly hear the bass with the end result that the bass was made much louder in the mix than would normally have been the case. It allowed the immaculate bass work of Chris to be heard and fully appreciated to the extent where it would always thereafter be regarded as an important typical characteristic of Yes music.

The front cover for the release of *Time And A Word* in England featured a surrealist black and white image of a naked woman by Lawrence Sackman but other editions had a color photograph of the band confusingly including new guitarist Steve Howe who had played no part in the recording. The image of the naked woman was later echoed in the cover painted by Roger Dean for the retrospective *Yesterdays*.

The *Time And A Word* album confirmed that Yes was becoming more sophisticated and increasingly drawing on eclectic musical influences. Some critics were wary about the use of the orchestra while others gave it a tick of approval. Reviewer Ed Nimmervoll wrote: "With Yes the group and the orchestra parts aren't separate or one incidental to the other. It's just flashes of everything, for moments, within the flow of a complete song. It's very complex music. One 'song' forms the opportunity for putting several ideas together. But they're able to control it. And I don't think it's ever really overdone. Or pretentious. It's fresh, lively, rich. Definitely a group to enjoy."[12]

The promotions for *Time And A Word* included a special performance by Yes at the Queen Elizabeth Hall, London in March 1970 with a twenty piece youth orchestra conducted by Tony Cox who had handled the orchestrations for the album. From all accounts, poor amplification marred the show but the concept of somehow expanding the sonic pallet of the band remained attractive to Yes. The band played a series of dates in Britain and Europe unencumbered by the orchestra but despite these efforts, *Time And A Word* failed to make a significant impact on the charts although it at least sold more copies than the first album.

"Sweet Dreams" (Anderson/Foster)

Sweet Dreams is a catchy and melodic song demonstrating that Yes could progress from covering songs such as "Every Little Thing" and produce a convincing original work in a fairly similar style with a real potential for wide popularity. "Sweet Dreams" was the 'A' side of one of the singles released from *Time And A Word* but unfortunately it never received the exposure it deserved and didn't find success on the charts.

Notable characteristics of "Sweet Dreams" are the upbeat, straight forward lyrics from Jon Anderson and the typically prominent and melodic bass from Chris Squire, complemented perfectly by Bill Bruford's crisp drums. The song has a pleasing hypnotic appeal that soon grows after a few listens and it is disappointing that Yes have seldom played "Sweet Dreams" in concert although it was thankfully included in the set list for the 2004 tour after a long absence.

Jon Anderson wrote "Sweet Dreams" with his old colleague from The Warriors, David Foster. At one point it appeared as though David was going to play guitar on the track until Peter Banks indignantly intervened but he still contributed backing vocals. Peter objected to the concept of an extra musician being brought into the picture and unfortunately, it only added to the brewing discontent surrounding his own role in the band.

In 1973 Chris Squire viewed the early Yes musical efforts as being part of a necessary learning curve: "We were kind of groping at vague ideas we had…But there's some beautiful moments on those first two albums and I still really like them…We even surprised ourselves with 'Sweet Dreams'. It's a very funky track."[13]

"Time And A Word" (Anderson/Foster)

The title track, according to Peter Banks, emanated from Jon Anderson wanting to produce a song with an anthemic feel similar to what the Beatles had achieved with "Hey Jude". Although "Time And A Word" certainly didn't attract attention on anything remotely like the scale of "Hey Jude", the melody is nevertheless very memorable in a song that is once again fairly conventional in format.

The lyrical content is an early example of the emerging positive philosophy of Yes that drew inspiration from songs such as "All You Need Is Love" by the Beatles. The message in "Time And A Word" was quite simple but heartfelt—the *time* was when we'll *get it together again* to *help the world go round* and *the word that will stop us going wrong* is *love.* (brief extracts from "Time And A Word" by Jon Anderson and David Foster; published by Cotillion, BMI)

As was the case with "Sweet Dreams", "Time And A Word" was a collaboration between Jon Anderson and David Foster who explained how both songs were written: "Jon and I sat down with a couple of guitars in (Yes manager) Roy Flynn's house, where we used to do a lot of stuff. We got hold of a little old Alba tape recorder—I remember it distinctly! We just played away and sang until something started going. We'd kick off each other. Jon would sing a line and I'd follow up with something that rhymed, and they just flowed. We didn't actually have to think about it. The songs were pretty straight from our heads, and on to tape. That's the way they came together; they were done in straight sessions, just one off. They weren't done over a period of time."[14] Unlike the studio recording of "Sweet Dreams", David this time actually played the acoustic guitar for Yes on the introduction to "Time And A Word".

The most obvious criticism of "Time And A Word" is that the musical conclusion doesn't quite live up to its full potential. The orchestra falls somewhat short of being totally satisfying as the song builds up towards the end and the available instrumental armory lacks the right elements to bring it off to perfection. It really demanded a more decisive and dramatic conclusion of the kind that Yes later achieved with "Starship Trooper" on *The Yes Album*. Notably the subsequent live performances of "Time And A Word" over the years (e.g. on *Keys to Ascension* in 1996) have been somewhat relaxed and low key, concentrating on the melodic elements and steering clear of any attempt at a big finish.

Jon Anderson said: "On the second album we tried to get together with other trade musicians and session men but they're so dumb about music, they're into making money and that was to our cost by not making a very interesting album. They weren't willing to swing at all, they just played note by note and counted how much a note cost, you know. It was very difficult..."[15]

"Then" (Anderson)

The music discussed so far has been relatively conventional and commercial in format but with "Then", an early prototype of the more progressive side of Yes was given a quick but searching test run. The dynamics of "Then" are dramatic, going from a mere whisper to full volume acrobatics. Some critics have said that the instrumental section in the middle of "Then" is somewhat bombastic but I'm more inclined to suggest that it is merely youthful exuberance led by a very impressive rhythm combination in Chris Squire and Bill Bruford.

Jon Anderson's vocals effortlessly fly above the instrumentation and the lyrics urge us to strive for a better world with an unambiguous central message that *love is the only answer, hate is the root of cancer* (brief extracts from "Then" by Jon

Anderson; published by Cotillion, BMI). In later songs in the years ahead the messages in Yes songs would become more sophisticated and be expressed more symbolically. It was during the recording of the *Time And A Word* album that Jon Anderson began to feel a certain peace of mind with a heightened spiritual awareness: "I was in tune with the ultimate being—God or whatever you want to use—and I came to terms with it personally. It is really music to praise (on *Time And A Word*). I mean next year I might turn into total mind dredging fears and write with the accent on depression."[16]

It is apparent on the early Yes albums that Tony Kaye's role on keyboards was generally a supporting one rather than as a soloist and he principally restricted himself to the Hammond organ. However, Tony certainly had a distinctive sound that Chris Squire would later refer to as that "swirling" Tony Kaye organ sound. It is an oddity that the promo video made for "Then" depicted a windswept Yes playing in an outdoor location at the seaside with Chris Squire on keyboards and Tony Kaye playing bass, even though in reality neither played those instruments on the record. To complete the somewhat misleading picture, Steve Howe is shown playing guitar in the video as he does for all of the promo videos for the album, even though he didn't join Yes until after the *Time And A Word* album was recorded. It was all somewhat indicative of changes and progress in the Yes camp.

◆ ◆ ◆

Time And A Word might not have topped the charts but it was an important musical stepping stone in Yes's career. The album revealed an impressive basic blueprint for Yes that with some further adjustments would take the band towards the exciting musical destinations it aspired to reach.

THE YES ALBUM

YES:
Jon Anderson—vocals, percussion/Chris Squire—bass guitars, vocals/Steve Howe—electric & acoustic guitars, vocals/Tony Kaye—piano, organ, moog/ Bill Bruford—drums, percussion.
ADDITIONAL MUSICIANS:
Recorders on "Your Move" by Colin Goldring
PRODUCED BY:
Yes & Eddie Offord
ENGINEERED BY:
Eddie Offord
RECORDED AT:
Advision Studios, London during the English Autumn, 1970 (except for "Clap" which was recorded live at The Lyceum, London)
RELEASED:
January 1971 (UK), March 1971 (US)
TRACKS:
Yours Is No Disgrace/Clap/Starship Trooper—a) Life Seeker b) Disillusion c) Wurm/I've Seen All Good People—a) Your Move b) All Good People/A Venture/Perpetual Change

The Yes Album was the third album recorded by Yes and it is generally regarded as being the first of their classic works. It sees the band making major musical progress and heralds the first personnel change with Steve Howe taking over on guitar from Peter Banks. It is significant that most of the songs on *The Yes Album* have consistently been performed on stage by Yes since they were recorded and it is notable that all of the songs were original compositions.

The greatest irony is that the band was generally in dire circumstances just prior to recording the album. Chris Squire said, "Everything around us—management, equipment, money—was in a complete shambles. But the main thing was that we were confident in our music. So we ignored everything else and hoped it would turn out okay. There was a unity in the band like the unity two years before, a unity that dwindled right off was somehow back again."[19] The appointment of new manager Brian Lane no doubt gave Yes some additional confidence when he helped to put the business aspects of the band back on course.

Yes set up camp in a house in the English countryside in Devon for a period of about three months during the summer of 1970 to write and rehearse the material that would become *The Yes Album*. The location provided inspiration and

Jon wrote the lyrics to the superb "Perpetual Change" while he observed the perpetual motion of nature in a nearby valley with an ever changing display of mist and rain. Yes were able to take advantage of the seclusion at Langley Farm and actually set up their equipment outdoors, recording their ideas onto a basic two track tape machine. The experience at Langley Farm resonated so deeply with Steve Howe that he later bought it and still owns it today.

Steve's arrival had a major impact on the music of Yes. Jon Anderson said of the change of guitarist: "…Peter Banks was slightly lazy and difficult to work with…as a band we didn't think that we should have to wait for different people's trips to get together."[20] Jon also remarked: "At the time Chris and I were still the strongest members of the band. But while we were away (in Devon) we suddenly realized that not only had we found someone who could replace Pete in the group but we'd found someone as strong as we were—which was really a surprise."[21] Steve made his mark on *The Yes Album* not only in terms of the overall Yes sound but also with his formidable individual ability as demonstrated by the inclusion of a live version of "Clap", his signature acoustic guitar solo piece.

Eddie Offord graduated from engineer on *Time And A Word* to co-producer for *The Yes Album* and he joined the band at Advision Studios in London for the recording sessions. Jon Anderson commented that Yes had originally wanted Paul McCartney as producer but they'd found as recording progressed that everything worked out more easily than expected with Eddie in the chair and he came up with some very good sounds.

The Yes Album had been a musical awakening that allowed Yes to adventurously race forward into uncharted territory. Steve Howe had initially felt worried that the band might have gone just a little too far in the pursuit of a unique sound when he first heard the album played on a mono record player but it was a concern that soon vanished. Lady Luck smiled on Yes when *The Yes Album* was eventually released. A national postal strike in England meant that the album charts were drawn from a narrower selection of record outlets than usual—predominantly from London where Yes had established a strong following. *The Yes Album* duly went to the number one position in the *Sounds* charts and in turn received even more exposure. The band consequently felt far more satisfied with their efforts after the disappointments of the first two albums.

Reviewer and musician Wayne Thomas wrote: "*The Yes Album* is a an absolute masterpiece in music from one of the finest progressive rock groups in the world today. It's very hard to categorize their music though. You could say they are all parts from all of your favorite groups put together or what the Beatles might be playing if they were all together. No one should miss this one! And just for the record—Yes are my favorite group after this record, no risk!"[22]

The cover for *The Yes Album* was a striking design by Jon Goodchild featuring frames from a roll of color film and the band is pictured in a somewhat surrealistic setting. It is noticeable in the photo that Tony Kaye was sporting a broken leg encased in plaster, an unfortunate result from Yes's vehicle having been involved in a head on traffic accident. Tony reportedly still pressed on with live performances despite the setback but evidently had to be carried on and off stage until he recovered.

Yes toured extensively to promote *The Yes Album* throughout Britain, Europe and importantly for the first time, America. Brian Lane had encountered quite some difficulty in securing the right opportunity for Yes in America but ultimately scored a tour supporting Jethro Tull. Chris Squire said: "We'd never worked with a band as amazingly big (as Jethro Tull) in our lives and for five weeks we were playing to between 15,000 and 20,000 people every day. The really strange thing was that having thought we'd got out there and nobody would know much about us, we were really strong in a few places like Philadelphia. The guy came out on stage and said 'The first band on stage tonight will be this new British band—Yes!' and about half the place went into uproar, because they knew about us from earlier albums and what we'd been doing."[23] It was an auspicious sign of things to come.

"Yours Is No Disgrace" (Anderson/Squire/Howe/Kaye/Bruford)

A staccato introduction immediately grabs the attention as this opening song on *The Yes Album* goes into full flight with a strong instrumental beginning. The galloping rhythm section is superbly complemented by the textures of Tony Kaye's organ and Steve Howe's flying guitar. It is already obvious that there is something special about "Yours Is No Disgrace" by the time the vocals enter. The inventive and sometimes abrupt changes and variations throughout the lengthy nine minute piece are deftly handled and carefully paced before it returns to a concluding full throttle version of the main original theme. The production is noticeably cleaner than on the earlier albums, allowing Yes to most certainly rock while also retaining a pleasing sense of lightness—power achieved by skill rather than heaviness.

Chris Squire said: "'Yours Is No Disgrace' is a song that we all had a part in. Jon had various lyrics and the tune, which we altered a bit when rehearsing it, and Steve had the basis of the guitar solo instrumental piece in the middle which he'd been playing around with a bit. And we all contributed to the arrangement. Tony Kaye was in the band then. He did pretty good on that song."[24]

There is no doubt that the contribution of Steve Howe takes Yes to a higher level. Steve's style has some similarity to that of Peter Banks but he is altogether a more expansive and dynamic player. However, Steve has acknowledged that he was fortunate to take up the reins from a guitarist as accomplished as Peter Banks who had already helped to establish a strong musical direction. The Steve Howe sound is very eclectic and is a distinctive product of a wide range of influences including classical, country, blues, rock, jazz and folk music. Steve said: "I'm fond of the 'Yours Is No Disgrace' solo on the original album, particularly because it was a breakthrough to be able to start working like that, overdubbing guitar parts, mixing parts, constructing a piece of music. I'd been wanting to do it for years but until I joined Yes, I didn't have the facilities. It was a 'studio-ized' solo because it was made up in different sections; I became three guitarists."[25]

The lyrical aspect of *The Yes Album* demonstrated an increasing maturity with Yes suggesting ideas or images that left room for the imagination of the listener rather than attempting to spell out every detail and sometimes words were primarily used for their sound value. "Yours Is No Disgrace" was written around the time of the Vietnam war and to shed some light on its the meaning, Jon Anderson said: "Very simple, people go to war, being in the position of war is not their fault, they have to…I mean…if all six of us are in the jungle with guns we've got to kill or be killed. There's not a disgrace, it's just something you put in an act of God or whatever."[26]

Chris Squire commented: "Essentially the lyrics to 'Yours Is No Disgrace' were Jon's though we changed a few of them about. There's some strange references. One line goes something like 'Lost in losing circumstances that's just where you are'—or something like that. And it's also relevant to the fact that at the time we were writing it, people had to go off to war. Like the ordinary Tommy soldier who was doing his bit, but not really sure why. Hence the title: 'Yours Is No Disgrace'. That's the basis of the lyric, the fact that we're controlled by forces up there—why am I killing this guy anyway?"[27] Chris went on to say that he was sure that people were starting to wake up to such matters but strangely enough more than 30 years later, the words of the song still ring true because the world is still facing very similar situations in times of conflict.

Jon Anderson elaborated: "'Yours Is No Disgrace' appeals to me. Now I really enjoy singing that. It makes sense to me—the possibility of hidden depths of the devil and hidden depths of the soul. The whole balance of the world is in fact between this evil and this good…My idea was a soldier crawling out of the mud, not wanting to be there, and if he was going to be dead tomorrow, why not rape and plunder and kill and fornicate? It's not his disgrace, it's the evil bastards who put him there."[28]

It is worth taking the time to listen intently to "Yours Is No Disgrace" to appreciate the attention to detail in what was a very strong and cohesive performance from Yes. The song is a rich mixture of musical ideas from three-part vocal harmonies to contrasting instrumentation, all emanating from the input of the different members of the band that the group as a whole worked upon and altered in the process of creating a very distinctive symphonic rock sound.

"I've Seen All Good People" (Anderson/Squire)

"I've Seen All Good People" is one of the most famous and easily accessible Yes songs. It actually consists of two songs linked together, the first part being "Your Move" which has received substantial radio airplay as a single over the years and the second part "All Good People" which is a dose of good time Yes rock music. The release of the "Your Move" single undoubtedly helped to attract many new Yes fans throughout the world.

"Your Move" has very unique sound with an opening burst of acapella vocals, distinctive acoustic guitar, a "bump" beat and a climax featuring dramatic church-like organ. Steve Howe was originally credited with playing a vachalia on the song but he discovered years later that the unusual lute-like instrument was properly termed a Portuguese 12 string guitar, his sister having obtained it during a holiday in Spain in the early 1960s. Steve commented: "*The Yes Album* is the first album where I got the chance to fulfill some of my guitar dreams of recording in a band where you could virtually do anything you want. The way that we did 'I've Seen All Good People' was the first time we'd experimented with not playing together but setting up a track so we all could individually add ideas to it and build up the arrangement in that way, as opposed to sitting together and playing"[29]

Although Jon Anderson doesn't write all of the lyrics for Yes, he writes the lion's share and his growing spirituality was reflected in "Your Move" by using the symbolism of a game of chess. Jon said: "It's just drawing parallels to the fact that there is a God."[30] "Your Move" exemplifies Jon's lyrical style of leaving the possibilities open for interpretation and Chris Squire commented: "'Your Move' is one of those multi-meaning songs. People can very easily refer to it as a game of chess but it isn't really that. In fact, we were in America playing at Staten Island—there's a lyric in the song which makes a reference to the queen—and this guy came up and said 'I've got to meet Jon Anderson. I'm the queen!' He said he knew exactly what Jon meant by the lyrics. That song really is one to interpret how one wishes."[31]

In "Your Move" the influence of the Beatles once again comes to the fore with the titles of two famous songs written by John Lennon being woven into the lyrics. There is a reference to "Instant Karma" in the line "*send an instant karma to me*" while "Give Peace A Chance" is mentioned in the underlying vocal line "*all we are saying is give peace a chance*". Alan White played the drums for John Lennon on the original recordings of both of those songs and under the circumstances, it couldn't have been more appropriate that he would later join Yes.

"All Good People" is an infectious song built around a bass riff written by Chris Squire. It's a showcase for his trademark Rickenbacker bass sound while Steve Howe's guitar solo on his prized Gibson ES175D is equally integral to the song. "All Good People" is as close as Yes gets to good time rock 'n' roll but it still has the unique trademarks of the band and the lyrics are essentially used for their sonic value. In the early seventies Chris Squire said: "'I've Seen All Good People' is just a nice lyric to sing over the particular chords that I had together there. It's not really much of a song; just a repeating riff that had a bit of a guitar solo. Some easy rock 'n' roll if you like."[32] Chris's description of "All Good People" is very low key, especially given that "I've Seen All Good People" suite is now regarded as a true rock classic.

"Starship Trooper" (Anderson/Squire/Howe)

"Starship Trooper" is an outstanding example of how Yes creates a song by combining the different musical ideas of the members of the band. The basic elements are a song by Jon Anderson ("Life Seeker"), a middle section by Chris Squire ("Disillusion") and a conclusion by Steve Howe ("Wurm"). An early version of "Disillusion" had been performed by Yes as part of a song called "For Everyone" and it surfaced on the "Something's Coming" album of Yes BBC recordings. Similarly, the riff for "Wurm" originally appeared in a song called "Nether Street" by Steve Howe's former band Bodast (see the "Mothballs" CD by Steve Howe).

Steve Howe commented that "Starship Trooper" had been a challenge to record because the arrangement was different to how it was originally conceived and it was never played in quite the same way on stage. Steve said: "We realized that it was quite good fun to have a song that we radically changed in the studio, either because we had hardly played it or we didn't know what do with it so we just arranged it there and then, much like 'Your Move'—we developed a way of recording which had nothing to do with being onstage. 'Starship Trooper' benefited from the same techniques—all the climbing and building business in the 'Wurm' section worked pretty well. But then again, Yes was a pretty good studio band!"[33]

"Starship Trooper" became a concert favorite for Yes fans, especially with its splintering instrumental finale titled "Wurm" which was the German name for the Ice Age. Chris Squire described "Starship Trooper" as a "tour de force" with a "very majestic long ending with great guitar from Steve and typical Yes arrangement."[34]

Jon Anderson developed the lyrical content of "Starship Trooper" after reading Robert Heinlein's book "Starship Troopers", a classic science fiction tale of politics and war. He felt that it was a strong song title and he envisaged the Starship Trooper as "finding the self and the soul and the light within".[35] Jon said: "There is a messenger within you that is always inter-reacting with the life form. There's that point in you within yourself that knows you. We call it God."[36]

◆ ◆ ◆

"The Yes Album" is certainly a classic record but Yes were in such a rapid state of development at the time that their subsequent live performances of the same material have frequently exceeded the studio originals. Live versions of songs from *The Yes Album* are included on the *Yessongs* album and can also be found on most of the band's subsequent live releases. Other recommended listening on *The Yes Album* is the excellent "Perpetual Change", while also worthy of mention is the often overlooked short track "A Venture" which tantalizingly fades out just as it seems to be reaching its peak.

FRAGILE

YES:
Jon Anderson—vocals/Chris Squire—bass guitars, vocals/Steve Howe—electric and acoustic guitars, vocals/Rick Wakeman—organ, grand piano, electric piano, harpsichord, mellotron, synthesizer/Bill Bruford—drums, percussion
PRODUCED BY:
Yes and Eddie Offord
ENGINEERED BY:
Eddie Offord, assisted by Gary Martin
RECORDED AT: Advision Studios, London in September 1971
RELEASED:
November 1971 (UK), January 1972 (US)
TRACKS:
Roundabout/Cans and Brahms/We Have Heaven/South Side Of The Sky/Five Percent For Nothing/Long Distance Runaround/The Fish (Schindleria Praematurus)/Mood For A Day/Heart Of The Sunrise

The *Fragile* album put Yes on the path to major commercial success with a high placing in the American charts and elsewhere around the world. *Fragile* was a large musical leap forward for Yes and Steve Howe commented that it was the time "when our creativity got so high."[37] The album marked the first involvement of Rick Wakeman on keyboards and of the artist Roger Dean, both of whom would make major contributions to Yes.

Chris Squire revealed that the title *Fragile* was itself a statement on the stability of a rock'n'roll band, the name having been suggested by Bill Bruford and it was no doubt inspired by the departure of former Yes members Tony Kaye and Peter Banks. Chris said: "We realized how fragile a band can be and we looked at the situation honestly. That's maybe why we're still together. The thing about a band is that every member has to think about the other four. The things one comes up against in this business, especially touring, are just outrageous."[38]

Roger Dean's vivid portrayal of a miniature world breaking up on the back cover of *Fragile* was certainly a different interpretation of the concept of fragility. The original idea of Yes was to have a piece of broken porcelain. There was a positive note in Roger's interpretation given that the intriguing spaceship in the cover painting appeared to be there to save the inhabitants and to take them to a new homeworld. Roger's artwork exhibited a stunning affinity with Yes's pictorial music and it seemed to depict another reality that was strange and yet somehow familiar. Aside from the considerable artistic merit, it was an eye-catching cover that was a most impressive visual marketing tool, especially when seen in the large format of the old twelve inch vinyl records.

Rick Wakeman felt some initial trepidation about joining Yes after he discovered with The Strawbs that life on the road in a rock band is "not always a bed of roses". Rick said: "Brian Lane phoned me up, I'd known Brian for ages...He said 'Here, I want you to come to my office, I want to talk to you'. I was very impressed because his office was very flash, very organized...And he just outlined what he wanted Yes to be. He said Yes are musically capable of being this and its my job to make sure they do. It's going to take time and I think you should be part of it...He said go along and have a listen to the band, a rehearsal with them. So what I decided to do was go along for like ten minutes, have a little play and then say 'I'll give you a ring'...I went down there at 11 o'clock in the morning and I left about nine at night! And during that period of time we wrote 'Roundabout'...When you get involved in the music you don't ask questions...I was saying I'd like to do this here—if you play that there and I do this here, then we can make this bit more interesting."[39]

As far as Jon Anderson was concerned, the arrival of Rick substantially enhanced the musical possibilities. Jon said: "When Rick joined it kind of opened up this slight barrier that we felt we had where we couldn't start doing heavy trips on record unless we could do it on stage. Bringing in Rick really helped us on and it has widened the color and scope of the music..."[40] Rick brought with him a tremendous armory of keyboard sounds with instruments such as the Minimoog, mellotron, organ, harpsichord and the acoustic and electric piano. By contrast, former keyboardist Tony Kaye had been reluctant to embrace the latest keyboard technology. Tony said: "In fact, one of the problems I had with the band then was that I did oppose the idea of using the new stuff that was coming out. I didn't like the mellotron and I didn't like the moog synthesizer...Maybe I was little afraid of it. Maybe the natural sounds of the acoustic piano and Hammond organ were what I wanted."[41]

Rick perceived Yes as going a step beyond the "heavy rock" of groups like Cream and The Who into "orchestral rock" which was more complex and cultivated but still with a similar level of raw excitement. It was music that was carefully planned but also allowed plenty of scope for the musicians to express their feelings. He witnessed the members of Yes working eighteen hour days in preparing and recording the music with each musician seeking to expand their role beyond the norm while demonstrating an ability to play material that seemed "frighteningly impossible".[42] It was a fertile creative environment for Rick to enter and he saw Yes as working in a classical manner to extract the most out of their ideas in "making the full use of melody by doing key changes, by doing rhythm changes, by changing the notes and the chordal structures underneath".[43]

As noted by Peter Clark in the *History of Rock*, the arrival of Rick Wakeman completed what many fans considered to be the definitive Yes lineup, combining "the mystic vision of Jon Anderson with an instrumental virtuosity capable of realizing it".[44] The exceptional talent of this lineup was such that the eclectic approach that began to flower on *Time And A Word* was developed to the point on *Fragile* where it became a seamless blend of diverse but perfectly compatible musical ideas. The music being made by Yes embraced all of the rich influences of the band members including rock, jazz, classical, country and whatever else seemed to fit.

The classical flavorings evident in pieces like "Roundabout", "Southside Of The Sky" and "Heart Of The Sunrise" were so well integrated that they sounded completely natural to the music. Amongst Jon Anderson's primary musical influences at the time were the classical composers Jean Sibelius and Igor Stravinsky who he regarded as the "kings of twentieth century music".[45] Sibelius provided Jon with the encouragement to have an orchestral feel with no obvious structure and subtle melody while Stravinsky inspired adventurous structure and strong melody. Both ends of the spectrum were evident in "Heart Of The Sunrise" and it is a prime example of where the influences of each composer came into play.

The format of *Fragile* was ground breaking in that it included a solo track by each of the five band members as well as songs featuring the entire band. This had essentially originated from the tight time schedule of about one month that Yes had to record the album and it was going to be easier to complete the record by adding the solo tracks. Of course, it also had the effect of highlighting the contributions of the different individuals to the group sound and some of the solo works are discussed later in this chapter in Classic Yes Solos. One thing to keep in mind with the writing credits for Yes songs is that they sometimes reflect who wrote the lyrics more than the music because the members of the band have sometimes made significant contributions to the music without necessarily being credited.

Consideration had been given at one stage to making *Fragile* a double album and for it to include an additional extended piece of music as the title track, along with some live recordings. Chris Squire had vague recollections that he did "write a piece of music called 'Fragile'" but it never made it onto the album and it was evidently never recorded.[46] A further interesting snippet is that the band's original title for "Long Distance Runaround" was "Corporal Salt" because it reminded them of a song on the Beatles album *Sergeant Pepper*.

As was the case with *The Yes Album*, the recording sessions for *Fragile* took place at Advision Studios in London with Eddie Offord taking on the dual role of engineer and co-producer. Eddie's ability was fast becoming very much appreciated by Yes and Chris Squire acknowledged learning more from him about recording studios than from anybody else. Chris explained that "a lot of unspoken things" worked because Eddie intuitively understood what Yes was trying to achieve.[47]

Yes toured extensively to promote *Fragile*, particularly in America, and live performances recorded on that tour of some material from the album ultimately appeared on the *Yessongs* live set. While many of the songs on *Fragile* became concert standards for Yes, the fan favorite "Southside Of The Sky" was very seldom played live, and never in its complete form, until the Yes *2002* tour of America when it received rapturous applause. "We Have Heaven" with its multi-tracked vocals was also never played live until that same tour, probably for the same reason that the band until then had not been happy with the live sound and there is no doubt that modern technology assisted Yes in perfecting both songs for performance on stage. Rick Wakeman commented that the latest technology enabled Yes in 2002 to perform songs such as "Awaken", "Close To The Edge" and "Southside Of The Sky" "better than we ever could have done when we first recorded them" although he cautioned that "the secret is actually to use the technology, not let the technology use you."[48]

In the *Fragile* era Rick gave some insight into what it was like to work with Yes: "It's not been an easy band to just slide into because we don't really mix socially—which is good really because I don't think music and social life mix very well. I mean we all argue after gigs anyway. The first time I met them I couldn't believe a group could argue so much. I thought we were about to split up...But then I found they just argue, everyone tells everyone else when they think they've played badly on a gig. They're all total individuals."[49] Fortunately there was no evidence on stage of any lack of harmony as Yes went on its way to becoming a star attraction with a reputation for hot live performances.

Rick summed up *Fragile* by saying: "Magic, a fantastic album. I've always said that. It really is a great album...it has all the ingredients...I was allowed the freedom to use quite a few keyboards. It was quite incredible because I could suddenly do all the things that were bottling up inside for years. When those sorts of things happen and they come out, it's very fresh."[50]

"Roundabout" (Anderson/Howe)

"Roundabout" is one of the all time great rock songs and if Yes has a signature song, this would have to be it. It is not only a song with immediate appeal but also contains many inventive ideas.

Jon Anderson and Steve Howe composed much of "Roundabout" while on tour with Yes in Scotland. The roundabout in the song was in fact a traffic roundabout encountered on that journey. Jon explained that they were driving in van from Aberdeen to Glasgow through a winding valley on a road with steep sides rising to the mountains. The low cloud cover gave the impression that the "mountains came out of the sky, they stood there". And then they drove past a large lake, "in and around the lake", with the knowledge that within twenty-four hours they would be home again to see their loved ones.[51] The lyrics of "Roundabout" lead the listener to consider several interpretations and yet the real explanation is very simple. The lyrics actually appear in the song as:

In and around the lake
Mountains come out of the sky and they stand there
One mile over we'll be there and we'll see you
Ten true summers we'll be there and laughing too
Twenty four before my love and you'll see I'll be there with you

—(brief extract from "Roundabout", written by Jon Anderson and Steve Howe; published by Cotillion, BMI)

"Roundabout" has many highlights and starts dramatically with a piano note that is played backwards, courtesy of manipulation in the studio. This is followed by a distinctive, classical-sounding acoustic guitar introduction before the driving rhythm section enters. It is notable that the acoustic guitar is kept fairly continuous throughout the song without sacrificing the rocking feel and it is interspersed with electric guitar. The organ and electric guitar solos towards the end burn with intensity and the massed vocal harmonies over the acoustic guitar provide a completely satisfying conclusion.

The bass guitar work on "Roundabout" illustrates the extent of the creative effort that Yes put into the recording. Chris Squire explained that he actually used two bass guitars for the track, his favorite Rickenbacker 4001 electric bass and a "very mellow old Gibson acoustic" that was miked and "ghosting the part an octave higher".[52]

To the surprise of the band, an edited single version of "Roundabout" was released and it proved to be very successful in giving Yes wide exposure. Strangely enough, the editing had never been discussed with Yes and Jon Anderson commented that while "it really worked and gave us a larger audience", it was also unsettling because "we didn't hear it until it came out and it really unnerved us to think that someone could wield those (editing) scissors".[53] It is interesting that Yes in recent years has played a shortened version of "Roundabout" with the middle section omitted as an encore in live performances. The band has also recorded a rearranged and shortened acoustic "blues-shuffle" version of "Roundabout" as a bonus track for the 2004 American release of *The Ultimate Yes* compilation album.

Yes immediately realized that "Roundabout" was one of their best songs and Steve Howe felt that they'd made one of the great rock epics while Jon Anderson said: "Whenever I hear "Roundabout" on the radio, I realize what a great recording it is. It's amazing to me!"[54]

"Heart Of The Sunrise" (Anderson/Squire/Bruford)

"Heart Of The Sunrise" is a quintessential piece of Yes music some ten minutes long and Chris Squire describes it as "pretty much a microcosm of Yes's talent" that is "almost a little symphonic". The characteristics that Chris highlights are "the fast, tricky, punchy beginning", the following "nice mellow song that allows Jon to stretch out" and the "moments where little odd things happen".[55]

Steve Howe described "Heart Of The Sunrise" as "a really powerful track and like many Yes arrangements it's strangely individual—we start with a big thing, drop down, build up then there's a song. It's clever how Rick's influence showed a lot on that album with what we called the "Rick-recapitulation" bit where we would go back and play fragments of previous segments interspersed with Rick's piano."[56] Rick Wakeman similarly considers "Heart Of The Sunrise" to be "one of the finest things Yes has ever produced or will ever produce."[57]

In relation to the meaning of "Heart Of The Sunrise", Jon Anderson said: "Whenever I sing it I always think about the people who are lonely in the cities, the people who are lost in big cities and they can't make cities work for them. There are millions of them."[58] Jon also commented: "When I work on music, I get a strange feeling at a certain point in time…I nearly always try to explain that before 'Heart of the Sunrise' because 'Heart Of The Sunrise' is that feeling I get…it's impossible to explain…but I get that feeling inside of completeness when we finish a piece of music and it rings true to my Chakra energy, my consciousness. That feeling I get is that Relayer system, that Christ system and it's something that you can't put your finger on."[59] When introducing "Heart Of The Sunrise" on stage during the Masterworks Tour in 2000, Jon said: "I used to feel this pretty strange energy around the studio. I wasn't quite sure what it meant but it was very sort of sharp and distant at the same time."

The lyrics to the powerful conclusion of "Heart Of The Sunrise" paint a vivid picture and I note that the words as actually performed for the studio recording differ slightly from those printed on the original album sleeve. The lyrics as performed are shown below with "wind" having replaced "sun" in the fourth last line:

Love comes to you then after
Dream on, on to the Heart of the Sunrise
SHARP—DISTANCE
How can the wind with its arms all around me
SHARP—DISTANCE
How can the wind with so many around me
I feel lost in the city

—(brief extract from "Heart Of The Sunrise", written by Jon Anderson/ Chris Squire/Bill Bruford; published by Cotillion, BMI)

In interpreting "Heart Of The Sunrise" and many other Yes songs, it is helpful to understand some of the symbolism involved. Generations of writers have used symbolism to add mystique or to sometimes obscure the true meaning of work so that it is less likely to be the target of criticism. Potentially controversial topics such as politics and religion have often been dealt with via symbolism. Of course, the relatively sophisticated lyrical approach of Yes with its frequent use of symbolism flies in the face of the more simplistic messages typically found in rock music, thereby confounding some critics who are more accustomed to finding an instant meaning. And to further complicate the situation, the lyrics of Yes sometimes reflect the use of words more for their sonic value than their literal meaning.

It soon becomes apparent after hearing several Yes songs that certain key words are consistently encountered and that there are many examples of symbolism in the music of Yes. The book by Thomas Mosbo *Yes But What Does It Mean* (Wyndstar 1994) provides a very useful insight into the symbolism used by Yes and in particular that used by Jon Anderson. Two of the most significant examples are that "sun" is used as a metaphor for God and "river" is used to symbolize life. As Mosbo points out, the resulting ambiguity in the lyrics doesn't indicate that there is no comprehensible meaning but rather it is one of the great strengths in Yes music to leave it open to the possibility of fresh interpretation.

Symbolism is one of the means by which Yes explores lyrical concepts not commonly visited in rock music in tandem with the pursuit of musical adventure. Jon Anderson is aware that lyrics can be a sensitive area but he's never flinched from delving into the spiritual aspects of life which is perhaps controversial to some people but nevertheless central to human existence and consistently paramount in Yes music. The subtlety of using symbolism can be seen to enhance the overall artistic value of Yes music.

It is fair to say that rock music was initially regarded as being of no serious or lasting value. Even though rock music has now been in existence for some fifty years and has already endured for much longer than most people may have at first imagined, it is still not necessarily regarded as generally being a serious form of music. It is consequently all the more significant that the music of Yes should emerge from the genre of rock music and be capable of being seriously appreciated on several different levels.

There is typically a profound, universal and positive message in the music of Yes but the point isn't thrust upon the listener and different interpretations are most certainly possible depending on one's imagination. It isn't even necessary to understand the lyrical message to appreciate Yes music because the music is more than strong enough to stand on it's own merits. For example, one might buy a Yes album such as *Fragile* just to hear Steve Howe play guitar or to hear Chris Squire play bass. These different levels of appreciation are important planks in the artistic success of Yes.

◆ ◆ ◆

Fragile was a major musical statement by Yes and it remains one of the greatest rock albums ever recorded. From the immediate appeal of "Roundabout" to the intricacies of "Heart Of the Sunrise", it is bursting with interest from the lyrics through the instrumentation, the subtleties, themes and variations. The album has a bright and energetic sound that is classy but also rocks and it deservedly captured an enormous worldwide audience. *Fragile* has now been released in the new DVD-Audio format that provides a high quality surround sound mix and includes the song "America" as a bonus track.

The chilling wind sound effects at the beginning of "Southside Of The Sky" bring to mind a memorable performance of that song at a Yes gig I attended in

Sante Fe, New Mexico in 2002 at the Paolo Soleri Amphitheatre. The wind sound effects of the song were stunningly brought to life when nature turned on its own show with a real storm that lashed the open air venue to provide an unforgettable way to experience a song about a group of mountain climbers who died in the cold on a windswept mountain but still found the warmth of heaven.

CLOSE TO THE EDGE

YES:
Jon Anderson—vocals/Chris Squire—bass, vocals/Steve Howe—guitars, vocals/Rick Wakeman—keyboards/Bill Bruford—percussion
PRODUCED BY:
Yes and Eddie Offord
ENGINEERED BY:
Eddie Offord, tapes by Mike Dunne
RECORDED AT:
Advision Studios, London during 1972
RELEASED:
September 1972
TRACKS:
Close To the Edge—a) The Solid Time Of Change b) Total Mass Retain c) I Get Up I Get Down d) Seasons Of Man/And You And I—a) Cord Of Life b) Eclipse c) The Preacher The Teacher d) Apocalypse/Siberian Khatru

Close To the Edge is arguably the finest album that Yes has ever made. It consists of only three pieces of music including the majestic title track weighing in at almost nineteen minutes and the entire album has an extremely rare magical intensity from the first note until the last. *Close To The Edge* was recorded at Advision Studios in London and cost 25,000 English pounds sterling to produce.

Rick Wakeman commented on preparations for the album: "We allowed four weeks for getting it all together, four weeks in the studios, two weeks for mixing and two for rehearsing. As for the material, Jon had all the ideas in his head and when we were in America, Steve and Chris used to plonk away and did quite a bit of work towards the compositions. Obviously Bill and I are at a disadvantage when it comes to rehearsing in hotels, so it couldn't really come together until we all got into a rehearsal room—but then it came together very quickly."[60] Chris Squire elaborated on the creative process: "It's a case of recording an album and then assessing it afterwards. We have very loose ideas at the beginning, mainly songs written by Jon, then we commence to put it through the machine. On this album some of the pieces of music have been spontaneous and we've decided to keep some of these, while others we've worked out as we usually do."[61]

Steve Howe explained how Yes developed the material from what was created in the rehearsal room into the final product: "We usually get in and work out exactly how we're going to go about doing the idea that we have mediocrely performed in the rehearsal studio. So most of the arrangements are done. We might expand things a little, you know, just open an idea up a bit more, because there's a great deal we learn about our music when we're actually playing it. We tighten it all up and tidy it up a lot."[62]

Reviewer Mike Channell said: "Yes has gone further into the realms of their music than any but their closest followers would have imagined. Their latest LP, *Close To The Edge,* is so musically complex it's hard to take the lot at the one sitting. But as you dig deeper and deeper into the brilliance of Yes, it becomes easier to understand and more obviously incredible…This LP is a raver. All tracks or rather both sides are brilliant. The complexity is at first a little startling but wait until you really get into it. Yes has taken itself into something completely new and incredibly exciting. A MUST!"[63]

Some other critics found the highly polished complexity of Yes a little too hard to take and a review by Ian McDonald stated: "They are not just close to the edge, they've gone right over it."[64] However, the reaction of the fans was the most encouraging aspect and the vast majority viewed the performance of Yes on this album to be outstanding, an opinion that only seems to have grown over the passage of time.

Rick Wakeman touched on the key to fully appreciating Yes music and the *Close To The Edge* album in particular—to listen to it several times. Rick said: "It takes a hell of a lot of to understand this album fully. In fact, it took me a long time to understand! I played it to some friends who really like the band and they listened carefully and gave constructive criticisms. After I played 'Close To The Edge' they asked me to play it again and again—about four times—because they couldn't take it all in one go. Basically the songs are simple and the arrangements are complex. I like Jon's lyrics, they do make you think and derive your own meaning from them."[65]

The outstanding cover created by Roger Dean for *Close To The Edge* was extraordinarily well suited to Yes's music. Roger's inspiration for the painting inside the gatefold cover of a mountain lake with a seemingly infinite capacity to feed a massive waterfall came from the lakes and waterfalls of the Scottish Highlands as well as the Angel Falls in Venezuela. In fact much of the work Roger has done for Yes over the years has been based around landscapes containing elements based on real places but rendered in a visionary manner that hints at science fiction and fantasy. It was also in this period that Roger designed the famous Yes "bubble" logo that first appeared on the cover of *Close To The Edge* and the band has continued to use it on and off to the present day.

The high regard that Yes had for producer Eddie Offord was evident in that his photo appeared on the back cover of the album in a way that suggested he was virtually a sixth member of the band. The spacious, widescreen, layered sound that Eddie achieved for Yes on *Close To The Edge* was certainly state of the art for the era.

Steve Howe summed up by saying: "*Close To The Edge* was very good for us. We were strong when we made the album. A group gets tested every time they bring out an album and I think we came up with the goods on *Edge*."[66] However, it took everyone by surprise when Bill Bruford decided to leave Yes as soon as the album was completed. Bill had become disenchanted with the amount of time it had taken to record *Close To The Edge* and he opted for a "musical cold shower" by joining King Crimson. He saw Yes as "a white kind of A major, diatonic, sunny kind of vocal group" compared to King Crimson which he characterized as a "nasty, minor key, playing group".[67]

"Close To The Edge" (Anderson/Howe)

On the preparation for the title track, Jon Anderson said: "We planned to do 'Close To The Edge'. We got together over a period of six months and worked out that we wanted to do this long piece of music. By the time we got into the studio we had a few ideas on hand but we didn't have the whole concept in our heads…but we had a rough idea of where we were going to."[68]

Herman Hesse's book *Siddartha* was the inspiration for "Close To The Edge". Jon Anderson said: "The song 'Close To The Edge' comes from reading Herman Hesse's *Siddhartha…Little Buddha* just go and see the movie, there was an old movie *Siddhartha* before but now its that handsome dude Keanu Reeves, he plays Siddhartha in the movie (*Little Buddha*). The idea was the search for self-realization…close to the edge of self-realization, I should have called it that, it would have made life a lot easier (laughs)…it's always delicate to talk about religious things…Most people are very spiritual anyway…they just keep forgetting it or they don't want to show it for fear of being put down."[69] The movie *Little Buddha* encapsulates the story of Prince Siddartha's search for enlightenment and not only brings into the focus the lyrical content of "Close To The Edge" but also acts as a pointer to the deeper meaning behind some other important Yes songs.

Jon also revealed: "A lot of the lines in 'Close To The Edge' are related to dreams or factual thoughts that I've had about the actual journey of life apart from reality. There is another journey if you're willing to accept it and be ready to enjoy it. So it obviously reflects things that I'm going into because I write most of the lyrics anyway and I sing them."[70] "Close To The Edge" is a prime example of Jon Anderson's approach to writing lyrics and several critics have referred to it as a "stream of consciousness". Jon said: "I just let go of trying to figure out how to write...I just wrote. So when I write, generally...lyrics...I just put them down, it just kind of flies in there, and there it is..."[71] As Jon explained to me recently, the different levels of meaning that can be found in the lyrics were amazingly not consciously implanted but instead came out of this process of spontaneous writing.

Steve Howe confirmed that the lyrics revealed something of the personal experiences of the band and Jon "found that he could write much more. He was writing wordy things because his life was not necessarily settled, it had a direction he was going in, as we all were. We stopped eating meat most of us, and we went vegetarian and started liking organic things and not eating chemicals or anything. I think it's coming out in our music".[72]

Although "Close to The Edge" ultimately has the most positive of messages, the lyrical maturity of Yes is evident in that it is acknowledged that darker times and experiences are all part of the journey of life. Of the "Total Mass Retain" section, Jon said: "It's got this deep, sad feeling for the mass rape of our planet, for the evilness that creates the wars, and there's no answer to these all these things. It's common sense in knowing what's right and what's wrong."[73] And of the "I Get Up I Get Down" section he said: "On 'Close' there are certain things that signify the answer is God—not through religion we've all been brought up on but a mass religion. I can see the possibility of bringing people together in the next ten or twenty years but the fact is at the moment there is the great hypocrisy of people doing battle to show their beliefs—it's ridiculous. In the middle of 'Close' about the two hundred women, there are parallels to Ireland—a woman seeing her child killed will obviously want to fight back. Religion is a weird concept now. Miracles aren't miracles today. Man being put on the moon is a miracle but nobody sees the miracle of life, of a simple hand. People go to church because that's the way their lives have been developed, so I'd never knock that. I do knock their lack of appreciation for other people's churches. That's why at the end of that track the cathedral organ goes crazy—religion as it stands is destroyed and there is hope for real understanding."[74] It is difficult to imagine a more incisive statement about the human condition and it still remains starkly relevant more than thirty years later.

Steve Howe played a major role in writing "Close To the Edge" and he commented: "By the time of 'Close To The Edge' we had a good idea of what the group was about and this was one of our most cohesively recorded albums. We came across all the ingredients we needed in America. There's this fiery guitar riff and the slow bit which I had written as a sort of chorus. Jon had written those wild verses and we just kept inventing. Rick's solo on the organ was actually a guitar part which sounded better on the organ—I was getting quite used to the idea of writing music which someone else played. This was the beginning of the Anderson/Howe song writing team which began with 'Roundabout' and had something really special and unique."[75]

On the Steve Howe Interactive CD-ROM, Steve explained the musical framework of "Close To The Edge": "Chris Squire always used to say that you had to have a good structure to have good improvisation. And when we constructed 'Close To The Edge', we used the idea of having improvisation at the very first onset of the song but it was leading to a theme that would prevail within the song itself. So 'Close To The Edge' took the form of improvisation and then a thematic approach. And that tune, which Rick plays in full chords later, seems to carry much of the essence of what 'Close To The Edge' was really all about."[76]

The spirit of invention and innovation pervaded "Close To The Edge" as Yes went about collectively finding the solutions to creating such an epic piece of music. The sound effects at the beginning and end of "Close To the Edge" proved to be one of the technical challenges to be overcome and Rick Wakeman estimated the loop tape running around the studio to be an enormous forty feet long. It was the kind of effect that in the present day would be readily achievable with high tech modern keyboards but in 1972 it was a substantial problem that required a brainstorming session and two days to solve.

The complete work gradually came together with numerous edits to the recording as the many inspired ideas were brought to fruition and added to the musical pot. The contributions of all five members of the band from the drums and bass through to the guitar, keyboards and vocals were superlative throughout. The strong themes ultimately culminated in an extremely powerful and uplifting finale with the band in full instrumental flight and the vocals soaring high above before melting into the fading bird-like sound effects. The key lyrics at the conclusion of "Close To The Edge" are:

Close to the edge, down by the river
Down at the end, round by the corner
Now that it's all over and done
Called to the seed, right to the sun
Now that you find, now that you're whole
Seasons will pass you by

I get up
I get down (repeated twice)

—(brief extract from "Close To The Edge", written by Jon Anderson and Steve Howe; published by Yessongs Ltd, ASCAP)

An interpretation of the conclusion is that the ups and downs of life, in other words the experiences of life, teach us about ourselves and in knowing ourselves we know God. This realization makes our souls immortal, so in the end there is no end—seasons will pass us by. The best advice in interpreting the meaning of Yes songs comes directly from Jon Anderson: "Remember it is all metaphors. When I wrote 'A seasoned witch could call you from the depths of your disgrace' (as the opening line) in 'Close To The Edge', the 'seasoned witch' was in fact our spiritual selves that is always capable of lifting us above whatever form of disgrace we might find ourselves in.'"

When talking generally about the music of Yes, Chris Squire commented that "the same message really applies to all of our music—I think it's a message of hope."[77]

"And You And I" (Anderson/Bruford/Howe/Squire)

"And You And I" is another classic Yes song. It starts deceptively with a quiet acoustic introduction using harmonics on the guitar before building to a soaring orchestral peak, dropping down again and then building to a dramatic orchestral conclusion rounded off delicately at the very end.

Rick Wakeman explained the process of writing "And You And I": "The theme is actually Bill's (Bruford) and Chris's (Squire). Bill had a theme which he played about with for three tours previously on the piano. It's quite funny how most drummers seem to be able to play the piano quite well…I mean, Alan (White) can play the piano quite well. Bill had this theme which he used to play and we rehearsed it in Una Billing's Dance School…The theme was quite strong but it needed a counter theme and Chris came up with a counter theme which went against it over the top—we worked on that for a long time. And it was a song that I think Jon had for quite a long time."[78] Rick also commented: "We tried to carry on the thing we did in *Fragile* which was lots of nice melodies. I mean you can have nice complicated structures but you can't have them without nice melodies. 'And You And I' was most probably one of the nicest melodic things that was ever done. It's a lovely track…I remember putting that together and thinking 'It's a magic song!' It just started really with a little simple chord sequence and a pulse on the bass."[79]

Steve Howe shed some light on how he approached "And You And I" from a guitar point of view: "When Yes were recording 'And You And I' it gave us an opportunity to use a lot of orchestral sounds but also get the twelve string guitar into play. It allowed me to really set the band up in a very restful almost sort of New Age way I suppose which is when you don't play very much and you leave a lot of spaces between it, it makes you sound real big in a way. I learnt a lot from doing the steel guitar, acoustic guitar as well as electric guitar on this particular number. Only in the middle do I get back to the regular six string guitar."[80]

As Jon Anderson explained, the structure of "And You And I" was difficult to finalize: "I think the hardest part (on the album) was on 'And You And I' because it had two speed trips going on. We had to put them together and that took the longest sorting out, we didn't know if we were just going to leave it as a two section piece or link it together. We finished up linking it together and it did work"[81]

Jon also spoke of the inspiration for "And You And I": "Just simply that political situations are getting exploited...too many politicians and not enough statesmen...it's all for the wrong things, the wrong ethics of life. It's nothing to do with the general people, it's to do with these people rising for power to be on par with other people, to keep up with the Joneses...to be as rich as and as important as...instead of thinking, well I'm in a situation where I can help and do things for people. I mean, we make our music for people. We also aim to be in love with it, which is a good thing and I think if politicians became in love with their gig, which is to organize and help the masses, then...you know, there's no love in politics. There's incredible developments happening in the world—I mean, science is marching on and slightly disregarding man, you know just charging away. If you get right down to the nitty gritty of life and what life is about, it's an incredible thing, it's a very magical thing. It has a purpose and that is to defeat evil...as evil be, you know. It's a challenge to learn, to know what God is, that's all—very, very simple."[82]

"And You And I" was another Yes song with influences from the writing of Herman Hesse based around the idea of self-realization. Both the preacher and the teacher in the lyrics are seeking the same inner spiritual truth but just as in "Close To The Edge", the suggestion is that traditional religions can unfortunately be divisive instead of bringing all people together in the universal light of God. When introducing "And You And I" on stage in Sydney, Australia in 1973,

Jon Anderson said: "It's a song about a dream, a dream of political science…about a lot of things to live by to create a better future for our children."

"Siberian Khatru" (Anderson/Howe/Wakeman)

"Siberian Khatru" closes the album and it's an opportunity for Yes to cut loose with some intense and dynamic instrumentation rather than to convey any particular lyrical meaning. The fast opening pace has Bill Bruford's snare drum driving along with Chris Squire's prominent bass while Rick Wakeman's work on Minimoog, mellotron, harpsichord and the rest of his keyboard armory is superb as the piece develops. Bill had become famous for his distinctive snare drum sound and it came out of the need for the drums to cut cleanly through the sound of the band to be properly heard. Bill developed a technique where he extracted the higher frequencies by using an open tuning and striking the snare drum towards the rim to achieve an ultra crisp sound.

Siberian Khatru became a favorite of the band to open their shows and it permitted Steve Howe to step out with some hot guitar solos. Steve explained that it was an innovative track for him as a guitarist because it was "the first time I started mixing steel guitar with regular guitar: steel solo, guitar solo, steel, guitar, et cetera."[83] Steve felt that "Siberian Khatru" was "ingenious" with its "three part harmony and big riff going on".[84]

As to the lyrics, Jon Anderson said: "'Khatru' is a word I made up in the studio and later I found out it meant 'as you wish'. I relate the track to that and you can take it exactly as you want."[85] The song is essentially a collection of vivid words and phrases that are used for both their sonic value and to suggest snippets of meaning, often in rapid-fire succession. In some respects, Siberian Khatru is a progression from a song like "I Am The Walrus" by the Beatles in its rich use of imagery. Yes sparks the imagination with lyrics such as *"Sing, bird of prey; beauty begins at the foot of you"* and *"Gold stainless nail, torn through the distance of man"* and one is inclined to mentally step into the "other reality" of the Roger Dean cover painting while listening.

"Siberian Khatru" is a Yes song to savor as intense, stimulating, pictorial music and it also rocks.

◆ ◆ ◆

Close To the Edge is a monumental and stunningly brilliant album. It is essential to listen to it several times to even begin to fully appreciate the music. Particularly in the large format of the old vinyl records, opening the vivid green gatefold cover was like entering another world. In my view the title track ranks as one of the most significant pieces of music ever recorded while "And You And I" and "Siberian Khatru" are nothing less than absolute Yes classics.

YESSONGS

YES:
Jon Anderson/Chris Squire/Steve Howe/Rick Wakeman/Alan White/Bill Bruford (on 3 tracks only *)
PRODUCED BY:
Yes & Eddie Offord
ENGINEERED BY:
Geoff Haslam, assisted by Mike Dunne
RECORDED:
On tour during 1972
RELEASED:
May 1973
TRACKS:
Opening excerpt from Firebird Suite/Siberian Khatru/Heart Of The Sunrise/Perpetual Change*/And You And I/Mood For A Day/Excerpts from The Six Wives Of Henry VIII/Roundabout/I've Seen All Good People/Long Distance Runaround*/The Fish*/Close To The Edge/Yours Is No Disgrace/Starship Trooper

Yessongs was the first live album released by Yes and it turned out to be a massive triple album affair in the vinyl record format with a spectacular cover designed by Roger Dean that included a booklet of color photographs of the band on stage. Although Yes had gained a reputation in some quarters for being a studio band, anyone who had seen one of their live shows could testify that Yes were undoubtedly at their peak on stage and this ability to deliver the most brilliant of live performances was all the more laudable considering the complexity of the songs. The recordings on *Yessongs* mainly came from the tour to promote *Close to the Edge* (starting in late 1972) but three tracks were taken from the earlier *Fragile* tour (in February 1972).

Chris Squire made the important point that the special energy on a live album originates from the presence of the audience and that the show as a whole is made up of the audience and band combined. *Yessongs* successfully captured that special energy and sold very strongly. Jon Anderson commented that *Yessongs* was "a Yes people's album. I didn't expect it to be a big hit, we put it out as cheaply as we could and I'm very surprised it's done as well as it has...Every band wants to put out a live album to show what they are capable of doing live."[86]

Roger Dean explained that the series of paintings on the lavish triple gatefold sleeve was an opportunity to tell a story using pictures. It was a journey through space that took the idea of the world breaking up on the cover of *Fragile* and followed the fragments through space until they landed and came alive on another planet like seeds. It exemplified Roger's approach to working with Yes in how he would use his imagery to "build a world where the Yes music seems to co-exist very well".[87] An interesting aside is that the blue painting known as "Pathways" on the front cover of *Yessongs* was walked on by one of Roger's pet cats while the paint was still wet and he salvaged the situation by turning the paw prints into clouds—a Japanese magazine later speculated as to whether wild animals were roaming in his studio!

It should be made clear that the technology behind a Yes show in this period was nothing less than cutting edge. In fact, Yes throughout it's career has been at the forefront of technological advancement in music and recording. The *Yessongs* era was a time when many bands had significant difficulty in successfully translating their studio sound to live performance because sound systems were still in the relatively early stages of development and so were many keyboard instruments. It was consequently mind boggling that Rick Wakeman would go on stage with Yes with a C3 Hammond organ, two mellotrons, two Minimoogs, a grand piano, an RMI electric piano and a custom built mixing device designed by the band's own lighting engineer, Mike Tait.

It was also fascinating and theatrical to watch Steve Howe utilize his impressive array of guitars, alternating from one instrument to another during and between songs to achieve just the right sounds when required. For example during "And You and I" Steve played a twin-neck electric guitar before switching to a steel guitar set up on a stand in front of him. By having all of the necessary arsenal of sounds available, Yes was able to superbly bring it's studio work alive on stage.

A Yes concert at the time of *Yessongs* extended well beyond the band simply playing their music and it was in sharp contrast to other groups who gave little thought to stagecraft. Mike Tait said: "The whole concept of Yes is to provide a show, something more than just music. We aim for the perfect compromise between music and entertainment. Lighting is an important part of the whole thing. It creates mood exactly as music creates mood...In 'Roundabout' for example, all the spots are on Steve Howe as he plays the opening solo. Then as the rest of the band comes in, the whole stage lights up to show the rest of the band there on stage with him. You can hear the audience gasp—it has that much effect on them."[88] The climax of Rick Wakeman's solo spot was a particularly memorable scene with smoke rising into the air around him and multi-colored lights reflecting from his glittering sequined cape while the sounds of explosions panned around the auditorium.

Yes were impressing people everywhere with their live performances and during the *Fragile* tour in America the enthusiasm was such that audiences in places like Rochester were jumping to their feet and applauding as soon as the band appeared on stage. At one concert in Syracuse, Chris Squire reported that Yes had to stop the show to restore order after many of the audience had crowded down to the front of the stage while others stood on their seats.

A review by Mike Channell captured the feelings of the audience in Sydney, Australia during the *Close To the Edge* tour in 1973: "English band Yes last night played the best musical concert I've seen or heard. And that's not including the incredible light show which accompanied the entire concert. Musicianship and stagecraft of Yes is beautiful...Rick Wakeman proved to be one of the few real masters of the moog synthesizer and mellotron in the world today...Steve Howe is a superb player of whichever of his dozen guitars he plays on stage...(Chris) Squire is one of the best bass-effects men around—his playing is a driving force...vocals are perfection...Jon Anderson's lead vocals were spot-on..."[89]

The normally down to earth editor of *RAM*, Anthony O'Grady, reminisced about the same Yes concert in Sydney—a full three years after it took place—and wrote: "This concert lifted into overdrive from the opening moments. There was a sense of wonder, a palpable feeling that the musicians were getting to grips with their instruments and music like pilgrims beating down the last straight to the Holy Grail...One was led into the music as if it were a procession into increasingly detailed, increasingly subtle patterns of fantastic detail—it was a gradual entry into a different time zone, with a steadily intensifying golden glow spreading out from the edges. Sounds like someone spiked the icecreams sure, but it happened. And not just to me but to everyone around us, as far as we could see."[90]

And so the scene has hopefully been set for *Yessongs*. However, the sound quality of the album was admittedly a little below the expectations of Yes. Eddie Offord toured with the band to supervise the recordings but found himself stretched between the mobile recording truck and doing the sound mixing for the audience, with the latter taking priority. Jon Anderson said at the time: "A gig now is like a big mixing studio and the audience is in the hands of the mixer. You can have a great mixer, or some dumb guy who doesn't know what he's doing and can mess up a good sound from the band. We're lucky in having Eddie Offord to mix our sound."[91]

Eddie admitted that he wasn't satisfied with the sound quality of *Yessongs* and given his mixing responsibilities, he didn't actually record most of the tracks himself. He also pointed out some of the difficulties in recording a live album:

"When you are making live albums with the band, it's very hard to get the perfect night. Most of the gigs are good but you get that magic about every fourth night."[92]

Drummer Alan White joined Yes just prior to *Yessongs* and he seemed to put his finger on any problem that might exist with the sound on the album: "Well the only part I'm not happy about in the live album is my drum sound. I always think that the drum sound indicates the quality of the recording and while this is a very well recorded live album, the sound just isn't mine. Our engineer Eddie Offord mixes our live gigs as well as our studio work and he gets me a fantastic sound both in the studio and on stage. When you try to record the sound we use for stage, you get a little mixed up."[93] The other relevant factor is that the mobile analog recording technology of the day would have been tested to the limit in trying to successfully make a live recording of a band like Yes with it's complex sound while retaining perfect clarity, balance and depth throughout. Nevertheless, *Yessongs* still makes for riveting listening.

"Firebird Suite"/"Siberian Khatru"

A recorded orchestral excerpt of the majestic "Firebird Suite" by Igor Stravinsky opens the album and the piece has over time become a firm favorite with Yes fans as an introduction for the band's live performances. One is tempted to think that such music by an innovative classical composer is a particularly appropriate choice for Yes but Steve Howe said: "We considered that aspect of it (laughs) but in the end it's not that Stravinsky is a contemporary composer. We had another piece of music before his and we'll eventually switch to another piece later. We use them more because they're a tape. In the case of the 'Firebird Suite' it happens to be in the right key and it was the first thing we could agree upon after seeing Grand Funk open with the one we had been using, the 'Theme From 2001'. The classical music acts as another introduction to our act and its viscerality enables the audience to get into our music quickly."[94]

"Siberian Khatru" provides the perfect opening song for Yes and it's full of musical action. It is soon apparent that Yes is able to successfully reproduce all of the essential sounds from the original studio recording including the more exotic instrumentation such as steel guitar, mellotron strings and harpsichord. While the fullness of the bottom end of the studio version isn't quite achieved, the live version more than makes up for it with excellent solos. This is especially so at the end where instead of fading out like the studio version, the live version powers forward with scintillating guitar from Steve Howe. Steve commented: "*Yessongs* has a couple of solos that I like, 'Siberian Khatru' for one."[95]

"Heart Of The Sunrise"

The performance of "Heart Of The Sunrise" on *Yessongs* is one of the highlights of the album. It not only has all of the precision of the studio version but also benefits substantially from the additional power and energy of being performed live. Jon Anderson reaches the high notes with ease and the whole band appears to almost magically ebb and flow with the demands of the song. The acid test is perhaps towards the end with the fast interplay between Steve Howe's guitar and Rick Wakeman's keyboards and the test is passed with great aplomb, underpinned by a very adept rhythm section in Chris Squire and Alan White. It is noticeable that when Yes is firing on all cylinders, the individual musicians tend to add small improvisations or variations that give the music added interest.

Reviewer David Pepperell wrote: "During the memorable performance of 'Heart Of The Sunrise' the lights almost took over the emphasis of the music. When Jon sang 'Sharp! Distance!' they flashed red across the whole stage and broke up into blues and greens that washed the scene in an ocean of color."[96]

"Close To The Edge"

The version of "Close To the Edge" on *Yessongs* is clear evidence that Yes could take a long and complex piece of music conceived in the studio and perform it totally convincingly on stage. The fire of the relatively youthful Yes comes to the forefront in the sweeping intensity of the opening section and it is particularly apparent again during the concluding "Seasons Of Man" segment through the aggressive playing of Steve Howe and Rick Wakeman. In relation to his guitar solo at the beginning of "Close To The Edge", Steve Howe said: "Somebody mentioned in a review that I never play the same solo in 'Close To The Edge' twice. In quite a few ways, it is always different, and that has a great deal to do with the audience. A lot of my technical striving, my improvisation, comes from them".[97]

Jon Anderson commented that performing "Close To The Edge" for the first time "was like we were playing all day. (laughs) We actually did a concert (in England) with Elton John and Mahavisnu Orchestra…and we went on stage and played 'Close To The Edge'. And it felt like forever because it was the first time we'd performed it in front of an audience, because if you can imagine, when you perform with an audience—you actually perform *with* an audience when you're on stage—they didn't know this music, it had just been released, it was hardly in the shops and we were playing it…so it felt slow to them, a long piece of music and it was like endless. But within six months we started playing it more and more and more, it became a natural event and that's when it started to take on that ascension...because when you make music that relates to a spiritual ideal, you're looking for that first and foremost on stage...and then you hope the audience are going to get it because if we don't get it on stage, then they're not going to get it."[98] When Yes played "Close To The Edge" in America for the first time, Steve Howe revealed that it was easier for the band to win over the crowd than in England because the audience had the opportunity to hear the album beforehand.

A live performance of "Close To The Edge" started with a revolving mirrored wheel being raised at the back of the stage and it reflected the spotlights in all directions as if to mimic the crescendo of bird-like sound effects at the beginning of the song. During the quiet interlude in "I Get Up, I Get Down", a dry ice fog enveloped the stage and the band stood there as if in suspended animation in the deep blue light. The mirrored wheel again came to life at the conclusion of "Close To The Edge" to accompany the fading sound effects before the stage finally fell dark. They were entrancing scenes for audiences who were astounded by the musicianship, the spectacle and the technology that was seemingly ahead of its time and it all ended with thunderous sustained applause.

"Roundabout"

On the *Close To The Edge* tour, Yes used "Roundabout" as a powerful ending to the main part of their set—the last song before the encores. Amplification at the time was not well developed for acoustic guitars and so the use of electric guitar throughout adds to the overtly rocking feel that is entirely appropriate for live performance. It is an example of Yes adapting a song so that it was suitable for performance on stage and it turns out that the studio and live versions are both very satisfying in their own right.

"Starship Trooper"

"Starship Trooper" was usually the last of the two encores played by Yes on the *Close To The Edge* tour. As with "Roundabout", the acoustic guitar sections were dispensed with in favor of electric guitar for live performance, the guitar in this case being a spectacular white Gibson twin-neck EDS 1275 with six and twelve string necks. The twin-neck was quite uncomfortable to use but it appealed to Steve Howe because it worked in with his multi-guitar approach and enabled him to have two guitars in one.

The live version of "Starship Trooper" mainly differs from the studio version during "Wurm". The build up is much more intense and Rick Wakeman's use of mellotron and Minimoog gives the piece a new dimension while Steve Howe's smoking guitar solo provides a stunning conclusion. Chris Squire commented that "Starship Trooper" wasn't played on stage until the *Close To The Edge* tour and he speculated that it might have been the influence of Alan White that helped to successfully translate the song into live performance.

Alan White gives Yes a more powerful rock sound than Bill Bruford who tends to have a more technical approach and it comes across when comparing the two drummers on "Yessongs". However, they are both excellent drummers in their own styles and Eddie Offord nicely summarized the situation: "Bill was basically searching for a little more freedom and less arrangement and Alan, who's one of the funkiest drummers around, needed to get into something a little more technical, different time signatures, paradiddles, all the rest. And so I think looking back it was good for both of them."[99]

◆ ◆ ◆

Coming in the wake of three highly inspired albums in *The Yes Album*, *Fragile* and *Close To The Edge*, the live *Yessongs* was the perfect way to chronicle the unforgettable shows that Yes had given in this era and to provide the fans with a lasting souvenir of the concerts. It is worth mentioning that the Japanese remastered high definition edition of *Yessongs* comprising 3 CDs in a miniature replica cardboard cover boasts a sound quality easily exceeding the standard 2CD release from the nineties that contained exactly the same music.

It should also be noted that the movie *Yessongs* doesn't contain all of the songs featured on the album and that some of the songs in the film are taken from different performances. The movie is available on video as well as on DVD in some countries but while the DVD picture quality is quite reasonable, the sound is disappointing and not up to the standard of the CD versions of *Yessongs*. Nevertheless, the movie *Yessongs* remains an important historical record of the youthful classic Yes lineup performing at its peak.

TALES FROM TOPOGRAPHIC OCEANS

YES:
Jon Anderson/Chris Squire/Steve Howe/Rick Wakeman/Alan White
PRODUCED BY:
Yes & Eddie Offord
ENGINEERED BY:
Eddie Offord, tapes by Guy Bidmead
RECORDED AT:
Morgan Studios, London in the late English Summer and early Autumn, 1973
RELEASED:
October 1973 (UK), January 1974 (US)
TRACKS:
The Revealing Science Of God/The Remembering/The Ancient/Ritual

The double album *Tales From Topographic Oceans* is the most controversial album ever released by Yes. It was viewed by many people at the time as being radical and indulgent because it consisted of only four inter-related songs, one on each side of the two vinyl records, and the lyrical themes were well removed from those normally found in rock music. Many critics savaged the album mercilessly when it was first released but some thirty years up the track, one is tempted to wonder what all the fuss was about. Yes had already clearly established that they were not a standard rock'n'roll band and *Topographic Oceans* was perhaps the ultimate expression of that fact. Whatever the musical positives and negatives may be, it appears that time has been kind to *Topographic Oceans* and the album somehow now seems much easier to digest so many years after it was recorded—perhaps an indication that Yes were well ahead of their time with this ambitious work.

Topographic Oceans was initially inspired by a meeting between Jon Anderson and ex-King Crimson percussionist Jaime Muir. It seems that Muir was one of those figures in rock music who acquired a reputation for being somewhat odd and he is said to have once run through the audience during a Crimson concert after having bitten a blood capsule, the red liquid bizarrely flowing from his mouth. After eventually departing Crimson, he left the music scene and became a monk. Jon Anderson said of the meeting: "And immediately I felt that I had to learn from him. We started talking about meditation in music—not the guru type but some really heavy stuff and he gave me some books of Shastric Scriptures. As I read them I became engrossed with the idea of making music around the concepts they spoke of, making a four part epic built around the four part themes of which I was reading."[100]

One of the books read by Jon titled *Autobiography Of A Yogi* by Paramhansa Yogananda was regarded as a classic of its type and a lengthy footnote on page eighty-three became central to the idea for the album. As noted on the album sleeve, the footnote "described the four part Shastric Scriptures which cover all aspects of religion and social life as well as fields like medicine and music, art and architecture". It followed on from Jon's earlier reading of other books with a spiritual message such as *The Journey To The East* by Herman Hesse and he began working closely with Steve Howe in developing the concept. Steve said: "*Topographic* had this Yogi thing. Jon and I were most probably the only members of the band—then and now—to be interested in meditation. It's something we usually don't talk about or share but I think it helps us put up with a lot of the craziness in our lives."[100] Jon added: "Because I was involved in something that took me over, I became a megalomaniac, I had this vision. I was driving everybody crazy including myself."[102]

The album was very challenging for Yes and relationships within the band were sometimes tested. Jon was asked during the recording sessions about how Chris Squire was coping with the situation and he said: "Chris is playing really well and he has a lot more understanding of our situation than he did...he found it hard in the middle of this album to see the point of it. It really is a lot of hard work. You see the concept of the album was mine and Steve's and I was more aware of the possibilities than the rest of the band. But it's worked out and everyone has accepted what I was talking about and got involved in it. People who didn't get on with *Close To The Edge* won't like this one either, unless they are prepared to sacrifice some time to get into it."[103]

Topographic Oceans was recorded at Morgan Studios in North London and was co-produced by Eddie Offord and Yes. The scenes in the studio were evidently amazing, with farmyard scenery being brought in including stacks of hay, white picket fences and a full size representation of a cow. It was organized by Brian Lane either as something of a joke or a compromise because Jon Anderson had wanted to record in the country. Jon said: "I'd wanted to record the album in a forest location I'd found. I'd wanted to bring a generator and some tents".[104] The idea from Jon's perspective was to create the right atmosphere because the album was "to do with the earth, to do with the ancient and revealing of all that is and trying to remember where we're from, why we're here...the ritual of life".[105] Steve Howe admitted that he was as responsible as anyone for the madcap scenes in the studio. He said: "I was as guilty as anyone else. We all enjoyed the craziness of it all, it wasn't just Jon. Our idols were Monty Python and we wanted that stupidity in our world. It was a way of lightening things up".[106]

Eddie Offord talked about the music during the recording sessions and described the "Revealing Science Of God" as "very uptempo and steamy, "The Remembering" as "a very sort of laid back and simple, very mellow", "The Ancient" as "very spaced-out with very spontaneous improvising" and "Ritual" as having "a nice steaming sound again".[107] The recording process as described by Eddie involved the four basic tracks being put down "more or less live, with everyone playing and a rough vocal. It took four weeks to do that and edit it".[108] Next came the painstaking job of overdubbing and tidying up the solos. Eddie explained that *Topographic Oceans* was the first time that he got the band in the studio to "all play together at the same time, because there was so much more happening, whereas on *Fragile* for instance, bass and drums were laid down and the rest overdubbed".[109]

Looking back on the album, Jon Anderson said that making *Topographic Oceans* was "a great experience" but Chris Squire was a little more circumspect: "It definitely was disorganized (laughs). It would have been a better album if we'd planned it better. Maybe it wasn't what people were expecting us to have done, or maybe it's not what we should have done after the success of *Fragile* and *Close To The Edge*, but I still think that it contributed a lot in terms of us sustaining a long career. It gave Yes another quirky kind of identity which has made it possible to spread out in different directions since then and even allowed us to go into a pop direction of *90125*. Part of the secret of Yes's success is that we haven't shied away from going a little bit out there as we did on *Topographic Oceans* or in a commercial direction as we did on *90125*."[110]

Rick Wakeman was sufficiently disenchanted by the album that it was a major factor in his decision to ultimately quit Yes after the subsequent tour. Rick's view was essentially that *Topographic Oceans* had "some great moments but not enough" and he felt that it should have been edited down from a double album to a single album.[111] Rick's disinterest was highlighted by the now famous incident in which he was hilariously caught eating curry on stage during a performance of *Topographic Oceans*. It seems reasonable to conclude that Rick's substantial solo success was also a factor in his decision to depart.

There was certainly a polarization of opinion amongst fans and critics about *Topographic Oceans*. Chris Welch of *Melody Maker* was a noted supporter of Yes and even he described it as "Yes—adrift on the oceans", "a fragmented masterwork" and "lacking in warmth".[112] It was representative of many other similar reviews that didn't hold back from giving Yes a resounding thumbs down. In contrast, reviewer Mike Channell brimmed with enthusiasm and wrote: "Yes—it's ear to ear brilliance. Yes is an incredible musical time machine and riding their *Tales From Topographic Oceans* is a trip and a half...All the simplicity and complex brilliance of *Close To The Edge* is continued throughout *Tales* but the compound of ideas is enlighteningly different...At first the feelings they've captured strike as strange, especially during the opening harmonic sequences...Yes is perhaps the most creative unit in modern music today. The scope of their mental and musical capacity appears unlimited. It bothers me to consider where this genius will terminate..."[113] Similarly diverse reactions were evident amongst the fans but regardless of what anyone might have thought, the album was still very commercially successful.

The main obvious difference in initially listening to *Tales From Topographic Oceans* is that the performance by Yes seems to be less intense than that on the preceding three studio albums. Jon Anderson expressed the view that *Topographic Oceans* was a "meeting point of high musical ideals and low energy".[114] Steve Howe said: "It's a lot less intense and it's the only Yes album I can play at home without having to drop everything to concentrate on the music. I'm talking to you now but if *Close To The Edge* was playing, I'd have to stop and listen. I couldn't relax doing anything else."[115]

The cover for *Topographic Oceans* was another creation by Roger Dean and it centred on some famous landscape features with the curious contradiction of fish swimming through the scene. Roger has explained that it was the only Yes album cover which he formulated in discussion with the band, mainly during the long flight he shared with them on the way to Japan while on the *Close To The Edge* tour. The landscape features include Brimham Rocks, the Last Rocks at Land's End, the Logan Rock at Treen, single rocks from Avebury and Stonehenge, the Mayan temple at Chichen Itza and markings from the plains of Nazca. It was a somewhat incongruous combination of topography and ocean—an effective solution totally in keeping with the album's title. In an internet poll conducted by Rolling Stone magazine in 2002, *Tales From Topographic Oceans* was voted to be the best album cover of all time.

The *Topographic Oceans* tour was as ambitious as the album itself. Roger Dean and his brother Martyn were commissioned to design and build a stage set for Yes and they produced highly imaginative fibreglass structures that were lit internally and externally. The effects were stunning and it was a ground-breaking concept in rock music stagecraft that was extremely successful in integrating the music with theatrical presentation.

Yes commenced the shows by performing all of the *Close To The Edge* album followed by all of *Topographic Oceans* and then a final encore of "Roundabout". As far as I'm aware, Yes is the only major rock band undertaking a large scale concert tour to have regularly performed a set list based around five highly arranged epic pieces of music, each of them approximately twenty minutes in length. However, the band ultimately elected to drop "The Remembering" from the latter stages of the tour, presumably to make the listening experience easier for the audience given the large amount of relatively new music.

When questioned about the *Topographic Oceans* album during the tour, Steve Howe said: "Re-creating you own personal experiences through music is one of the hardest things in the world. We leave it to the audience to supply anything they might feel is missing. When we laid 'Close To The Edge' on the audience, we didn't worry about whether they were going to get the full meaning. Music conjures up different ideas to different people, and I don't really feel that it's necessary that everybody interpret what we do in the same way. We're trying to be pictorial—like Dvorak or Stravinsky if you will."[116]

"The Revealing Science Of God" (Anderson/Howe/Squire/Wakeman/White)

"The Revealing Science of God" is the first of the four pieces of music on the album. Steve Howe said: "People usually laugh when they hear that Jon and I saw side one of *Tales From Topographic Oceans* as being a pop song. That song has got all those intros and then 'what happened to this song we once knew so well?' To us, this was an accessible song like 'Roundabout'. We had written it about things that had happened to us but we thought that it translated quite well universally. Originally, side one was twenty eight minutes long but we cut six minutes from it—it was still too long for a pop song though! We had so much space on that album that we were able to explore things which I think was tremendously good for us...Side one was the most commercial or easy listening side of *Topographic Oceans*..."[117]

"The Revealing" starts off in quite unexpected form with a chant-like vocal build up, a sort of variation or development from the crescendo of bird-like sound effects at the beginning of "Close To The Edge". The eventual dramatic entry of Alan White on drums propels the music forward and Steve Howe's exotic guitar riff is a memorable theme. There is arguably somewhat of a doldrum factor in the middle of "Revealing" but the final sections are increasingly dramatic and Rick Wakeman's searing synthesizer solo is one of his absolute best.

Commenting on the meaning of "The Revealing Science Of God", Jon Anderson said the song is about "the revelation of God and the enjoyment of knowing there is a God and why things happen in life, like a patchwork quilt."[118] The title in itself is more self-explanatory of the lyrical content than is usual for Yes and Jon once lamented that he should have simply called it "The Revealing" in an effort to avoid too many unwanted questions about the obvious religious connotations. It is a song about the search for the knowledge of God as the ultimate source of all that exists and of how we shouldn't forget the experiences and magic of the past in our pursuit of the self-awareness required for that realization of spiritual truth.

It is particularly interesting that Yes played "Revealing" on the first leg of their *2002* American tour. Given earlier controversies, one might have expected Rick Wakeman to be circumspect about any material from *Topographic Oceans* but he played the music enthusiastically. Rick commented he was aware that many fans liked the song and he was consequently happy to play it.

◆ ◆ ◆

While *Tales From Topographic Oceans* is less intense than say *Fragile* or *Close To The Edge*, the live performances of "The Revealing Science Of God" and "Ritual" in recent years have seen Yes adding new dimensions and extra energy to these epics, the live version of "Revealing" on the *Keys to Ascension* CD and DVD being a good example.

"The Remembering", the second part of *Topographic Oceans*, includes some of the best moments on the album although it is admittedly a little slow to warm up in the opening stages. The third part, "The Ancient", is probably the most challenging to listen to but the going gets easier as the piece progresses and the concluding section featuring solo acoustic guitar and the song known as "Leaves of Green" is quite beautiful.

The fourth and final part of the album, "Ritual", tends to be somewhat long winded on record but it was a genuine showstopper when performed live on the *Masterworks* tour in 2000, the *Yessymphonic* tour in 2001 and the *35th Anniversary* tour in 2004. Even high quality live recordings such as on the *Yessymphonic Live* DVD don't seem to quite do justice to "Ritual" with the mind blowing drum segment towards the end.

Of all the Japanese remastered high definition editions of Yes albums, *Topographic Oceans* ranks as the most radically improved with far greater depth and presence. One Yes fanatic was evidently so keen to obtain a copy that he paid

$1000 on Ebay but I can only imagine how he must have felt when a second edition of the same item was released a few months later at the regular retail price!

RELAYER

YES:
Jon Anderson/Chris Squire/Steve Howe/Patrick Moraz/Alan White
PRODUCED BY:
Yes and Eddie Offord
ENGINEERED BY:
Eddie Offord, tapes by Genaro Rippo
RECORDED AT:
Chris Squire's home studio using Eddie Offord's mobile equipment in the late English Summer and early Autumn, 1974.
RELEASED:
November 1974 (UK), December 1974 (US)
TRACKS:
The Gates Of Delirium/Sound Chaser/To Be Over

Relayer was the follow up album to *Tales From Topographic Oceans* and it was the first with new keyboardist Patrick Moraz in place of Rick Wakeman. It saw Yes take a more conservative approach in format by reverting to the same three song framework as *Close To The Edge* but there was nothing conservative about the music and it is one of the most adventurous albums ever made by the band.

Relayer was recorded in a period of four months at the home studio of Chris Squire using equipment provided by co-producer and engineer Eddie Offord. Chris's studio was only half completed at the time and Eddie brought in his own equipment that he'd assembled for mixing live sound on the road and which could also be used for recording. After the disruption surrounding Rick's departure, Eddie perceived that *Relayer* represented a more settled period for Yes with Alan White having had some time to become accustomed to the band and with the arrival of "this crazy Swiss guy" Patrick Moraz.

On joining Yes, Patrick said: "When Yes called me, they knew I was not exclusively signed to anything. I was still involved in (the band) Refugee, but it wasn't happening. It wasn't essential music. It was interesting but we had management problems, we had a record company pushing us for more commercial things, and I felt that I was ready to leave, to suffer by starting over again, when Yes called me."[119]

Jon Anderson explained that the basic concept behind *Relayer* was to create a major stage show: "By then we realized that there was a key to stagecraft, stage production, theatre and music and color. And we'd sort of been dragging Roger Dean along with us—the stage design was brilliant. From a stage point of view, we discovered more to music than just making music, there's a lot of theatre and that's what the *Relayer* album personified, a major show, a major visual art. I think we did some great shows and it cost us a fortune because we were travelling around with like tons of equipment trying to put on *Aida* at every gig."[120] The stage show reached a peak on the 1976 tour with the spectacular "Crab Nebula" stage set that was designed by Roger and Martyn Dean and it conjured up the image of a giant, moving, three-headed alien crab.

The cover of *Relayer* was designed by Roger Dean and it took the form of a magnificent painting of a fortified city, the idea originating from a drawing that he had done in 1966. Roger has said that the *Relayer* cover is one of his favorite paintings and that Jon Anderson came up with the album title after seeing the picture. Somewhat unusually for Roger, he eschewed the use of bright color and it's a very apt approach given the subject matter of war in the album's epic centerpiece, "The Gates Of Delirium". Roger explained that he was fascinated by the crusades in the middle ages and it led to him doing the painting for *Relayer*, essentially a castle with some degree of influence from Tolkein. The armed horsemen in the picture are leaving on a quest and the presence of the serpent is suggestive of conflict between forces of good and evil.

Relayer saw Yes adopting a more intense approach than on *Tales From Topographic Oceans*. Reviewer Bernie Tier wrote of *Relayer*: "It is definitely the heaviest thing Yes have done with most of the added weight coming from Steve Howe's amazing guitar—especially on 'The Gates Of Delirium' side. Being the first album with new keyboard player Patrick Moraz one would have thought the biggest change would have come from that direction. He definitely plays a little heavier than Wakeman and fits in well..."[121]

It turned out that *Relayer* was another Yes album that drew mixed reactions. Author Dan Hedges described *Relayer* as "nerve-shatteringly futuristic" and as having "a cold alien edge".[122] Rick Wakeman wasn't moved and said: "I'll be very honest, I don't think I could have played a note on *Relayer*. I bought the album and I couldn't understand it...(but) I've met people who have gotten into the album".[123] In contrast, some fans who liked *Relayer* declared it to be the best Yes album ever.

If nothing else, *Relayer* demonstrated that Yes were in no uncertain terms continuing to extend the boundaries of their music. The performance of the band was frequently awesome and today the album is generally regarded as a very significant part of the sequence of great Yes albums from the seventies. Steve Howe acknowledged that the music on *Relayer* is "particularly complicated", not only in terms of the overall structure but also in how it was arranged with small differences in bars and beats here and there.[124] It was music that was interesting for such exceptional musicians to create and at the same time was also enticing for an adventurous audience.

Relayer would prove to be the only studio album that Patrick Moraz recorded with Yes. Patrick said: "I didn't feel all that comfortable playing with Yes, because there was something not right in the way they interacted. Some feeling of uneasiness. But I went to see them rehearse and it was incredible. I had seen them play before and didn't think their music was very alive. It sounded dead. But seeing them rehearse 'Sound Chaser' (from *Relayer*), I thought they were incredible. Plus I had never seen anything like them before. There were armies of roadies, and they were rehearsing into a twenty four-track tape recorder. It took a lot of courage for me to get up and play along with them…Being in a band like Yes, there was always someone around telling me to try this instrument or that instrument. I lost a lot of money in 1975 because of that kind of thing…I eventually left Yes because it was like a big festival of egos. There was never any conference on what was artistically important. It was always economical."[125] Yes seemed to have a slightly different view of Patrick's eventual departure as revealed by Jon Anderson's comments in the review of the *Going For The One* album.

An entire Yes show from the *Relayer* era is captured on the *QPR* video and DVD that was recorded at the Queens Park Rangers soccer stadium in London in 1975. While the picture quality is good, the sound varies from very satisfactory to diabolical. The release was not approved by Yes and the sound quality is at its worst in the first half of the concert where it is clearly apparent that the mix isn't balanced and key instruments are sometimes almost inaudible. However, there is some hope that a properly mixed and fully authorized version might appear in the future because the previously lost multi-track master tapes were recently handed over to the band. The performances are nevertheless excellent and the songs include the entire *Relayer* album together with many other Yes classics.

Other high quality performances of material from *Relayer*, but with much improved sound quality, include the 1976 recording of "The Gates Of Delirium" on the *Yesshows* 2 CD set and the 2001 recording of the same song complete with orchestra that graces the *Yessymphonic Live* DVD/video.

"The Gates Of Delirium" (Anderson/Howe/Moraz/Squire/White)

"The Gates Of Delirium" is a true Yes epic and it clocks in at just under twenty-two minutes in length. It essentially consists of an instrumental introduction followed by a song and then an instrumental battle of stunning proportions before finishing with the most peaceful and calming of songs.

By way of background to "The Gates Of Delirium", it was the first time that Jon Anderson had walked into a session with Yes and presented an idea for a complete epic. Jon explained what the music was about: "It was about war. When I wrote it, we were getting into the last throes of the Vietnam war. And in a way it was a statement about that. It said that war is this kind of thing that everyone gets sucked into…you're slaying our people, we'll slay yours…and we will burn the children's laughter. And the theme of war, that was the driving force and there was a lot of hot metal flying about. And the music got very crazy, it's like a void and out of this void rises this form which controls war, and it's like a demonic form. The devil, if you like. And this form has been watching the war, glad it's happening…and the music crashed at the end and out of that rises a very gentle stream of sound and goes into a very delicate kind of lyric…'Soon oh soon the light, pass within and soothe this endless night' like at the end of a long tunnel, there will be light and things will become clearer at the end. Everything will return to peaceful ways. It's an optimistic view but you have to go through this violent tangle to get there."[126]

With the additional benefit of having seen Yes perform "The Gates Of Delirium" live in recent years, I offer the view that it is one of the great Yes masterpieces. It is superb, dynamic, rock music theatre that ultimately has a positive message to communicate. The instrumental introduction is typical Yes and the song that follows could be described as being a progression from the likes of "Total Mass Retain" on *Close To The Edge*. The real listening challenge is in the subsequent instrumental section that features some brilliant musicianship and it has taken many listeners quite some time to initially digest it. It will help to think of it as being a musical battle with the different instruments attacking and responding until finally reaching the point of collapsing in chaos before the glorious and soaring sounds of victory at the end of the battle segment.

The concluding "Soon" segment is very much the calm after the storm with light emerging after the darkness of war and it is one of Jon Anderson's finest melodies with his voice floating beautifully over the silky smooth steel guitar of Steve Howe. Jon has said that he originally envisaged "Soon" as "being performed by five keyboard players but Steve felt that he wanted to add his steel guitar".

If anyone had the notion that Yes was merely a sunny, Utopian band, then "The Gates Of Delirium" completely dispelled it. The positive philosophy of Yes isn't lightweight and there is a deep perception in Yes music of the universal struggle of life. The affirmation provided by Yes is that there is light and it can come out of even the most adverse of life's circumstances. In "Gates" Jon Anderson lyrically burned the laughter of the children and there was a terrible war but in the end the light prevailed. The realization is that the war was futile because everyone suffered. The closing words of "The Gates Of Delirium" are: "*The Sun will lead us, Our reason to be here*". To know God is our reason to be here and our experiences have helped us to see the light and find the way.

One critic suggested that "The Gates Of Delirium" could have been condensed into a three minute song to deliver the same message but such comments completely miss the point. "Gates" was intended to make a statement as an elaborate theatrical experience of the mind and much of what was communicated was conveyed through the images that the music created.

◆ ◆ ◆

When Yes performed "The Gates Of Delirium" for the first time in twenty-four years during the *Masterworks* tour in 2000, the band appeared somewhat surprised by how much the fans have grown to appreciate the piece. Indeed, it is one of the most exciting Yes songs to experience live. Whether the re-formed classic Yes lineup will perform "Gates" remains to be seen because Rick Wakeman has not played it in the past. However, the prospect of Rick tackling this challenging music and bringing his unique brilliance to it would certainly warm the hearts of a good many Yes fans.

For further listening from *Relayer*, I highly recommend "To Be Over" which Steve Howe says is one of his favorite Yes songs and it's probably the most accessible song on the album. The remaining piece is "Sound Chaser" which features some astonishing playing at breakneck speed and although it might be just a little too over the top for some tastes, it's a crazy musical ride that should be experienced.

GOING FOR THE ONE

YES:
Jon Anderson/Chris Squire/Steve Howe/Rick Wakeman/Alan White
PRODUCED BY:
Yes
ENGINEERED BY:
John Timperley, assisted by David Richards
RECORDED AT:
Mountain Studios, Montreux, Switzerland in late 1976 and early 1977
RELEASED:
July 1977
TRACKS:
Going For The One/Turn Of The Century/Parallels/Wonderous Stories/Awaken

Going For The One was the long awaited new studio album from Yes after a gap of some two and a half years. The intervening period had been devoted to touring throughout the world and also to solo projects.

Jon Anderson explained the background to *Going For The One*: "At the time of our last American tour I was thinking about the sort of album that we wanted to do to follow up *Relayer* and I decided we wanted a very kind of celebrational feel to it. We had gone through a very long 'inside' period at the time of *Topographic Oceans*, when we were looking very deeply at ourselves, and with *Relayer* we were still in that feeling of being a band that could try anything without the commercial pressures. We then decided that we wanted to do an album of the best of Yes music, an album that would show the band working towards an easier outlet, a more listenable, more approachable music."[127]

Yes decided to record what became the *Going For The One* album in Montreux, Switzerland at Mountain Studios and the big change was the departure of keyboardist Patrick Moraz who was replaced by the returning Rick Wakeman. Jon commented: "He (Patrick) realized that he was not really getting off on what we were doing for the new album. I felt his first year with the band had been hard work for him but a good time. However, the way we were working on the new album was to get on and play the music rather than discuss it too much. We found that we had four people moving towards something and one not quite making it, which meant we had to start talking. Patrick said to me that he wanted to leave—Chris told him it wasn't in the contract—and we agreed to try things for another week. After that, he was not very sure what was going on and I said if that was the case, it was probably best if he left".[128]

Yes had talked about Rick Wakeman some two months earlier and speculated that after his extended period of solo work that he may have had the desire to work with top class musicians again. Rick told the story of his return to Yes: "It came about the beginning of November (1976) when they'd been here (in Montreux) for about a month just getting things together. They phoned me up and asked me if I'd like to come over. I came over and listened to some demos that had been put down and I was really knocked out because it was back to the (style of music on *Fragile*)...that knocked me out immensely. The sort of music that I could feel part of and play and really offer".[129]

The *Going For The One* project also saw two other notable changes in the Yes creative team. Firstly, Hipgnosis designed the album cover instead of Roger Dean and although the double fold out cover was undeniably impressive, it was somehow not totally satisfying for the Yes purist who tended to prefer Roger's "other worldly" approach. The front cover depicted a naked man looking up at the looming skyscrapers of civilization. The second change was that John Timperley engineered the album in place of Eddie Offord with Yes handling their own production. It soon dawned on Steve Howe and Chris Squire that the valuable contribution of Eddie was sorely missed but it was too late and unfortunately the production values suffered with the result being reflected in a less satisfactory sound.

The return of Rick Wakeman added significantly to the positive atmosphere in making the album. Alan White said: "I loved making that album (*Going For The One*). We all had such a tremendous time. It was such a happy period in the band's life when Rick came back to the fold and was playing really great—I think there's some really creative moments. And that's what that album means to me, the joining back to the fold of Rick Wakeman and the happiness of all that."[130]

Chris Welch seemed to capture the general feeling with his review of *Going For The One* in *Melody Maker* and saw it as "a classic Yes album" marking a "triumphant return".[131] Rick Wakeman was similarly enthusiastic: "It really is an exciting album. It's just like 'Fragile' was done...Gone is what I would call any self-indulgence that came from me or any of the other lads in the band. It's down to good songs and good arrangements...The album gives me the same buzz that *Fragile* and *Close To The Edge* gave me and more. Excellent album".[132]

As always, however, not everyone was happy and some critics no doubt preferred the then newer sounds of Punk rock. Critic Wayne Elmer wrote: "Despite Wakeman's return, Yes still sound like a bunch of art school rockers who awoke one morning to find their record was a hit and spent the next eight years trying to figure out why."[133] Regardless of what any of the doubters may have thought, *Going For The One* proved to be a winner for Yes by topping the album charts in England and the band was firing on all cylinders on the subsequent highly successful tour.

Jon Anderson gave his views on how he saw Yes in 1977 after the release of *Going For The One*: 'There is more energy in the band than ever before. And more enjoyment and optimism. We're a very contented band. Happy that we're still here and still playing together after all these years...Around the time of *Topographic Oceans* we were accused of playing games with people, of being cynical. But that wasn't the case. We were very serious about that album. I believe that one day it will be recognized as a very important part of our contribution. Certainly for the new album we reverted to the way we used to do things. But it wasn't really a backward step. We didn't panic. We just put together the album that seemed right for now...A lot of the New Wave bands resent us and I can understand that. To them, we must be a million miles away. Like creatures from outer space."[134]

In many respects one can listen to the music from *Going For The One* in much the same way as *The Yes Album*, *Fragile* and *Close To The Edge*. It is unquestionably progressive and distinctive but also quite accessible music.

"Going For The One" (Anderson)

The title track opens the album and it's high energy rock with obvious commercial appeal. Jon Anderson said: "The title track 'Going For The One' shows one side of Yes. It is a real rocker and the band is playing hard kicking rock, really steaming, and I was singing about being a jockey, then about going in a boat down the Grand Canyon river. I realized that the first two verses were rather tangled up and people might not know what they were about, so I put in the explanatory third verse."[135] Jon's reference in the third verse to his search for a "punch line" in his "cosmic mind" was a reminder that he did have a sense of humor and that Yes music wasn't always meant to be terribly serious.

Even the critics seemed to like the song and reviewer Phil Manzie wrote: "The title track 'Going For The One' is sheer, exhilarating, immediate rock brilliance. No pastoral interludes or extraneous themes—just a single minded concentration on the thumping beat, with beautiful descending and ascending bass lines, vibrant piano and searing slide guitar."[136]

The searing guitar was indeed a feature with Steve Howe playing steel from start to finish. Steve said: "'Going For The One' was recorded in '77, the early days of the Punk movement, and was one of the wildest things we had done ever! Maybe we just needed to get it out of our system like we did with 'South Side Of The Sky' on *Fragile* or side four of *Topographic* or 'Sound Chaser' on *Relayer*. The title track of 'Going For The One' was pretty over the top…"[137]

"Turn Of The Century" (Anderson/Howe/White)

In complete contrast to the title track, "Turn Of The Century" is a delicate and beautiful song with superb acoustic and electric guitar from Steve Howe and sensitive piano and electric keyboards from Rick Wakeman. Jon Anderson's voice effortlessly glides over the top of the instrumentation.

The lyrical approach on "Turn Of The Century" is somewhat different to many Yes songs in that a specific story is told, admittedly with a rather magical twist. Jon Anderson explained that the story was about a sculptor who created a statue of his lady after she died during the winter: "The story was triggered off by *La Boheme*, which is a great opera, and I wanted to develop the story to the point where the music would take over. The point of the story is that he puts all of his love into the statue and it comes to life. It is an old Greek tale, and in putting it to song I wanted to become more of a storyteller. I have gone through the phase of cosmic, interplanetary thoughts as they came to me, and I felt I needed to get much more involved in the business of storytelling. Through 'Turn Of The Century' I was trying to find the key to unlock that vast door."[138]

The lyrical ideas for "Turn Of The Century" originated from Jon but it was Alan White who came up with the main chord sequence while Steve Howe made his contribution by further developing the chords. "Turn Of The Century" gradually builds to a dramatic climax but still remains light and melodic to colorfully bring the story alive.

"Awaken" (Anderson/Howe)

The epic final track on the *Going For The One* album is "Awaken", albeit relatively short as full scale Yes epics go at fifteen and a half minutes. When performed live, however, it is usually about three minutes longer with the band slightly extending those sections that invite improvisation. "Awaken" is highly regarded by many Yes fans and it is also known to be a favorite of Jon Anderson who variously describes it as "the best piece of Yes music", "a beautiful piece of music in structure and form", the "most exciting piece of music to play on stage", "a totally different thing altogether than most music of the last hundred years" and having "everything I would desire of a group of musicians in this life".[139]

"Awaken" is a dramatic and mystical musical odyssey that is a profoundly spiritual experience. Author Thomas Mosbo described "Awaken" as being a song where the listener might actually "see the face of God".[140] When talking about spirituality, Jon Anderson referred to reading *The Finding Of The Third Eye* by Vera Stanley-Adler and touched on the essence of "Awaken": "It's an energy (spirituality) that's dormant in a lot of people but it's 'awakenable' as in the song 'Awaken'…it's an awakenable gland, the pineal gland…now we are starting to re-learn how easy it is to re-contact the oneness of being, the oneness we call God".[141]

The lyrical content of "Awaken" is another instance of Yes making a complete departure from the usual subject matter of rock music and it brings us back to one of the great strengths of Yes music in that ideas aren't forced upon the listener because of the artistic way in which they are expressed. This approach makes the Yes message universal and it consequently transcends personal beliefs. It is left up to the imagination of the listener to make an interpretation but there is a meaning to be found by anybody choosing to do so. And of course, the music alone in "Awaken" is magnificent in itself featuring an array of brilliantly played electric and acoustic instrumentation. Chris Welch's review in *Melody Maker* described "Awaken" as containing "more sheer music making" than "a whole catalog of albums".[142]

"Awaken" is an excellent example of how Yes works in composing music by drawing on ideas from the various members of the band.[143] The first element was the main guitar riff in the "Awaken Gentle Mass Touch" section (starting at 1m 30s into the track) that was written by Steve Howe. It gave Jon Anderson the idea of "doing the song as a verse" and he asked Rick Wakeman to come up with an introduction. Rick wrote the introduction on piano using some ideas that he'd been working on with Jon when they'd been playing Celtic harp and organ together at St Martins Church in Vevey near Montreux. Steve then added a "flowing sound" to the introduction using his steel guitar (starting at the 35 seconds mark) to accompany Jon's sensitive vocals.

The "Awaken Gentle Mass Touch" section included a remarkable guitar solo from Steve (starting at 2m 50s) who revealed: "The very beginning of that solo was worked out in advance. It was originally going to be part of a solo guitar piece. When we were actually arranging 'Awaken', the basic riff of that solo was first used on the demo but intended for the beginning of the song…When we change things around in the studio, I very often end up putting in the bits that have been taken out—not necessarily in their original form or location, though."[144]

When it came to the "Workings Of Man" section (starting at 5m 10s), Steve worked with Jon and devised a chord sequence that contained "every major chord you could play" and for added interest, Jon suggested stopping on certain chords. Not to mention that the minor chords also changed in different places. In the quiet middle section of "Awaken" (starting at 6m 35s), Yes took a completely different approach and actually recorded Jon and Rick playing harp and organ respectively in St Martins Church while the rest of the band played along with them in the studio in Montreux some five miles away. It was an innovative idea made possible by the high quality underground telephone lines in Switzerland. The key to the climax of "Awaken" in the "Master Of Images" section (starting at 10m 35s) came from Chris Squire's idea to "slow down the chords". It provides the platform for the music to go to infinite heights with towering church organ, soaring steel guitar and celestial choral effects.

"Awaken" was clearly a very collective effort by Yes and Rick Wakeman commented on how the song writing credits for the album were determined: "Everyone contributed. We've given up trying to break it down on album sleeves. If Jon wrote the words, it's put down to Anderson or whatever. We sort out the problems of how we 'split the dole' afterwards (laughs)…Nobody worries, they know when they do their bit, they're doing it for a piece of music". [145]

Live versions of "Awaken" can be found on the *Union Tour Live* DVD (from 1991), the *Keys To Ascension* CD and DVD (from 1996), the *House Of Yes* CD and DVD (from 1999) and the *Yesspeak* DVD (from 2003) as a bonus audio track. All are very good performances of "Awaken" although it should be noted that the *House Of Yes* version features Igor Khoroshev on keyboards and he does a commendable job in interpreting Rick Wakeman's keyboard parts. "Awaken" was performed during the *2002* Yes tour of North America and the 2003 *Full Circle* tour and it was undoubtedly a highlight of the shows.

◆ ◆ ◆

Going For The One contains some truly classic Yes music and for further listening I'd recommend the very melodic hit single "Wonderous Stories" which is one of the best Yes songs in a short format. The remaining track on the album that hasn't been mentioned so far is "Parallels" but unfortunately the original album version sounds somewhat weighed down by church organ—unlike the more dynamic live version on the *Yesshows* CD. Steve Howe once said that the studio version of "Parallels" had a "disgraceful" amount of echo on it because the acoustics of the room it was mixed in didn't permit Yes to properly adjust the sound.

In fact, the overall sound of the *Going For The One* album is generally below the usual standards of Yes which is a pity given the excellent quality of the music itself. The live recordings of the songs from *Going For The One* consequently tend to show the material off to better advantage. Nevertheless, the Rhino 2003 remastered and expanded edition of *Going Of For The One* represents very good value with the addition of extra tracks including an early version of "Awaken" titled "Eastern Number".

TORMATO

YES:
Jon Anderson/Chris Squire/Steve Howe/Rick Wakeman/Alan White
PRODUCED BY:
Yes
ENGINEERED BY:
Geoff Young & Nigel Luby, assisted by Peter Woolliscroft & Pete Schwier
RECORDED AT:
Advision Studios and RAK Studios in London
RELEASED:
September 1978
TRACKS:
Future Times/Rejoice/Don't Kill The Whale/Madrigal/Release Release/Arriving UFO/Circus Of Heaven/Onward/On The Silent Wings Of Freedom

Tormato was released in 1978 and it was the year that marked the tenth anniversary of Yes. It is fair to say that the subsequent extensive concert tour, the aptly named *Tormatour*, would prove to be far more significant than the album itself.

Jon Anderson described *Tormato* as "a sort of combination of ideas without anyone really driving the project" and he acknowledged that the band lacked "a good producer"[146] Jon had been very much the prime mover behind the initial ideas for much of the Yes music created in the seventies and one journalist even dubbed him "The Hippy With The Iron Hand" due to his single minded determination to put everything he had into creating Yes music. Perhaps after sensing a change in prevailing musical tastes with New Wave music riding high in the late seventies and also taking on board the very considerable musical growth of all the members of Yes, Jon decided to take a less central role when it came to recording *Tormato*.

During the sessions for the album, Jon reflected on the previous ten years with Yes: "It's been crazy fast. We had a great time last year with the hit album (*Going For The One*) and single ("Wonderous Stories"), and now it's coming up for our tenth year together, it's such a kick to feel so strong together...So much has happened in the last ten years—I can't believe it all sometimes. But I can't lay back yet. I don't believe we have done everything possible. The main thing is we're still going. We've still got a chance of making it! We've kept soldiering on and I don't regret a thing that has happened. We've had to struggle with the forces all around us, and nobody thinks the same way within the band. It's still a bit like being at school in a way..."[147]

Despite Jon's enthusiasm, the recording sessions for *Tormato* weren't totally successful. Steve Howe said: "The last album we made in those ten years with Rick and Jon, *Tormato*, was rehearsed more in the recording studio than anywhere else because things were getting very strained and painful. This meant in effect, that we rehearsed less and although *Tormato* doesn't suffer from dreadful arrangements we definitely lost the sense of production on it. Although 'Madrigal' and 'On The Silent Wings of Freedom' are okay, we had a flatter sound than usual. We were trying to produce ourselves and we sometimes paid the price."[148]

Chris Squire commented on how Yes approached *Tormato:* "There was a time when tracks were laid down to evolve upon and it was a case of music growing out of music. But now, on this album, we've got a pretty clear idea of the end product to start with. We rehearsed over twenty-five songs before we started to record. And we're hoping to record as much of that material as possible."[149]

However, the absence of a good producer eventually became all too apparent. Eddie Offord was unavailable and Rick Wakeman felt that the potential of *Tormato* had been severely stifled by poor production. He pointed to "Arriving UFO" as a track that wasn't given every opportunity to shine on record. Alan White agreed that *Tormato* wasn't the greatest Yes album but commented that it was a favorite of people in some parts of America who thought it was remarkable and would ask to have their copies autographed.

Perhaps the strangest element of all about *Tormato* was the album cover. It was another creation by the Hipgnosis group and it left many fans wondering what it was all about. The front cover featured a tomato splattered across a photo of a man standing in the countryside holding divining sticks. Chris Squire said: "Did anyone ask Groucho Marx why they called it *Duck Soup*? It was a question of getting the sleeve design associated with a place in Devon (England) called Yes Tor, which is in the middle of a firing range, miles from anywhere. When we saw the photographs of Yes Tor, somebody threw a squashed tomato at them, and the result was photographed for the cover. I wish I could come up with a really good line to explain it!"[150] It's been said that Aubrey Powell of Hipgnosis wasn't happy with the look of the photos and consequently threw the infamous tomato. There is little doubt that it was inspired by the popularity of Punk rock at the time but it was a misguided attempt at marketing because it had little to do with Yes music.

It is profoundly ironic that Yes in the late seventies incurred the wrath of the Punk movement and was lumped in with many wealthy, established acts to be branded as a "dinosaur" band. For starters, the history of Yes clearly shows that the band had to struggle to survive in the early years and almost never made it through to become successful. Most importantly, the adventurous epic rock music of Yes was in many respects far more radical than any Punk band could ever have imagined and therefore couldn't logically be seen as representative of "the establishment". The prime difference was that Yes just happened to be musically sophisticated, had the talent to draw large audiences and used their position to make a positive statement, as opposed to the three-chord aggression and erupting angst of the Punks. Jon Anderson said: "People forget...We were just like any other band starting out. No money, cheap digs, sleeping in the van. It was no easier for us than anyone else. Just because we made a bit of money later on, we became targets for all those people who wanted to slag off everyone who'd become successful. But we worked for it. Nobody gave us our success, we earned it...There was no reason for us to feel ashamed".[151]

When *Tormato* was released in 1978 in the era of Punk it was readily apparent that the music critics were becoming more cynical and prejudiced than usual towards a famous band like Yes. It was reflected in one review of *Tormato* which more or less criticized the fast songs for being fast and the slow songs for being slow. It was the kind of time where it would have been difficult for any Yes album to be an outright winner, much less one that was of uneven quality. *Tormato* contains several good ideas but for the most part, the ideas aren't fully realized. The highlights include "Future Times", "Release Release", the quiet "Madrigal" and the love song "Onward"—the best version of the latter probably being the live recording on *Keys To Ascension*. The instrumental introduction to "On The Silent Wings Of Freedom" is pure classic Yes but the rest of the song doesn't quite live up to the early promise.

Fortunately the *Tormatour* made any criticism of the album seem insignificant and the main talking point was the ingenious revolving stage that was designed for Yes by their lighting engineer, Mike Tait. The stage deck was 8.5 metres (twenty-eight feet) in diameter and consisted of sixteen segments that could be easily disassembled for transportation. At ground level on the circumference of the stage were wheels that ran in a track and allowed it to revolve, the whole set up weighing about six tons. Mike explained the concept: "It was actually quite natural for them. Playing end-of-hall you'd have the drums and keyboards at the back and the three vocalists across the front with Jon in the center. The only change required to play in the round was to put the keyboards opposite the drums with the vocalists inbetween. They used that kind of configuration in rehearsal anyway. Jon was raised up a bit in the center...It was driven by one motor only, on one of the wheels on the outside, with the center pin being the only part secured to the ground. It went around about three times and wound the multicore snake (stage electrical wiring) around the center pin; it then went back the other way three times and unwound the snake. The audience never noticed the change in direction as it turned out; everyone used to ask how I did it".[152]

Apart from the main platform of the stage where Yes performed, there was also a lower level that rotated and it was packed with people and equipment unseen by the audience. The lower area was fitted out comfortably with carpets and chairs but everyone had to sit down because the height clearance was only 1.5 metres (five feet). There was also a trapdoor to allow equipment such as guitars to be passed up to the band and it helped to ensure that virtually the entire stage surface was playing area. The major advantages of the revolving stage were that it allowed the audience to get closer to the band on all sides and it also permitted ticket prices to be increased because there more well located seats available, making it possible to earn an extra $10,000 to $15,000 per show according to Mike Tait. The downside for Yes was the security problem in getting to and from the stage. After considering the possibility of a tunnel, the band simply decided to take their chances by walking down the aisle through the audience with the inevitable result that fans would reach out and try to grab them as they went by.

The *Tormatour* appearance of Yes at Wembley Arena in London was reviewed in *Melody Maker* by Karl Dallas and he stated that it was unlikely that any band since the Beatles had elicited such a noisy response as Yes and that the revolving stage had resulted in "communication at a level which baffles belief and is even a little frightening", making it "a good thing, therefore, that their motives seem entirely benign".[153] Tellingly, Yes didn't play all of the songs from *Tormato* on the tour. Prior to one of the shows at Madison Square Garden in New York in front of 20,000 people, Chris Squire said: "We're not doing all the new songs on the concerts. We do 'Future Times', 'Don't Kill The Whale' 'Circus Of Heaven' and 'Release Release'. We've been trying to work in 'Arriving UFO' but we've not actually played it yet. We've done eight concerts in a row now so far and we've had a lot of teething problems and the revolving stage is crazy!"[154]

It can reasonably be concluded that *Tormato* is not the most important album in the Yes catalog but it still has some interesting moments. A visual record of a show from this era is provided by the *Live In Philadelphia 1979* DVD/video that features one hour of highlights from an "in the round" show at the Spectrum. It appears as though it was made for television and both the sound and pictures are not of the highest quality.

"Don't Kill The Whale" (Anderson/Squire)

"Don't Kill The Whale" was released as a single and it showed Yes seeking to deliver a more direct lyrical message with a fairly straight ahead rock approach to the music. Chris Squire came up with the musical sequence and Jon Anderson developed the lyrics from some personal poetry that he'd been writing.

Rick Wakeman pointed out that "Don't Kill The Whale" showed how Yes cared about the environment and the world in general a long time before it became fashionable to do so. Chris Squire said: "It rocks really nicely but it's not a heavy song. We just wanted to make the point that they should stop the factory ships. Men have hunted whales for a long time, a thousand years, but the factory ships…well people don't need it. Let's not kill off all the whales. That's what we're saying. But Yes aren't getting heavily into it. It's a track off the album and we've got lots of different songs…This isn't a concept album. We had a glut of those in the seventies, which was not a bad thing. But we have a lot of young people come to see us and we want to keep the music wide open."[155]

Although "Don't Kill The Whale" saw Yes taking a more direct approach, Steve Howe explained that he was still looking to do something different with his guitar work: "I usually improvise my fills in songs. 'Don't Kill The Whale' from *Tormato* has some quite strange fills going on alongside the vocals. I was playing 'The Les Paul' which was the top model in the range—that guitar has made some special appearances. On 'Don't Kill The Whale' the guitar might be pretty odd but that's really fairly typical of me—I would always try to do something a little different or a little sideways."[156]

"Don't Kill The Whale" didn't have a big impact as a single but it was, interestingly enough, dusted off by Yes and played during the *2002* tour in America with quite remarkable rocking power.

"Release Release" (Anderson/White/Squire)

"Release Release" is generally regarded as one of the best tracks on *Tormato* and the second line of the song *rock is the medium of our generation* essentially tells what it was about. During the recording sessions for the album, Chris Squire said: "(Yes music is) the product of five guys who were approximately twenty years old in 1968. We're the children of that time. That's the single factor that makes Yes music…The album (*Tormato*) doesn't have a title yet but some of the songs…are titled, like 'Anti Campaign' (later changed to 'Release Release') which is about rock as the medium of our generation, which it is. People have become very educated about sound and the average rock concertgoer is very fussy about how their music is presented. You can get fans who quote frequency cycles at you, especially in America. Rock as a business has set itself standards that are a lot higher than many others, in its attempts to entertain. And we're making music for the whole world now."[157]

"Release Release" is a fast rocking song that is easy to listen to with an infectious melody. The middle section features a short drum solo and guitar solo that are executed with a deliberate hint of familiarity so as to suggest they are symbolic of rock music as the medium of our generation—even though the accompanying background crowd noise was strangely enough recorded at a soccer match. The music picks up to furious velocity after the solo interlude with the vocals riding high above the urgency of the instrumentation and the speed of Rick Wakeman's ensuing synthesizer work is stunning. It is a potent reminder that part of the genius of Yes is that the same musicians who created the epic grandeur of "Awaken" on *Going For The One* are equally capable of producing the full throttle rock of "Release Release" on *Tormato* and they demonstrate the ability to take each of these diverse pieces of music to the highest possible level.

Steve Howe commented that there was a definite sixties influence in his guitar work on "Release Release" that was powerful and didn't rely on blues guitar for inspiration. It is the same kind of approach that he has adopted on other tracks such as "Shock To The System" on *Union* where Yes sought to achieve a heavier rock feel. Steve reflected on the *Tormato* and philosophically said: "We used up each other's energy I think. There was a refueling needed. I think with Rick going and coming back...by the time we'd done *Tormato*...although it had several good tracks on it...I know that Ahmet (Ertegun, head of Atlantic Records) particularly liked 'Release Release'—he said to us, 'If all the album's like that, it'll be fantastic!' And we said, 'Yeah, it's all like that!'(smiles) And of course, we never made albums that were all like one thing."[158]

The review of *Tormato* in *Melody Maker* by Chris Welch proclaimed "Release Release" to be "the hookline on the fastest, funkiest, piece of rock 'n' roll Yes have ever produced."[159] Given that "Release Release" was a definite bright spot on a mediocre album, it was very surprising that it was only played live on a small number of dates on the *Tormato* tour and not at any time since. Alan White was the main writer of "Release Release" with Jon Anderson and he seemed to shed some light on the "mystery" when he explained that it was such an energetic handful to play on stage that it simply left the band out of breath.

◆ ◆ ◆

The Rhino 2003 expanded and remastered edition of *Tormato* presents the album in a better light than ever before with the addition of ten bonus tracks from the same era including previously unreleased material and a hidden track right at the end. It swells *Tormato* to almost double its original length at just under eighty minutes and it seems to be a better balanced effort all around. It shows that Yes wasn't short of the right musical building blocks but still suggests that the band needed a producer like Eddie Offord to coordinate their efforts in order to achieve the best possible results.

DRAMA

YES:
Chris Squire/Steve Howe/Trevor Horn/Geoff Downes/Alan White
PRODUCED BY:
Yes; backing tracks produced by Eddie Offord
ENGINEERED BY:
Hugh Padgham, Ashley Howe & Peter Schweir; tape operator George Chambers
RECORDED AT:
The Town House, Roundhouse and RAK Studios in London
MIXED BY:
Gary Langan & Julian Mendelsohn
RELEASED:
August 1980 (UK), September 1980 (US)
TRACKS:
Machine Messiah/White Car/Does It Really Happen?/Into The Lens/Run Through The Light/Tempus Fugit

Drama is the most unique album recorded by Yes by virtue of the fact it is the only album on which Jon Anderson does not appear as lead vocalist. The album was most appropriately titled given that it was recorded in a volatile period in the band's history after the acrimonious departure of both Jon Anderson and Rick Wakeman.

The new members of Yes in vocalist Trevor Horn and keyboardist Geoff Downes, otherwise known as pop duo The Buggles, were the most unlikely replacements imaginable. They'd had a worldwide hit single with "Video Killed The Radio Star" and gave the journalists plenty of fodder with headlines such as "Pop Goes The Cosmos" (*Sounds*, August 1980), "Macrobiotics In The Plastic Age—Music's Most Unlikely Marriage…Yeggles" (*Juke*, July 1980) and "Tales Of Topographic Buggles" (*RAM*, July 1980). The Buggles had started out being called The Bugs, a name that was derived from the Beatles. They shared the same manager as Yes in Brian Lane and after having written a song they felt would be suitable for the band, the duo were invited down to the studio where their involvement in *Drama* soon became a reality.

The mood of Yes fans with the departure of Jon and Rick and the arrival of The Buggles was one of stunned disbelief. The rift in Yes began during recording sessions in Paris in late 1979 and it became apparent that personal relationships were beginning to unravel when serious disagreements in the musical direction escalated. Steve Howe explained that because the music wasn't right, it became impossible to carry on and he elaborated on the musical differences: "It wasn't right for Jon in the instrumental way and it wasn't right for us in the lyrical way. It wasn't right overall in a directional sense...We didn't want our music to be folky, in the sense that we have powerful musicians at our fingertips and not utilizing them. But one of the styles that Jon was introducing to Yes over the years, when we were trying to mould and reshape it and found it wasn't really going to work, was the softer, more gentle and lyrical sort of music. We've always done a bit of that—'And You And I', 'Turn Of The Century'—there's always been those things but they have to be very dramatic, in contrast to something extremely the other way, something big and sizeable, weighty. I think we were just feeling that we were going in more of a strong direction and we wanted a very marginal amount of this gentle, passive music, very marginal relief."[160]

Despite the potential for complete disaster, *Drama* was a much more cohesive effort than *Tormato* and it featured some strong music with a more direct, pop-influenced rock emphasis than any Yes album since the early seventies. It is true to say that the soul and beautiful voice of Jon Anderson was definitely missed but Trevor Horn and Geoff Downes nevertheless did a commendable job and the album sounds very fresh. It was mainly recorded at The Town House in London and the production by Yes was the best since *Topographic Oceans*, undoubtedly assisted by the return of Eddie Offord who worked on the backing tracks. The main recording engineer for the album was Hugh Padgham who went on to have great success in co-producing Genesis.

As explained by Chris Squire, the band had the aim of "re-inventing the Yes idea" and they looked towards *The Yes Album* as an appropriate model. Chris commented that he worked hard along with Steve Howe and Alan White to "make sure the music was pretty happening".[161] Alan's view was that *Drama* had "a lot of credibility", "a lot of great playing and a lot of great music on it"[162] Steve looked at *Drama* as "picking up a thread" that had been lost in the not too distant past.[163] *Drama* had the authentic appearance of a Yes album with the cover having been created by Roger Dean, albeit with a more "dramatic" look than usual with a stormy background. Roger conceded that it was somewhat different to the earlier Yes covers but pointed out that it was still a landscape with a "strange feel to it" in common with his previous work for the band.[164]

Geoff Downes indicated that the new lineup had adopted a very unified approach and it was "a situation where everybody was putting in their ideas and creating the kind of music that comes out of five people's ideas".[165] A number of songs had already been written before the arrival of Geoff and Trevor who also brought material to the table. When asked to compare *Drama* to previous Yes albums, Geoff said: "Well I think in some ways it's better, mainly because we spent a lot of time in getting it right. The other guys (in Yes) that I met never used to on the previous couple of albums. They used to throw them together...it's obviously a lot more contemporary."[166]

Some critics were very kind to the new Yes album and reviewer John Gill wrote: "Apart from a few breathers, they instill *Drama* with a frightening intensity rooting themselves firmly back into rock 'n' roll. Needless to say, it's no plain boogie but their unique amalgam of orchestral construction and gargantuan rock spirit. They've recaptured the romanticism of old, and are once again dealing in that timeless and idiosyncratic quality that defines the best of Yes. They've condensed their sprawling artistry into a dense-yet-diverse album that hangs perfectly together."[167] Other critics agreed and John Hall said: "The marriage works well with an early Yes, not a latter day Buggles sound on this album called *Drama*."[168]

As might be expected, not everyone was convinced about the merits of *Drama* and reviewer Michael Smith stated: "The main problem with this album is that with the influx of energy and ideas brought by the two new members, the material is trying too hard to recapture the old enthusiasm in a time when the bulk of the audience consider their time to be passed. The arrangements are jagged and cumbersome in many places, not least the opener 'Machine Messiah', but there are new ideas, the playing is still superbly skilled; there is a lot of energy and the band is playing as a band again."[169] Jon Anderson's view from outside the band was that *Drama* was "a very well produced album" and although he "didn't relate to it very strongly", it made him realize how much he enjoyed being in Yes.[170]

As usual, Yes toured to promote the album and the revolving stage was used on the opening American leg of the tour. Chris Squire explained that the tour had already been sold out before the change in lineup became known and that Yes had taken the punt to go ahead with the shows without offering ticket refunds, a strategy that luckily attracted only minimal bad publicity. They played to an enthusiastic capacity crowd at Madison Square Garden and John Gill in his review wrote: "New York's teenagers shelled out their dollars and got an amazing performance. Would you be surprised to be told they lit matches, jumped up and down, waved giant Yes flags, screamed, stomped, yelled their love? Some sections of Madison Square Garden resembled those scenes of hysteria from the early Beatles newsreels."[171]

Yes were very happy with the tour in America but the reception was not always positive in England. It ultimately became very apparent that the Yes fans weren't going to accept Trevor Horn as lead vocalist in place of Jon Anderson. Steve Howe said that Yes at first felt that they'd managed to pull it off without

Jon and Rick in the lineup and that the band was "going on exactly the same", at least until the audiences in England "started shouting stuff out (that was very negative)".[172] Chris Squire commented: "There was one particular night when I remember him (Trevor) singing 'And You And I' really really well, but to be honest it wasn't always up to par".[173]

"Machine Messiah" (Downes/Horn/Howe/Squire/White)

"Machine Messiah" opens the *Drama* album and in format it is a typical Yes mini-epic of about 10 minutes in length. However, the real surprise element is the additional heaviness in the music, particularly from Steve Howe's guitar, and the contrast of this with the lighter moments makes for an effect that is all the more menacing. The listener needs to have a slightly readjusted approach to accommodate the additional heaviness but it achieves the right atmosphere because the subject in "Machine Messiah" is alienation and it is lyrically a few shades darker than most Yes songs.

Trevor Horn was primarily responsible for the lyrics on *Drama* and he successfully creates some intriguing images although the Yes positive philosophy championed by Jon Anderson is pretty much absent, a very notable omission because there is nothing really uplifting from that perspective. There isn't an obvious light at the end of the tunnel with the Machine Messiah of the *singular eye* that we ask to take us *into the fire*. It is more a faint hope that we'll perhaps be delivered from our circumstances with *All of us standing in line, All of us waiting for time* and *Maybe we'll change, Offered the chance* (brief extract from "Machine Messiah" written by Downes/Horn/Howe/Squire/White, published by Topographic Music Ltd, administered by WB Music Corp, ASCAP and Island Music Ltd).

Trevor Horn had been very concerned about joining Yes with the knowledge that he was going to have to go onstage and do justice to classic Yes songs like "Starship Trooper". However, at the same time he was excited about working with such talented musicians and was amazed to be in band that could write "Machine Messiah" in only one day. Geoff Downes commented that "Machine Messiah" was the song on *Drama* that best represented the integrated input of Yes and The Buggles and he felt that the band should have gone more in that musical direction.

Steve Howe agreed with the proposition that the new Yes lineup on *Drama* could have gone further in fully using the ideas of The Buggles: "I think we pulled it off and we did get positive feedback from crowds and the critics, but our aim was to get a Yes thing with two new people. I was hoping it'd be a bit more radical when we started recording it but not everyone had the same vision of trying to make it different, so in the end it sounded like a Yes album rather than something different. Perhaps we didn't give the new guys the leeway for their ideas".[174]

Reviewer John Gill wrote: "'Machine Messiah' buckles side one open, swooping in at crazed speed and stating itself like a fiery manifesto. Mountainous collapsing noises and abrasive/phased guitar sweep you into the maelstrom, leaving little time for second thoughts...It's a very busy cinemascope piece, themes restating themselves all over the shop like a Roeg movie, and serves as an excellent opener."[175] Michael Smith in his review commented on Trevor Horn's contribution and said: "He is obviously as interested as (Jon) Anderson in the lack of human communication today, which is light-weight pop rambling when wrapped in *The Age Of Plastic* (by the Buggles) and pure pretentiousness when presented as Yes on 'Machine Messiah'. The lad as far as most critics are concerned can't win. But a lot of Anderson's lyrics were gibberish to most people, so why should the new Yes change that—they can't write simply love songs after all."[176]

In summary, "Machine Messiah" has all the variations that one normally expects to find in Yes music, although with a heavier approach to underline the band's aim to produce weightier compositions—probably with an eye to the prevailing musical climate of New Wave music.

"Tempus Fugit" (Downes/Horn/Howe/Squire/White)

The title of "Tempus Fugit" means "time flies" and was derived from Latin. Steve Howe revealed it was something of a send up of Chris Squire who had developed a reputation amongst the Yes members for always being late. There was certainly nothing tardy about the music in this instance and there was a quintessential Yes feel about the urgent, exciting pace of the song with strong bass lead and the deftly handled punctuation-like changes although it also had a dash of Punk influence to make it a modern song for the era. It was a relatively short outing for Yes of just over five minutes to close the album but it was potent and arguably worthy of being deemed a Yes classic.

Steve Howe explained that "Tempus Fugit" was a song being developed prior to the arrival of The Buggles: "In just a few weeks Alan, Chris and I had played most of *Drama*—we were playing 'Tempus Fugit' as a very powerful rock guitar trio and it worked okay! But when we heard the keyboards and quirkiness of Buggles we thought that would be far better for us—we needed some new blood that was quite different. By coincidence, Trevor had a voice similar to Jon's but he also had great production and song writing skills…I thought *Tormato* was a bit of a wobbly album but I was always keen on *Drama*."[177]

Chris Squire's bass guitar brilliantly contorts and sprints its way through "Tempus Fugit" with awesome force while the drums of Alan White superbly underpin the rhythm and Steve Howe's guitar glides overhead before pouncing. Trevor Horn nimbly dances through the vocal lines with ease while Geoff Downes provides thick textures on the organ that hark back to the earliest Yes albums. Indeed, "Tempus Fugit" contains the same kind of thrilling musical energy that had made Yes famous. It is definitely worth checking out the promo video of "Tempus Fugit" on the *Yes Greatest Video Hits* video/DVD.

"Tempus Fugit" was a powerhouse when played live and particularly because it featured the word "yes" in the lyrics, it provoked a great reaction from the audience. Unfortunately it hasn't been played on stage in full by Yes since the *Drama* tour although Chris Squire has often included snippets of it in his bass guitar solo spot. In 2002 Steve Howe was reported to have said that Jon Anderson was open minded about singing "Tempus Fugit", so perhaps it might make an appearance in a Yes set list at some time in the future.

◆ ◆ ◆

Jon Anderson is irreplaceable within the framework of Yes but in saying that, it doesn't detract from the work of Trevor Horn on *Drama*. Rather it is the enormous talent of Jon and the extraordinary warmth that he brings to Yes music that is impossible to duplicate and it is therefore inevitably missed when not present. Much the same can also be said about the other members of the classic Yes lineup but the lead vocalist of any band is naturally one of the most immediately recognizable characteristics of the sound. With that proviso, *Drama* is a very good Yes album from the cover right through the performance, compositions and production.

Steve Howe, Chris Squire and Alan White all put in thoroughly excellent performances. While it is true that Geoff Downes is not as gifted as Rick Wakeman, he does a more than satisfactory job. The material on *Drama* lacks the uplifting, positive lyrical content of many of the best Yes songs from the earlier albums but bridges the gap to some extent by sheer dynamism. In addition to "Machine Messiah" and "Tempus Fugit", I also recommend "Into The Lens" and "Does It Really Happen?" as very worthwhile Yes songs. Some of the previously unreleased tracks from the aborted sessions in Paris with Jon Anderson and Rick Wakeman are included on the *In A Word: Yes* compilation and on the Rhino expanded & remastered edition of *Drama.*

90125

YES:
Jon Anderson—vocals/Chris Squire—bass guitars, vocals/Trevor Rabin—guitars, keyboards, vocals/Tony Kaye—keyboards/Alan White—drums, percussion, vocals
PRODUCED BY:
Trevor Horn
ENGINEERED BY:
Gary Langan; additional engineering by Julian Mendelsohn & Stuart Bruce, assisted by Keith Finney
RECORDED AT:
Sarm Studios, London in the English Spring and Summer, 1983
RELEASED:
November 1983
TRACKS:
Owner Of A Lonely Heart/Hold On/It Can Happen/Changes/Cinema/Leave It/Our Song/City Of Love/Hearts

In some ways the *90125* album was even more radical than *Drama* in departing from what had been the perceived progressive musical style of Yes. The music was simplified and much more mainstream in character with far fewer Yes idiosyncrasies than any previous album. This may have partly come about by accident given that the basis of the album was conceived when the band was still called Cinema before Jon Anderson returned to the lineup. Nevertheless, this change of direction for more overtly commercial territory alienated some long time Yes fans while at the same time attracting many new fans who preferred more conventional rock music with more obvious popular appeal.

Atlantic Records boss Ahmet Ertegun made it clear to Yes that a hit single was essential this time around and he charged Chris Squire with the responsibility of making sure it happened. Chris said: "Ahmet Ertegun, came down to the studio and said, 'We have to have a hit single this time. You have to work on it; it is your responsibility, Chris, to make sure it happens.' And fortunately we did."[178]

Although Jon Anderson was back in the band for *90125*, the lead vocals were often shared with new guitarist and vocalist Trevor Rabin. Trevor brought with him a commercially orientated, popular rock music approach and his guitar style was far more orthodox and hard-edged than that of Steve Howe. Chris Squire explained that the songs were mostly fully written before Jon returned and although it wasn't really the plan to reform Yes, he could see that the music "could be much much better" with the right vocalist.[179]

Jon Anderson had just returned from the south of France with the intriguing idea of establishing a band with Rick Wakeman and Keith Emerson before he received the call from Chris. Jon said: "Chris gave us a call, asked if I'd like to hear some of the music he'd been working on, because they felt they were going somewhere but it wasn't really taking off...So we popped down to the local pub, he played me a tape, and it just excited me, the overall prospect of working on that music. But I said to Chris at that first meeting, if I start singing on top of this, it's gonna sound like Yes. Because obviously the dominant rhythm section and vocals were very complementary to what Yes was all about."[180]

90125 also saw the return of Trevor Horn but this time as producer rather than as the lead vocalist, and it seemed to help to steer the album in a commercial, pop-influenced direction. Chris Squire said: "We were actually playing simpler music. I know basically my own playing on the album is a lot simpler, but for a reason, to have a modern version of Yes."[181] Tony Kaye was another ex-Yes man who unexpectedly returned to the fold on *90125* but his keyboard contributions to the album were minimal because most of the keyboard work was done by Trevor Rabin. According to Rabin, "Tony and Trevor (Horn) didn't seem to get on. Also Tony's not very familiar with the new gear. He's a great Hammond (organ) player, but as a far as the new, computerized keyboards go he's not really into that."[182]

Tony Kaye played a more significant role on the ensuing tour but he made some pertinent observations about the kind of sound Yes were seeking on *90125*: "We knew that the album would have to be somewhat simple, so we kept it very dimensionally sparse. We wanted it to be more modern sounding; we wanted to appeal to an audience that the Police or the new Genesis would appeal to. It couldn't just be old Yes fans and the same old dirge, yet at the same time we knew it mustn't sound like Styx or Journey, those kind of American bands with vague English roots. Yes's music kind of dictates that you take a very orchestral approach, though. We're doing a lot of stuff from *The Yes Album* (on stage)—'Yours Is No Disgrace', 'I've Seen All Good People'—and when I went back and listened to the old tunes I realized how orchestral it was. You have to have thick textures going on in those songs, so the trick became to get that bigness, but to make it very precise, very spiky. That was the challenge."[183]

Respected keyboardist and electric violinist Eddie Jobson of Curved Air and U.K. fame had tantalizingly joined Yes for a few days but quit in frustration when told that he would have to share the stage with Tony on the *90125* tour. Despite careful editing, an occasional glimpse of Eddie can still be seen in the promo video for "Owner Of A Lonely Heart". As it turned out, Yes's keyboard technician Casey Young added extra keyboard effects to the live sound during the *90125* tour from his keyboard rig set up off stage out of view of the audience. Casey said: "I do a lot of vocoder parts, vocal reinforcing, with Emulator sampled effects and brass parts here and there."[184]

Trevor Rabin played a major role in writing the music for *90125* and he had a huge number of stockpiled demo tapes from which to select material. Trevor made it clear that as the new guitarist in Yes he felt no pressure at all to sound like Steve Howe: "None whatsoever. And I think it would be a big mistake. Obviously we're gonna be doing old stuff on the road. The first thing I did was I learned all Steve's bits and changed parts so it was me and not him, although obviously parts like in 'Roundabout' (sings) gotta be the same. To be quite honest he was never one of my favorite guitarists. He's got pretty good technique. Tch, gotta be careful what I say here! I was with Kissinger before I came over! I think one good thing is my guitar playing is so different to his."[185]

Especially with his late entry into the project, Jon Anderson's creative input to the music on *90125* was far less than it had been for the Yes albums of the seventies although he did change some of the lyrics where he could get everyone to agree. Jon made some interesting observations about the commercial direction of *90125* and commented that Yes took the approach of complying with the current trends in music rather than adventurously exploring new ground: "There was a time when musicians had to develop technique a bit better. And it's like everything new, you always overdo it. I think that's why we had technoflash rocking, because to learn the balance, to find their levels, a lot of musicians had to go through the barrier, rise above it and play the fastest sort of lick with the pianist doing exactly the same with harmonies in thirds, fifths and ninths. Now you just program your computer and it's done, no big fun any more. I think we're in a nice lull at the moment. The handclap, dancebeat, Trevor Hornisms, if you like...There's a lot in music today that's all production and recording technique, there's not many stylists like there were in the sixties and early seventies. We'll probably come to that when recording advances have settled a bit...Maybe we've just jumped on the bandwagon and said, okay, as a group we can sit with everybody else in the driving seat...But it certainly isn't ahead of anything, it's along with it. I'm not sure that you're going to have a breakthrough along the lines we're moving".[186] Jon elaborated that a band should be able to survive on the strength of its music and ability to perform on stage rather than have to rely on the fickle support of the media to achieve the next hit single. It was a scenario that seemed to have more appeal for Jon and perhaps he was biding his time for circumstances to change.

Trevor Rabin suggested that *90125* contained its share of complex music: "Hopefully we've modernized the technoflash thing a bit. I mean the instrumental track 'Cinema' starts out in eleven-eight, goes to seven-eight, then three-four, but it comes out pretty naturally because we all like playing. It's streamlined, but definitely not simple, some of it is highly arranged. I think the whole thing was to try something that was really new."[187] According to Trevor, there was also a twenty minute track called "Time" that was being worked on before the return of Jon Anderson but intriguingly, it was apparently never completed and perhaps it was felt that it didn't fit the style of the rest of the album.

To go with the new approach of Yes on *90125*, the cover was a sleek, minimalist, computer generated design by Garry Mouat of Assorted Images. It featured a silver background with a dash of fluorescent color in the centre emblem, with no sign of the familiar classic Yes logo designed by Roger Dean. To complete the transformation, the album also spawned some remixed versions of the songs in the 12 inch vinyl format to cater for the discos and dance clubs—notably the dance mix of "Owner Of A Lonely Heart" and similar remixes of "Leave It".

While it was all too much to bear for fans of the earlier very progressive Yes music, *90125* became the biggest selling Yes album ever and the simpler and more orthodox sound received positive press. Reviewer Geoff Barton said: "Whatever you might feel about this Yes resurrection (Anger? Despair? Sick to the stomach?), taken as a package and pushing preconceived notions to the back of your mind, this is really a remarkably good 'comeback' album…Throughout the first few tracks the signs are that Yes have consciously toned down the inaccessibly 'progressive' side of their nature and opted for an altogether more straightforward approach. Of course the lyrics remain saturated with patchouli oil and there are moments—Anderson's acapella activities during 'Hold On' and the clever-clever Oriental opening to 'Changes', for example—when Yes do threaten to overstep the mark. But overall it's a happy compromise. It's such a shame therefore that the group couldn't quite restrain themselves enough for the duration of side two. Self-indulgence creeps in immediately with the too-flash instrumental 'Cinema', a hyper-involved relic from the previous incarnation of the band. And follow on cuts 'Leave It' and 'Our Song' unfortunately stay in the same rut; marvelously accomplished, immensely ingenious, stunningly played stuff, to be sure…but utterly soulless."[188]

The concert tour to promote *90125* turned out to be highly successful for Yes although it was delayed by two months after Trevor Rabin was injured in a freak accident in a hotel swimming pool. Trevor was on a short vacation in Miami and while lazily floating in the pool at the Fountainbleu Hotel, a lady said to be of large proportions came hurtling down the pool slide and crashed on top of him causing a ruptured spleen. After eventually recovering from emergency surgery and finally setting out on the tour, Trevor said: "We'll be on the road for an entire year, and each show is still a buzz. Jon told us right from the start, let's go out and prove that Yes are a damn good live band, not a dinosaur coasting on past glories. It wouldn't have mattered if the LP (album) hadn't done well or anything, because the priority was to present Yes as a very good live act."[189]

The video/DVD *9012 Live* is a good document of the highlights from a live performance of Yes from this era showing them in action on their new sloping stage, although the fifties-style movie footage inserted at various points might not be to everyone's taste. The producers Charlex evidently felt that the movie footage was an appropriate theme given that the band was originally going to be called Cinema and the instrumental piece of the same name from *90125* actually opened the show.

"Owner Of A Lonely Heart" (Rabin/Anderson/Squire/Horn)

"Owner Of A Lonely Heart" was the most successful single ever released by Yes and it reached number one in the massive U.S. market. However, the musical style was quite alien and not representative of Yes at all, being completely out of step with the rest of the musical output of the band up to that point. Jon Anderson said: "Love lost, love won, or it could be happening…someone looking for love. These are supposed to be the three main options for a hit record, aren't they? Which one's 'Owner Of A Lonely Heart' then? I don't know!"[190]

"Owner" was mainly written by Trevor Rabin and he was surprised that Yes decided to record the song: "It'd be an understatement to say that Yes had changed—can you imagine early Yes trying something like 'Owner Of A Lonely Heart'? (laughs) I wasn't even going to give the song to them because I thought it was so unsuitable, I was going to save it if ever I worked on a solo album. I was just playing them a tape of some songs I'd written and put on tape, and by chance it stopped on 'Owner' and they said, 'What's that? It sounds interesting.' And I said 'No, honestly you won't be interested.' But they insisted; just as well really, because it was just the right sort of song to make the statement they wanted to make from the beginning—this new Yes wasn't just a feeble re-run of what went on before."[191]

Perhaps the most familiar Yes aspect of "Owner" was the prominent bass line although it was, paradoxically enough, written by Trevor Rabin. According to Trevor, he wrote it while in the toilet because he liked the sound there! As Chris

Squire pointed out, the bass line is simple but it cleverly "swings very well at the tempo we did it".[192] Yes made the most of modern technology in recording the track and even Jon Anderson's voice was electronically processed to make it sound like a trumpet in certain places while Alan White's fills on drums were enhanced using a Fairlight computer keyboard instrument to give them a digital sound as though they were coming through a megaphone.

Looking back on "Owner" fifteen years later in 1998, Jon Anderson gave it some very insightful perspective. He sat with an acoustic guitar on his lap and sang parts from three songs that were number one hits—"Owner Of A Lonely Heart", "Twist And Shout" and "La Bamba"—all to the same rhythm and same chords on the guitar and exclaimed: "It's the same song!" Jon explained that he knew "Owner" was going to be a hit as soon as he heard it because it was very well produced and was simple. He clarified that "a pop record has to be, to reach many people, has to be simple but universal and unfortunately Yes music isn't based on simplicity. It has to have more sophistication and if you're working with Steve Howe and if he plays (a simple chord), he gets very bored because he's a magnificent (guitarist)...and if you're working with Rick Wakeman or now with Igor Khoroshev the keyboard player, you can't give them simple (music)...you can give them simple things but it's nice when you can explore different musical areas. So when we did *Big Generator* which was the next Yes album, I got tired because it was trying to find that hit record and if you're trying to find a hit record—forget it, it will never happen!"[193]

"Owner" earned Yes some good reviews, particularly from critics who were not previously enamored of the band. Reviewer Geoff Barton said: "I was never a big Yes fan. Indeed, once in the dim distant past, I can recall a girlfriend dragging me along to see 'em perform *Tales From Topographic Oceans* at London's Rainbow Theatre and being bored to tears. But that splendid new single 'Owner Of A Lonely Heart' piqued my interest about the band's reformation and I simply had to investigate further. The beginning is good. 'Lonely Heart' kicks off *90125*...A jaunty, clever slice of Americana, spiced up by a plethora of Trevor Horn ABC-style production shrieks, it's Adult Orientated Ecstasy."[194]

The success of "Owner" gave Yes some respite from the vacuous criticism often aimed at the band by hostile critics whose tastes usually didn't seem to extend beyond the latest pop music fad. Chris Squire said: "What I've learned from 'Owner Of A Lonely Heart' is the wonderful thing of people going, 'Is that Yes? Really?' I like that. It's especially good for all the fans who stuck with Yes for the right reasons—people who'd been written off by others who'd say, 'Oh, he's into that old Yes shit.' When 'Owner Of A Lonely Heart' came out, those people could say, 'Have you heard my band's new single?'"[195]

The live versions of "Owner Of A Lonely Heart" with Rick Wakeman (*Union Tour Live* DVD/video, 1991) and Steve Howe (*House Of Yes* DVD/video/CD, 1999) have appreciably more instrumental bite than the original studio recording. The version on *9012 Live* with Trevor Rabin and Tony Kaye is also spirited and it features an instrumental introduction from "Make it Easy", a Rabin song recorded by the Cinema lineup in early 1981 but not included on *90125*. "Make It Easy" eventually appeared on the *Yesyears* boxed set compilation and is a bonus track on the Rhino expanded & remastered edition of *90125*.

"It Can Happen" (Squire/Anderson/Rabin)

"It Can Happen" is one of the few tracks on *90125* that has a sound close to that which is normally associated with Yes. Perhaps the primary reason is that Chris Squire was the main writer of the song and he composed it on piano quite some time before it was eventually recorded for *90125*.

Trevor Rabin came up with the introduction and his use of an electric sitar sound on "It Can Happen" immediately brings to mind Steve Howe who very distinctively used the instrument on a number of famous Yes songs including "Close To The Edge". The lyrics also show a welcome return to a more overtly uplifting positive message, reminding each of us that our undesirable situations can be redeemed: *"You can mend the wires…You can bring your soul alive.*

"Leave It" (Squire/Rabin/Horn)

"Leave It" was the second single released from *90125* and essentially it's a commercial song that seemed to be aimed at finding Yes a wider audience. The gimmicky promo video that accompanied "Leave It" was made in eighteen slightly different versions. It was directed by Godley and Creme who were the hot video producers at the time but I suggest that only the most desperate fanatics would wish to seek out all of the versions—one was right side up, one was upside down and so on. The version appearing on the *Yes Greatest Video Hits* video/DVD is a combination of the other seventeen.

Trevor Rabin wrote "Leave It" with Chris Squire and while there was no specific inspiration for the lyrics, the basic idea of the song was to achieve a high tech sound using voices as instruments. Trevor came up with the melody while Chris developed the bass line and it was recorded using multi-tracked voices to create a vocal extravaganza. After some hesitation about the drum sound, it was ultimately decided to use a drum machine to add to the high tech feel rather than Alan White's conventional drum kit.

The demo of "Leave It" was the first song that Jon Anderson heard before deciding to re-join Yes for *90125*. Chris Squire played the tape to Jon who said: "The first one he played was 'Leave It' and I said, 'This is great'. He thought it was good too but that it needed another voice added to it...Music isn't a risk, it's an adventure and I decided to try it for an album and a tour".[196]

"Hold On" (Anderson/Squire/Rabin/White/Kaye)

"Hold On" was another song from *90125* that was mainly composed by Trevor Rabin. Trevor explained that it was written prior to his involvement with Yes when he was thinking about recording a solo album. The song was essentially about his indecision—he was holding on.

"Hold On" is a straight forward rock song with strong vocals but the fairly orthodox rock guitar sound and the lack of any lead keyboard activity arguably leave it sounding a little pedestrian. However, the vocal harmonies imploring all of us to "hold on" are undeniably impressive.

◆ ◆ ◆

After experiencing and understanding the complex, classic Yes music of the seventies, it is somewhat difficult to listen to the more conventional music on *90125* with the same degree of enthusiasm. Opinions will vary about *90125* and it must be acknowledged that it achieved tremendous commercial success, but the fundamental problem remains that the unique Yes sound and sense of adventure was substantially muted. Jon Anderson's creative input had clearly been minimized, Trevor Rabin's guitar work had a more ordinary hard-edged rock sound and there was little in terms of incisive lead keyboard work.

The success of *90125* and the "Owner Of A Lonely Heart" single would ultimately become something of a double-edged sword, posing the important question as to whether Yes should continue to pursue commercial acceptability or revert to its adventurous progressive roots. Nevertheless, *90125* contains some interesting tracks and I'd recommend "Our Song", "Cinema" and the excellent "Hearts" as further examples.

BIG GENERATOR

YES:
Jon Anderson—lead vocals/Chris Squire—bass guitar, backing vocals/Trevor Rabin—guitars, keyboards, backing vocals/Tony Kaye—keyboards/Alan White—drums, percussion
PRODUCED BY:
Yes, Trevor Rabin, Paul De Villiers & Trevor Horn.
ENGINEERED BY:
Paul De Villiers, Alan Goldberg, Dave Meegan, Trevor Rabin, John Jacobs, Paul Massey & David Glover with various assistants
RECORDED AT:
Lark Recording Studios, Caramati, Italy; Sarm Studios, London; Air Studios, London; Southcombe Studios, Los Angeles; Westlake Audio, Los Angeles; Sunset Sound, Los Angeles
MIXED BY:
Trevor Rabin
RELEASED:
September 1987
TRACKS:
Rhythm Of Love/Big Generator/Shoot High, Aim Low/Almost Like Love/Love Will Find A Way/Final Eyes/I'm Running/Holy Lamb (Song For Harmonic Convergence)

After a long gap of almost four years, *Big Generator* was released as the follow up album to *90125*. It generally followed the style of *90125* with a definite leaning towards with music with commercial potential but with a harder and tougher guitar orientated sound. The cover for *Big Generator* was another design by Mouat who also did *90125* and it was a simple affair with just the name of the album and the band in large colorful lettering. The colors for the cover varied depending on whether it was the CD edition in yellow and hot pink or the vinyl record edition in green and mauve.

Chris Squire and Trevor Rabin indicated that the intention was to make *Big Generator* similar to the Beatles *Abbey Road* album in that separate songs were to be linked together. Trevor said: "Before we started, we thought a lot about *Abbey Road* as a model. In the sense that, if we come up with an idea, why pressure ourselves into making it a song? Just have it there. If you can't come up with a chorus, don't throw it out because it's not a complete song and don't put a bad chorus around it; just leave the chorus out. So it evolved into an album with long songs, ranging from four to nine-and-a-half minutes."[197]

There were serious obstacles in bringing the recording of *Big Generator* to fruition with disagreements and technical problems. Recording started out at Lark Studios in Italy using an engineer recommended by Trevor Rabin and then adjourned to Trevor Horn's Sarm Studios in London before finally being completed in Los Angeles. Trevor Horn commenced as the chief producer but was eventually usurped by Trevor Rabin who finished it off and there was an unusually large contingent of recording engineers associated with the project. Trevor Horn did most of the production work on the backing tracks but he maintains it was impossible to get the band to agree on the music because they were always arguing amongst themselves and nothing was ever finished.

Trevor Rabin had a slightly different take on proceedings but agreed that there were problems: "There were certain personal problems but mostly it was a musical thing. The band had a very clear understanding of what we wanted to do on this album, and we thought the producer had the same understanding—that obviously wasn't the case. He was pulling it in one direction, us in another, and nothing ever got sorted out…I just said, 'Stop, let's go back to L.A.' I'm on home territory here. I have a 24 track studio at home and I can check things out there…One of the reasons this happened, was the success of our last album (*90125*). There was a lot of apprehension going into it, so it's not so surprising that it didn't work out."[198]

As to the technical problems, Trevor Rabin recalled that the band recorded "I'm Running" at Sarm Studios and the drum sound proved to be so unsatisfactory from an engineering point of view that Alan White had to later completely re-record his part. Chris Squire remembered numerous arguments between producers and engineers as to the technical merits of the latest electronic gadgetry without much progress being made on the album. In fact, Chris and Alan had recorded their bass and drum parts some two years before *Big Generator* was released. During the mixing of the album, Chris said: "I realized—but certain other people didn't—that going to Italy to save money was the start of doing it wrong. Inevitably, when you try to do anything to save money, it ends up that because it's cheaper it's not the best place to be…So we had to redo stuff in London, and other people weren't happy with Trevor Horn doing it there, either, so we ended up doing it in L.A.! The most sensible thing would have been if we'd never left here (L.A.) in the first place; then the album would've been finished a year ago".[199]

Similar to *90125*, most of the keyboard work on *Big Generator* was done by Trevor Rabin and not by Tony Kaye. The keyboards were generally confined to textural work with no real attempt to incorporate adventurous solos and the potential of the music was consequently stifled. According to Trevor Rabin, Trevor Horn had said that he didn't want Tony Kaye playing keyboards and perhaps it was just another part of the general atmosphere of disagreement that riddled the whole creative process for the album.

After *Big Generator* was finally completed, the reaction from the fans was mixed. Similarly, not all members of the band were happy with the album or with the creative process that it involved. After the ensuing *Big Generator* tour, Jon Anderson again decided to leave Yes because he felt that he'd been relegated to merely being the singer in the band with little say in the creation of the music. Steve Howe's view at the time from the outside was: "With *90125* and *Big Generator* we—they—went for what Yes was, but they didn't have the time—or take any time—to be explorative. So they had a song, and hey, bang, it's a song! Well, Yes did that with 'Wonderous Stories' or 'Your Move', but very often we wanted to join it up—say with 'All Good People'. Or 'Wonderous Stories' went into 'Awaken', which compensated for its lightness and was longer."[200]

Big Generator contained some good ideas that didn't always reach full potential and the proposed linkage of the tracks in the style of *Abbey Road* was not strongly apparent. The longer more complex tracks such as "Final Eyes" and "I'm Running" had the hint of classic Yes music about them but stopped short of being totally successful. The guitar work of Trevor Rabin dominated the soundscape of the album but sometimes it didn't seem quite clean enough as in the acoustic passages of "I'm Running" or it was too heavy as in the crunching sections of the title track "Big Generator". Nevertheless, the two singles "Rhythm Of Love" and "Love Will Find A Way" were impressive commercially orientated efforts and received considerable exposure.

Trevor Rabin held a positive opinion of *Big Generator* and liked it as much as *90125*, picking out "Shoot High, Aim Low as being the equal of any track on the earlier album. In contrast, Chris Squire felt that the balancing and mixing of the sound on *Big Generator* had been inferior to that of *90125* and indeed, his bass didn't come across with its customary power. The mixing had been left in the hands of Trevor Rabin and Chris has subsequently acknowledged that they "didn't see eye to eye on how things should be mixed".[201] The version of the title track "Big Generator" that appeared on the U.K. and Australian release of the *Ultimate Yes* compilation was remixed by Paul Fox and it is a considerable improvement on the original with a better balanced sound all around including less guitar and more prominent bass, demonstrating how important the mix is to the final product.

Looking back on the musical environment of the eighties in which both *90125* and *Big Generator* were made, Jon Anderson commented that it was the era of the video artist with little emphasis on live performance: "In the eighties a lot of music was made like a package. You had your music, you had the video, and a show: 'If we have a hit we will put on a show.' Give us a break! So what you had was musicians and singers becoming video artists. You put them on stage and they lasted about half an hour, and like an hour later it's difficult! There were very few bands that could hold an audience for more than an hour, simply because they didn't do the years on stage or in the clubs…There wasn't the growth of great stage-presence musicians as you had in the seventies…So we (Yes) are very fortunate. I really appreciate that there is an audience waiting for us to record and do shows."[202]

Trevor Rabin conceded that much of the material from *Big Generator* didn't translate well into live performance and again, it was probably symptomatic of a troubled project. Chris Squire's perspective on *Big Generator* was: "It's the 'Hootie & the Blowfish' syndrome. They never stood a chance after their first album of ever looking successful again. *90125* sold almost nine million worldwide, so when *Big Generator* only did a couple it was perceived as a failure. Doing extremely well with one project is almost a curse for what is to follow."[203]

"Rhythm Of Love" (Kaye/Anderson/Rabin/Squire)

"Rhythm Of Love" opens the album and it is a bright, upbeat song with a Beach Boys style vocalized introduction before the beat is laid down in no uncertain terms by Alan White and Chris Squire. It's a compelling mixture of melody and rhythm without ever becoming too heavy. It's a song certainly far removed from the likes of "The Revealing Science Of God" but still readily identifiable as a Yes song with commercial potential. "Rhythm Of Love" was released as a single and there was also a mix on twelve inch vinyl to cater for the dance clubs.

Trevor Rabin was the main instigator of the song and he explained that it was about sex as the "Rhythm Of Love", being a cheeky tease and departure from the cosmic lyrics of Jon Anderson. However, the "Rhythm Of Love" doesn't really come across as raunchy but instead has a more sing-a-long kind of feel. The promo video though does lean towards being suggestive but the images seem second rate and distinctly un-Yes like.

As author Bill Martin points out in *Music Of Yes* (Open Court, 1996), Yes always seems to be capable of writing a commercial song like "Rhythm Of Love" but they never made an entire album in that vein because Yes at heart remains an adventurous band—even if "Big Generator" wasn't the definitive expression of their progressive nature. Jon Anderson saw the likes of "Rhythm Of Love", "Love Will Find A Way", and "Almost Like Love" as strong chorus ideas from Trevor Rabin although not necessarily central to the concept of Yes. However, Jon took a pragmatic approach and decided that he couldn't "really change what was imprinted on everybody's mind" in the band, so he would "sort of lyrically dance around the idea of that".[204]

"Love Will Find A Way" (Rabin)

When the *Big Generator* album was released in the vinyl format, "Love Will Find A Way" opened side two and it was virtually a bookend to "Rhythm Of Love" with both being bright, commercial songs. Additionally both songs featured brief orchestral introductions and in the case of "Love Will Find A Way", it was somewhat reminiscent of the Beatles on "Eleanor Rigby".

Trevor Rabin originally wrote "Love Will Find A Way" for Stevie Nicks of Fleetwood Mac but both Chris Squire and Alan White liked it and insisted that Yes record it instead. It was a song with a strong hookline and pleasing harmonies but Trevor admitted that some Yes fans felt that it was too much of a departure from what Yes was about.

The promo video for "Love Will Find A Way" on the *Yes Greatest Video Hits* video/DVD is one of the best and classiest that Yes has made for a single. The video swings between Yes looking at their glossy best on stage in the video studio and scenes of the band sitting around a camp fire while singing.

"Holy Lamb (Song For Harmonic Convergence)" (Anderson)

"Holy Lamb" is a fairly simple song written by Jon Anderson and it is closer in musical style to his solo work than most of his material for Yes with lyrical content that was obviously more cosmic than the rest of *Big Generator*. Although Trevor Rabin felt that *Big Generator* was in many respects amongst his best work for Yes, he mentioned "Holy Lamb" as being a weak track and confessed that he had no idea of what a "harmonic convergence" was.

The real significance of "Holy Lamb" here is that it starkly reveals the difference between Trevor Rabin's mainstream lyrical style and Jon Anderson's quest to be adventurous and to delve into lyrical areas not normally explored in rock music. Jon explained that "Holy Lamb" was about a special event that occurred in 1987 which didn't receive wide publicity but was to do with the ancient energies of the Earth: "What happened was each sacred site…there are twelve sacred sites on the planet—the Vatican is one, the Pyramids, Ayers Rock (Uluru), Mount Fuji, Machu Picchu, the Four Corners of Arizona, Bimini which is near

Florida—there are twelve of these sacred places...and what it is, is a sort of energy point for this planet, so the energy was like as though the Earth was plugged in again to the universe. The Indians say in the next ten years we will realize the potential and destiny of mankind—that's their prophecy and what they believe in. It's in the Bible—Chapter 14, Revelations—that day has occurred; it was August 16 & 17, 1987. It was called 'Harmonic Convergence'. Since then the weather is changing, there is an overall change of atmosphere around the planet. There is a definite openness and awareness that something is slowly but surely changing. Japan is actually in financial control, technology is very Japanese orientated. The Red Indians say that maybe it is their spirituality that will come through to give us a new breath of life about what Christ's consciousness really means. These are things that are happening around us now. It's a good time to be alive!"[205]

◆ ◆ ◆

A number of long time Yes fans don't like *Big Generator* and yet in some ways it is more musically satisfying than *90125*. One senses more input from Jon Anderson on "Big Generator" than on *90125* but Jon clearly wished to be far more influential in the final outcome and it led directly to his departure from Yes for the second time. It is difficult to escape the fact that the Yes lineup on *Big Generator* although certainly talented, was simply not capable of the same brilliance as the classic Yes lineup and couldn't match the profound epics from the seventies. All of that said, I've heard a hot live performance of the unheralded "Almost Like Love" from the *Big Generator* tour and it was surprisingly effective. It is further evidence that even the less celebrated Yes albums have yielded some exciting musical moments.

ANDERSON BRUFORD WAKEMAN HOWE

ABWH:
Jon Anderson—lead vocals/Steve Howe—guitars/Rick Wakeman—keyboards/ Bill Bruford—acoustic and electronic drums
ADDITIONAL MUSICIANS:
Tony Levin—bass/Matt Clifford—keyboards, vocals/Milton McDonald—rhythm guitar
PRODUCED BY:
Chris Kimsey & Jon Anderson.
ENGINEERED BY:
Chris Kimsey & Chris Potter, assisted by Steve Orchard & Rupert Coulson
RECORDED AT:
Air Studios in Montserrat and London
MIXED BY:
Steve Thompson and Michael Barbiero, assisted by George Cowen
RELEASED:
June 1989
TRACKS:
Themes—a) Sound b) Second Attention c) Soul Warrior/Fist Of Fire/Brother Of Mine—a) The Big Dream b) Nothing Can Come Between Us c) Long Lost Brother Of Mine/Birthright/The Meeting/Quartet—a) I Wanna Learn b) She Gives Me Love c) Who Was The First d) I'm Alive/Teakbois/Order Of The Universe—a) Order Theme b) Rock Gives Courage c) It's So Hard To Grow d) The Universe/Let's Pretend

The album *Anderson Bruford Wakeman Howe* was very well received by Yes fans because it represented the reunion of four of the best and most influential musicians to ever be part of Yes. This particular grouping was not legally permitted to call itself Yes but there is no doubt that the public perceived ABWH as in fact being the real Yes under a different label.

Jon Anderson explained that he wanted to "make a different kind of music" to that which he'd been involved in with Yes on *Big Generator* and "the kind of very heavy guitar-oriented type of band that that was becoming". Jon elaborated that he didn't have the freedom on *Big Generator* to use his imagination to the extent he would have liked and it led him to contacting Bill Bruford, Steve Howe and Rick Wakeman, a move that started to open certain doors. Jon found that the members of ABWH were all "very happy to swap musical ideas" and everything began to quickly fall into place.[206]

Rick Wakeman commented that the members of ABWH had a most formidable track record in working together and wanted to take up where they'd previously left off: "For some unknown reason, this particular combination of musicians is quite frightening. It's weird, because Jon, Bill, Steve and I only actually played together for two and a half years. But during that period, we were four-fifths responsible for *Fragile*, *Close To The Edge* and a considerable amount of *Yessongs*. That's pretty terrifying. We were also aware that when Jon, Steve and I did some things together in the latter years of the seventies, something special was going to come out. So when we started this project, however people might accept it, we knew that this strange chemistry was going to produce something that would excite us...There were certain things that we did set out to do when we first discussed the possibility of getting together again. We wanted to have the musicianship of the seventies and what we called proper writing while utilizing the technology of the eighties. We all felt very strongly that the eighties will probably be remembered, more than anything else, for its surge of technology, which has been so powerful that musicianship has been sadly lacking".[207]

The *Anderson Bruford Wakeman Howe* album turned out to have some fine musical moments and the only element really missing from the classic Yes sound was Chris Squire's inimitable bass guitar although Tony Levin proved to be a very adept substitute. Oddly enough, the album featured additional musicians in Matt Clifford on keyboards and Milton McDonald on guitar but their contributions seemed to be minimal and unnecessary. It appears as though they were brought in at points where Rick Wakeman and Steve Howe were unavailable due to other commitments. The music included some typically complex and ambitious songs in the classic Yes style that were about ten minutes in length, interspersed with some shorter pieces. The highlights included the intense "Fist Of Fire", the emotionally powerful "Birthright", the solid rocking "Order Of The Universe" and the trilogy "Brother Of Mine". An edited single version of "Brother Of Mine" received considerable airplay on radio and assisted the album in selling very satisfactorily.

Rick Wakeman explained that ABWH had adopted the classic Yes approach in creating extended pieces of music with substantial depth: "Jon (Anderson) always wanted people to get what they wanted from music. We all feel that you should be able to listen to a piece of music and enjoy it. If you just want to listen once when it's on radio, that's great. If, however, the mood takes you to get a bit more out of it, then there's no reason why you shouldn't be able to put headphones on and go deeper into the music. And if that depth hasn't been planted there by the musicians, you can't go looking for it. It's like trying to scuba dive in three feet of water: it all looks the same from the surface, but you need great depth to get something more out of it. Now, you know as well as I do that people really do want to get something out of music. People don't change over the years. In every generation, there are people who want a lot from their music. The problem is that I don't think the eighties have given that to them."[208]

The *Anderson Bruford Wakeman Howe* album was mainly recorded at Air Studios in Montserrat but Steve Howe added his guitar parts at Air Studios in London. Steve subsequently expressed a great deal of dissatisfaction with the final mix of the album because he played a major role in writing the music and yet it was astonishingly apparent that there was relatively little guitar work on the album. The record label Arista had appointed Steve Thompson and Michael Barbiero to mix the album and they did so in America with evidently no reference to Steve Howe during the process. The global route of the project might not have been helpful to the final outcome, particularly given the fact that the album was recorded over a massive sixty-four tracks before overdubbing commenced. Input from all of the key musicians at the mixing stage would surely have been invaluable.

Steve Howe viewed the mixing fiasco as "some super, high-power, techno-wizard mixers" who "started interfering" with the sound he'd tried to create for the album. He called it "pretty catastrophic" and points out "the record's awfully guitar light; I didn't play like that, it was worked at the mix stage". [209] It should be noted that the version of "Fist Of Fire" which appears on the *In A Word: Yes* compilation is a different mix to the album version with considerably more guitar being evident, probably giving a good idea of the type of mix that Steve had envisaged for the entire album.

Despite the imperfections, many fans felt that the *Anderson Bruford Wakeman Howe* album was the best new Yes-related product to emerge for several years. Rick Wakeman viewed it as "a good album because it had a modicum of spontaneity" and he felt that it had "some wonderful strengths" in songs such as "Brother Of Mine" and "Order Of The Universe".[210] The album cover featured spectacular new paintings from Roger Dean, the front cover depicting an imaginative structure that had originally been a proposal for a building in the desert of Arizona. An excellent promo video was put together for 'Brother Of Mine' incorporating an animated sequence using the image from the front cover and the video included unconventional, almost primal dance-like sequences featuring actors wearing colorful face painting, the designs on their faces having been created by Roger Dean based on his earlier work illustrated in the book *Magnetic Storm*. An amusing aspect was the ABWH album's original catalog number of 90126 that was a satirical response to the earlier *90125* album by Yes.

ABWH toured extensively to play both the new music and older Yes songs to great acclaim from very enthusiastic audiences. Promoters wisely pushed the Yes aspect in publicity for the tour, emphasizing the tag of *An Evening Of Yes Music Plus*. Given their pedigree, it must have been frustrating for ABWH in not being able to simply call themselves Yes but Jon Anderson put on a brave face and said "the music we made together as Yes is very important to us" but "I always feel that I'll make Yes music" and "I have no regrets at all having left the band (Yes)".[211] Steve Howe expressed similar views, saying: "I never thought of calling it Yes. I don't think we needed to because we never particularly wanted to go back to anything. We're not carrying the Yes banner, even though we live up to it, nurture it, guide it and continue to deal with whatever ashes are left from past remnants of it. I didn't want to call it Yes to make everything really easy for us—not that life was meant to be difficult. But greed or possessiveness or jealousy are not things I want to be part of. So I say, good luck to Chris (Squire) and to Ahmet (Ertegun, head of Atlantic Records) with Yes. All's fair in love and war."[212]

Bill Bruford pointed out that ABWH on stage were joined by Milton McDonald on guitar and Julian Colbeck on keyboards because the music was quite complex to play live and "we're not all on a machine, it's not a sequencer band where you press a button and the Madonna show starts".[213] Jon Anderson commented that Bill Bruford had an important role in recording the *Close To The Edge* album but had not actually played the music live until the ABWH tour some seventeen years later, making it a special feeling to finally perform it. The reactions from audiences astounded ABWH and Steve Howe recalled that "every time we played a Yes track, it was like ovation" with "And You And I" attracting such a deafening response that Bill remembered the band being "flattened by a blast of whooping and hollering like you've never heard in your life!"[214]

Some of the critics agreed with the enthusiastic audiences while others just didn't appear to grasp what it was all about, seemingly because of the complexity of the music. Critic John Mackie wrote of the show at the Pacific Coliseum in Vancouver that it must have a been a treat for Yes fans because the band "recreated the old hits to perfection" but they were "about as visually exciting as watching paint dry" because "playing those complex mini-suites takes concentration" and for the most part "the musicians just sort of stood there riffin' away".[215]

A full show from the ABWH tour was filmed in 1989 at the Shoreline Amphitheatre, Mountainview in California for viewing on pay television. It was released on video/DVD as *An Evening Of Yes Music Plus* and is regarded by many fans as one of the finest examples of Yes related musicians on film with excellent performances and camera work, the shots at times focusing on members of the audience carrying large "Yes" banners. The superb Roger Dean stage set is a visual treat and the band is quite animated, with one of the highlights being Bill Bruford's brilliant solo spot played on his sophisticated electronic drum kit. Tony Levin played bass on the tour but missed the Mountainview show through illness and was replaced by Bill's friend Jeff Berlin at very short notice. The soundtrack is also available on CD and at one point a combined CD/video set was available.

Another video/DVD worth seeking out is *In The Big Dream* which is a collection of promo videos for the ABWH album along with footage from the recording sessions. Amongst the selections are the "Brother Of Mine" video and an excellent, extended version of "I'm Alive" (the concluding section of "Quartet") which was released as a single but unfortunately wasn't included on the album in that form.

"Brother Of Mine" (Anderson/Bruford/Wakeman/Howe/Downes)

The song "Brother Of Mine" was effectively the centerpiece of the *Anderson Bruford Wakeman Howe* album and it exemplifies what the band was setting out to achieve. It is music in the classic Yes style with strong melodies and lyrics that emphasize a positive view of life while the complex instrumentation and arrangements cover a wide range of sounds and moods all within the scope of the piece.

Steve Howe played a major role in creating the main musical and lyrical themes for "Brother Of Mine". He contributed a core of musical ideas that he had written before the recording sessions for the album and those ideas were subsequently adapted by the band to become part of the three part mini-epic song. Steve's original song "At The Full Moon" became the basis for the first part of "Brother Mine" titled "In The Big Dream" while similarly, his original song "Never Stop Learning" written with Geoff Downes became the basis for the chorus of "Long Lost Brother Of Mine" in the third and concluding part. It is fascinating to listen to Steve Howe's original versions on his *Homebrew* album and to make the comparisons. The creative process was a prime example of how the members of Yes, or in this case ABWH, collaborate and combine their individual ideas.

Steve explained that he originally wrote "Never Stop Learning" about his own brother who had years earlier gone away to Australia and lost touch. As to "At The Full Moon", it was associated with a dream that Steve had in Devon during a full moon and it was about "waking up one morning and finding that the world had changed, not physically, but mentally. The one thing we hadn't thought of! We're always destroying things; people blowing each other up; but suddenly things change through the mind. So thinking was different, telepathy was there, and it was a sudden shock to find that things had changed, but not physically".[216] Steve elaborated that his ideas tend to be on a more personal level whereas Jon Anderson takes the concepts and expands them to make them more universal in context.

In this case, "Brother Of Mine" sees Jon in typical fashion leaving the lyrical door open for different interpretations. On the one hand, it could be viewed as the reunion of four musical brothers but according to Jon, it was in reality about a person with a narrow outlook who didn't see themselves as being part of the singular whole of humanity, the positive interpretation being that the long lost brother can always return to the fold. The implication taken further is that individual religious, political and economic differences are far less important than the overriding common good of humanity.

"Brother Of Mine" featured an interesting combination of newer and older sounds with Rick Wakeman using modern digital keyboards as well as the more familiar Minimoog from the seventies that had been MIDIed. The musical complexity of "Brother Of Mine" was underlined by Julian Colbeck when he described the requirements of performing the song on stage in his role as additional keyboardist supporting Rick. Julian variously spoke of "a dozen or more (sound) patch changes", "probably four megabytes worth of triggered samples" and "a myriad of key, tempo and basic time changes" over some twelve minutes.[217] It points towards the very considerable effort required to perform and create the music of ABWH and Yes. It is all the more remarkable when it is realized that at each gig during the *An Evening Of Yes Music Plus* tour, ABWH was on stage playing complex Yes music for in the vicinity of three hours in giving some one hundred shows in fifteen different countries on three continents in the space of just eighteen weeks.

◆ ◆ ◆

This album by ABWH was like a breath of fresh air after some of the uninspiring rock music that had been released during the eighties and many dedicated Yes fans preferred it to the musical direction being pursued by Yes on *90125* and *Big Generator*. On the downside, Chris Squire's bass guitar work is definitely missed and it is frustrating that more of Steve Howe's guitar was not permitted to shine through in the mix. Nevertheless, the music on the *Anderson Bruford Wakeman Howe* album is very worthwhile indeed.

UNION

YES:
Jon Anderson/Chris Squire/Steve Howe/Trevor Rabin/Rick Wakeman/Tony Kaye/Bill Bruford/Alan White
PRODUCED BY:
Jonathan Elias, Jon Anderson, Steve Howe, Trevor Rabin, Mark Mancina, Eddie Offord, Billy Sherwood
ENGINEERED BY:
Brian Foraker, Chris Fosdick, Buzz Burrowes, Steve Howe, Trevor Rabin, Eddie Offord, Stan Katayama & Billy Sherwood, with various assistants
RECORDED AT:
Studio Miraval, Le Val, France; Studio Guillaume Tell, Paris, France; Sarm West, London; Record Plant, Los Angeles; Vision Sound, New York; Platinum Island, New York; Langley Studios, England; The Jacaranda Room, Los Angeles; Cherokee Studios, Los Angeles
RELEASED:
April 1991
TRACKS:
I Would Have Waited Forever/Shock To The System/Masquerade/Lift Me Up/Without Hope You Cannot Start The Day/Saving My Heart/Miracle Of Life/Silent Talking/The More We Live—Let Go/Angkor Wat/Dangerous (Look In The Light Of What You're Searching For)/Holding On/Evensong/Take The Water To The Mountain

Union is one of the least popular Yes albums amongst both the fans and the members of the band. It was the result of an amalgamation between *Anderson Bruford Wakeman Howe* and the so-called "Yes West" band consisting of Chris Squire, Alan White, Trevor Rabin and Tony Kaye. Unfortunately the somewhat uneasy alliance between the two groups under the Yes banner was the subject of strong influence from Arista Records in terms of musical direction. The subsequent tour was the one bright spot, providing fans with the novel experience of seeing an eight man Yes lineup perform on stage together.

Rick Wakeman explained how the *Union* lineup grew out of the stand-off between Yes and ABWH: "It got really silly. It was a case of 'Who owns Yes? Who owns the name? Who owns the band? Who owns the recording contract? Who owns yer left leg?' It was so stupid. Then along came Larry Magid..."[218] Magid had been involved in promoting Yes on their first American tour in 1971and he put an idea to Jon Anderson while the ABWH tour was taking place in 1989, a proposal that involved covering all of the costs for an eighty-five date world tour if the reunion of both ABWH and Yes could be agreed. The respective management teams led by Brian Lane for ABWH and Tony Dimitriades for Yes West cemented the partnership deal and Rick was in no doubt as to the motivating force behind it: "If you want me to be brutally honest, those parties are really only interested in one thing, and that's their slice of the financial cake."[219]

The *Union* album was only made possible after Yes agreed to change record labels. Tony Kaye said: "I'd guess that the most complicated thing was for us to join with the record company that really wanted to put out the album. We (Yes West) were on Atco (a division of Atlantic Records), and they were given an opportunity to do it, but they didn't want to, while Arista was very enthusiastic, and they had ABWH. So we had to leave a record company we had been with for twenty-five years to join something new."[220]

The band members expressed varying degrees of uncertainty going into the project and Steve Howe was concerned about the future of ABWH after so much effort had been put into establishing the band. Trevor Rabin also had misgivings but went along with giving it a try. Chris Squire commented: "Jon and I had been talking about the idea of getting this big lineup together for a couple of years. But when the reality of it came up and my manager came to see me with it, I kind of went, 'Oh no, not really.' Knowing the cast of characters, I was concerned about how certain ones would react with others but it seems to be going okay. Even in rehearsals, a lot of my fears were dispelled."[221]

Jon Anderson was attracted to the vision of a large combined Yes going out on tour but he still faced the dilemma between obtaining exposure for his work and striving for the adventurous music that was closest to his heart: "If we're just releasing happy, commercial songs on the radio, it's because the business won't accept anything other than that. So, to get songs on the radio, you have to work with someone who can write those sort of songs and Trevor (Rabin) was perfect. But I'm thinking that on the next LP (album), I'll bring a lot of musicality out. It shouldn't be done too quickly. But if we make one more album in the nineties and it's a beautiful album, it'll be worthwhile."[222] Jon further explained that "Yes is an idea of making music rather than just a list of specific people. It's still trying to be adventurous under the tight reins of the record company. It's an MTV world. No matter how hard you try to stretch your muscles, musically speaking, you have to be attuned to that".[223]

None of the eight musicians in Yes were happy with the *Union* album and they openly expressed their dislike for it. ABWH had been busily putting together material for their second album when it suddenly became the basis for *Union*, with four tracks from Yes West tacked on. Bill Bruford saw *Union* as a disastrous album born out of business dealings in order to maximize financial returns but paradoxically, it fared no better than the earlier ABWH album with 750,000 copies sold. The music on *Union* was the result of a great deal of political interference at various levels and was tremendously expensive to make, costing some $2 million. Ironically, Steve Howe's solo guitar track on *Union* titled "Masquerade" was recorded at nominal cost in his home studio and received a Grammy nomination. Steve commented: "Everything about that record was political—dealing with the producer, the record company, the band members…A lot of people had to be kept happy."[224]

Jon Anderson unfortunately realized too late that the production of the album had become something of a nightmare and he said: "I wish I had stuck to my guns and been the overall producer. But I didn't, I let everyone else produce it and it became a mess."[225] Indeed, it was incredible that such a large number of people worked on the project and even Eddie Offord was involved with the production of two of the four Yes West tracks. However, there was little musical interaction between ABWH and Yes West except for Jon Anderson singing on all of the tracks and Chris Squire supplying backing vocals for three of the ABWH songs. Tony Levin still played bass for ABWH instead of Chris. Jonathan Elias was primarily responsible for producing all of the eight ABWH tracks and in an astounding turn of events, he evidently deemed it necessary to bring in a host of additional keyboard players and an additional guitarist (Jimmy Haun) to record the album. It is bewildering to learn that Steve Howe and Rick Wakeman had most of their work on *Union* altered and replaced by Elias using session musicians, a fact that didn't become known to them until after the album was actually released.

Rick Wakeman commented: "When we were told that we could all get together legally and play, Arista wanted the album finished hastily. The problem was that Steve Howe and I had a lot of other heavy commitments, so a lot of our stuff was stuck in the computer (as MIDI data) and had not been transferred to digital tape. That, sadly, gave the producer a lot more carte blanche than he should ever have had in editing what I'd done, even to the extent of changing what I'd played, because it was so easy: you just had to sit there and play with the little mouse, and things come and go…For example, my personal arrangement of playing 'Shock To the System' bears no resemblance to what was on the record…Well, Jonathan Elias, who I wouldn't have trusted with a food mixer, was the producer. Basically, though, the whole thing got out of control. When I was unavailable, they just steamed away. The thing that annoyed me more than anything was that even if you're unavailable to come in and do things, there are such things as telephones for consultation on the pieces of music you're involved in. I want the next Yes production to be done in house or I'm out. If there's any talk from Arista that they want to give the producer license to do what he likes, they'll be one keyboard player short. That's very important: I want the next Yes album to be a Yes album."[226]

Jonathan Elias for his part has alleged that communication problems at the time between the different members of the band essentially made it difficult to create the album under the circumstances that existed. While it is possible that there may have been some truth to those claims, it also appears to be true that he didn't really understand the creative processes of the group. Rather than managing the creative input from the musicians and sorting out the best ideas, decisions were obviously made that weren't consistent with the aims of the band.

The entry of session guitarist Jimmy Haun into the project at the behest of Elias and Arista was particularly puzzling. The record company had claimed that Steve Howe's guitar parts were unacceptable because there was too much soloing and yet Steve's instrumental album *Turbulence* released in the same period as *Union* was quite excellent. Indeed, some of the music on *Turbulence* was used as the basis for the songs on *Union*, including for instance Steve's tune "The Inner Battle" that became part of the Yes song "Silent Talking". One can only conclude that whatever motives were driving those responsible for the production of *Union*, it had little to do with any attempt at achieving an album with a definitive Yes sound.

That view is further reinforced by a recording that is purported to contain the original demo tracks for *Union* and it confirms that many of the Yes trademarks were originally in the music but eliminated from the final album mix. For instance, the track "Without Hope You Cannot Start the Day" originally had a guitar solo in the middle before it was edited out and "Take The Water To the Mountain" became a fully-fledged song with a guitar solo before it was, for some reason, edited down to the short version on *Union*. Additionally, there was an extremely good commercial song called "Touch Me Heaven" that wasn't even selected for the album, a curious decision that completely baffled Steve Howe and Bill Bruford.

The *Union* tour was a much more successful undertaking than the album. Most of the shows on the world tour were performed from a revolving stage wherever it could be accommodated at the particular venues, the stage completing some ten revolutions during the course of each show. The typical set list was top heavy with Yes's most popular songs from the seventies and eighties with usually only two new songs from *Union* in "Shock To The System" and "Lift Me

Up". The audience response to the show in Quebec, Canada was so explosively enthusiastic that the crowd refused to leave at the end and the venue management had to ask Yes to play a second encore—after the road crew had started dismantling the stage and after Steve Howe had already left the venue and was heading back to the hotel. Martin Townsend reported in *Vox*: "At the end after one encore, the Quebec audience won't stop cheering, stamping and clapping. The row builds into one sound: an oscillating drone, and there's a feeling of riot in the air".[227]

However, the reality of having two guitarists, two drummers and two keyboard players on stage inevitably led to some disquiet and frustration in the ranks. Steve Howe commented: "When we really behaved ourselves there were some great great disciplined shows on certain legs of the tour. But believe me, there were other legs where people just went overboard. There was spotlight stealing and a lot of crawling around and posturing on the floor of the stage. If you're in Yes you have to have more style than that".[228]

Jon Anderson was disappointed that attempts to play "Close To The Edge" as an eight piece lineup were thwarted when some members of the band weren't cooperative but rationalized that the whole *Union* experiment was worthwhile by concluding that it provided the opportunity to play the epic "Awaken" as an extended group. Jon said of "Awaken": "It's my favorite Yes piece of music, the best attempt we ever made to restructure new form, new age, aggressive music. It was always performed very well on tour and it has always been a great spiritual experience. I think it's a great song to bring into the nineties with a little power".[229]

In the final analysis, the *Union* album still contains some interesting music but the potential was undoubtedly and seriously compromised somewhere between the conception of the material and the final production. The album cover by Roger Dean at least gave it the look of a Yes album although the CD booklet was so crammed full of credits for the myriad of people involved that there wasn't even room for the lyrics of the songs. The highlights of the album included "I Would Have Waited Forever", "Shock To The System", "Miracle Of Life", "Silent Talking" and "The More We Live—Let Go". One track written by Trevor Rabin titled "Saving Your Heart" had a very light weight pop feel and would certainly be a contender for the least Yes-like track on any Yes album.

The *Union Tour Live* DVD/video contains highlights of the show performed at the Shoreline Amphitheatre, Mountainview in California on 8 August 1991. Unfortunately the band didn't use the revolving stage for that show but the picture and sound quality is quite satisfactory and a good performance of "Awaken" is included.

"I Would Have Waited Forever" (Anderson/Howe/Elias)

"I Would Have Waited Forever" is the strong opening track on *Union* and it was one of the songs recorded by ABWH. It has a characteristic Yes sound featuring a memorable guitar riff and strong vocal harmonies with additional backing vocals from Chris Squire. Steve Howe said that "I Would Have Waited Forever" "very much has the Anderson-Howe look about it. There's a lot of structure from me, a more ethereal 'Brother Of Mine' feel, if you like, in which it keeps making transitions. The track is very Howe and the lyrics are very Anderson."[230]

The main guitar riff in "I Would Have Waited Forever" was taken from a piece called "Sensitive Chaos", a powerful instrumental track on Steve's solo album *Turbulence*. The title was inspired by a book called *Sensitive Chaos: The Creation Of Flowing Forms In Water And Air* by Theodor Schwenk that was published by the Rudolph Steiner Press, an organization dedicated to education with a philosophical and spiritual perspective. It was a book that combined aesthetics with science to emphasize the nature of water and its link with life. Steve's notes on the album sleeve of *Turbulence* elaborated on his thoughts behind the music in "Sensitive Chaos": "A tumbling rock lands on the sand, only for a while, until the sea reaches it and moves it on, perhaps toward deeper underwater terrain. Change, often resisted but hard to ignore, challenges our ability to adapt. And only those who adapt survive to make their dreams come true". It provides a vivid image when listening to the same musical theme transplanted into "I Would Have Waited Forever". A video about the making of the *Turbulence* album was released under the title *The Turbulent Plan.*

The bizarre twist comes from session guitarist Jimmy Haun who claims that at the request of producer Jonathan Elias, he did all of the guitar work that now appears on "I Would Have Waited Forever", apart from a portion near the beginning and the solo right at the end that are the remnants of Steve Howe's parts.

In common with many Yes songs, "I Would have Waited Forever" was originally written in an unusual time signature but in this case, it was later adjusted to be predominantly in 4/4. Rick Wakeman commented: "It always stems from how it feels. Oftener than not, we'll record it down, and then somebody will go 'What bloody time signature is that?'...I believe that the original piece was in 12/8. If I remember correctly, while we were running it through that way, it didn't sit. The fact is that we can handle 4/4 for an awfully long time because we're all accustomed to it. 12/8 is very difficult to handle for a long period of time. It can become almost comical. I believe that we reverted to 4/4 because that gave us more flexibility, but the ending and the fade sat nicely in 12/8".[231]

"Lift Me Up" (Rabin/Squire)

"Lift Me Up" gained a significant amount of airplay on radio as the main single from the *Union* album and was written by Trevor Rabin and Chris Squire. Trevor has commented said that the lyrics were deliberately written to come across as somewhat indefinite and the song was partly about a homeless person who looks up to the sky for help, to be lifted up and helped out of his predicament. It was originally intended to be a song on one of Trevor's solo albums and Chris suggested some changes to the lyrics after hearing it.

The lead vocals on "Lift Me Up" were mainly handled by Trevor with backing harmonies from Chris Squire and Jon Anderson. It doesn't sound like a typical Yes track with the notable absence of lead vocals from Jon along with the obviously commercial nature of the song.

◆ ◆ ◆

The manipulation of the music on *Union* in the production phase without reference to the Yes musicians was disgraceful to say the least. The best sounding track is probably "The More We Live—Let Go" and it is very significant that it was produced by Eddie Offord who had a clear vision of what Yes music should sound like. More than anything else, the *Union* album underlines the lack of artistic freedom that Yes had in this era as opposed to the early seventies where the members of the band could do exactly as they wanted and achieved such amazing results.

TALK

YES:
Jon Anderson—vocals/Chris Squire—bass guitar, vocals/Trevor Rabin—guitars, keyboards, vocals, programming/Tony Kaye—Hammond organ/Alan White—drums
PRODUCED BY:
Trevor Rabin
ENGINEERED BY:
Michael Jay & Trevor Rabin
RECORDED AT:
The Jacaranda Room, Los Angeles and A&M Studios, Hollywood
RELEASED:
March 1994
TRACKS:
The Calling/I Am Waiting/Real Love/State Of Play/Walls/Where Will You Be/Endless Dream—a) Silent Spring b) Talk c) Endless Dream

Yes went through a period of uncertainty after the *Union* tour and Arista boss Roy Lott suggested that the eight man lineup should be more flexible and consider working in different groupings of say two, five or eight musicians depending on whatever a particular piece of music required. It appears that the idea had little appeal to most of the band with the exception of Steve Howe who felt that it had the potential to promote more interaction amongst the musicians. The decisive move came when long time Yes associate Phil Carson, formerly with Atlantic Records, decided to set up his own record label Victory Music and signed a deal with the *90125* lineup of the band. At first it appeared as though Rick Wakeman might be involved but it ultimately transpired that Rick, Steve Howe and Bill Bruford were excluded from the project. The musicians who were out weren't happy and as it turned out, neither was a large chunk of the Yes fan base.

The *Talk* album was mainly recorded in Los Angeles at Trevor Rabin's home studio known as The Jacaranda Room, with Trevor handling production as well as assisting with engineering. The recording process was very innovative in that it relied heavily upon computer technology. Chris Squire said: "We had been working on ideas for a couple of years, so as soon as we signed the deal with Victory we were ready to go. This record is different because it's the first time Trevor, who was also the producer, wrote together with Jon (Anderson) from the outset. When we did *90125* and *Big Generator*, Jon came in very late and added only a few bits to what we had. For this record, I stepped aside in those areas to allow that union to happen. I only have a couple of writing credits but I'm very happy with what Trevor and Jon came up with. Mark Of The Unicorn came up with Digital Performer and we were really the first people to use it to record everything onto the hard drive. We didn't use any tape, except in a couple of cases to add some vocal overdubs and harmonies. Other than that, all voices and instruments were recorded direct to the computer. Personally, I've never liked the sound of a bass guitar coming off a digital tape machine, I would always feel that serrated edge. So I was amazed when we first started recording bass through this system because it came back sounding better than tape."[232]

Trevor Rabin explained that the argument in recording onto tape had always been about whether analog or digital was superior but with both now producing high quality results, recording with computers had changed the equation yet again. Trevor said: "What's relevant is having the ability to manipulate things and to allow the creative process to work without being held like a noose to tape recorders which work in a specific way in a linear form. With (computer) hard drives you can grab things. With regard to drum tracks you can grab the best drum track and put it where you want, so you can really retain spontaneity."[233]

As to the creative process for *Talk*, Trevor decided that in his role as producer he would have to set the direction for the project. He arranged to spend some time with Jon Anderson to write new material and the two stayed at a beachside motel in San Clemente just south of Los Angeles where they recorded their ideas onto cassettes. Jon Anderson was much happier with *Talk* because he was more deeply involved in writing the music. Jon said: "When two people work together, they create a third event, something neither could on his own. We created this together and that's what Yes has always been about…The music is a clear message of love, power, freedom, spiritual energy and love of life. And that's what Yes music has always been about for me."[234]

Trevor Rabin's approach in the studio was aimed at achieving spontaneity and he commented: "My intention was to just let it roll and not think too much about it; just let it happen and forget about the rules. There were times when someone would say, 'It doesn't sound very Yessy.' To that I would reply, 'Good, let's keep it.'…Yes has always been about change and musical evolution."[235] Despite the positive comments from Jon and Trevor, however, the feedback from Yes's new record company Victory Music suggested that *Talk* wasn't a totally coordinated effort because the members of the band contributed their "individual parts" rather than being together in the rehearsal room and in the studio to create as a unit. Trevor has also more recently admitted that he had disagreements with Jon both during and after the recording of *Talk*.

Talk comes across as being very much a vehicle for Trevor Rabin in terms of creation, production and playing with his guitar work appearing to be heavier and more prominent than ever. While the fifteen minute epic "Endless Dream" is arguably the best and most adventurous work attempted by this particular Yes lineup, the band nevertheless seemed to be somewhat lackluster and the rhythm section of Chris Squire and Alan White often sounded pedestrian when compared to earlier Yes albums. At times *Talk* appears almost as though it were a Trevor Rabin solo album with the members of Yes making guest appearances. Trevor's long list of credits included production, engineering (with Michael Jay), music and lyrics (with Jon Anderson), guitar, vocals (sharing lead with Jon Anderson) and keyboards (Tony Kaye only played Hammond organ on three tracks). It was a level of artistic domination that would have been unthinkable in earlier incarnations of Yes.

The musical style of *Talk* with it's heavy guitar emphasis as exemplified by the metallic introduction to "State Of Play", arguably took the sound of the band so far from home ground that it ceased to be uniquely that of Yes. It was a departure that might have been welcomed by some but it generally drew a very mixed reaction from the fans because it was in some ways the antithesis of the classic Yes sound. Even the album cover had appeared to veer off course with a design by Peter Max who had previously created artwork for the Grammys, the Superbowl and the 1994 soccer World Cup. It was a simple white cover with a new Yes logo but it looked as though it was a somewhat unfortunate punk version of Roger Dean's famous logo from the seventies.

Chris Squire looked back on *Talk* and conceded that because the album was recorded using experimental technology, it came across as somewhat "inorganic and not very Yes-like". He added that Trevor Rabin was "very much the guiding light" in going down the route in working with the new computer technology. [236] Chris further commented: "We were pioneering a lot of systems that are involved with that kind of recording. Although the actual playing is sometimes impersonal, a lot of the music is very good and Jon sings well."[237]

Steve Howe from his position in exile from Yes wasn't a fan of the heavy Rabin guitar approach and said: "I didn't get off on it really because I thought it was too hard and *Big Generator* was too hard and *Talk* was too hard, too tough and in a way too ordinary for me. Although there was some clever things in *Generator*, all three albums had clever things in them, they didn't seem to have much Yesness in them."[238]

The *Talk* tour featured the novel innovation of Yes broadcasting its performances in stereo within the auditorium at each show and it was possible to listen on headphones. Billy Sherwood made his live debut with Yes on the *Talk* tour and provided additional guitar and backing vocals. However, the reversion to the *90125* lineup and the musical style of *Talk* saw album sales and concert attendances plummet—the Yes fans had spoken and they weren't happy with the direction of the band.

The influential fanzine *Yes Magazine* published by Doug and Glenn Gottlieb printed an editorial headed "Change They Must" and it went straight to the heart of the problem, the headline being a play on the title of Jon Anderson's then new solo album "Change We Must". The editorial said that "you don't dismiss three of the principal architects of the Yes sound in Steve Howe, Rick Wakeman and Bill Bruford without some serious repercussions" and that the domination of Yes by any one member as occurred with Trevor Rabin on *Talk* wasn't "the band we know and love as Yes". It went on to say that true Yes music resulted from a collaborative effort of all band members working closely together and that the chase for hit singles should be abandoned. The bottom line was that it urged for Steve Howe and Rick Wakeman to be brought back into the band to once again create the complex, classic Yes music that came from the heart and had established the Yes fan base in the first place.[239]

To their great credit, Yes agreed with the sentiments expressed by *Yes Magazine* because it accurately reflected what the majority of the fan base was thinking. Jon Anderson explained that he knew the editorial to be right and that it had been very difficult in the eighties to make music that kept everyone happy, the crux of the challenge being to balance the commercial requirements of the music business with the continuing pursuit of musical adventure. Given the promise of a new beginning, it turned out that Steve Howe and Rick Wakeman agreed to return to Yes.

The listener needs to be prepared for the generally harder rock sound achieved by Yes on *Talk*. Apart from "Endless Dream" which incidentally wasn't included on the "In a Word: Yes" compilation, the highlights of "Talk" include "The Calling", "Real Love" and "Where Will You Be".

"The Calling" (Rabin/Anderson/Squire)

"The Calling" is the seven minute opening track on "Talk" and it was also released in edited format as a single that received considerable airplay on American radio. In addition to the standard album cut, a lengthened version of the song appeared on the Japanese edition of the album and also on some editions of the single.

Trevor Rabin explained that the music for "The Calling" was "written around the guitar riff" and that lyrically it was "just calling out for everyone to get together."[240] Trevor wrote the lyrics with Jon Anderson who said that they were trying to convey "the idea that we're going to tour the world with this song and we're going to sing to so many people...Everywhere I go are Yes fans. It's just amazing."[241] "The Calling" is a very accessible song with jangly but powerful guitar and strong vocal harmonies in the rousing choruses.

Chris Squire revealed that his dual role of playing bass guitar and singing backing vocals with Yes as on "The Calling" required quite an amount of practice: "Sometimes a (musical) passage can be pretty challenging, but I've been doing it for so long it's like riding a bike. It's all just practice. I always learn the playing bits first, so as soon as they become second nature, I concentrate on getting the vocals tight...We just sat down and listened to the songs (on *Talk*) and then came up with our own parts. Sometimes suggestions were made, but we all trust each other after so much time together. 'The Calling' is fun to play live. It's a good example of separate vocal and bass lines going at the same time which leads to some tricky spots."[242]

◆ ◆ ◆

Trevor Rabin demonstrated in his time with Yes that he was certainly a multi-talented musician but the central question is whether *Talk* is great Yes music. Some people like the *Talk* album very much and it does have its moments but I'm of the view that Jon Anderson and Chris Squire undoubtedly made the right decision to subsequently pursue the path of classic Yes.

Keys To Ascension

YES:
Jon Anderson/Chris Squire/Steve Howe/Rick Wakeman/Alan White
PRODUCED BY:
Yes & Tom Fletcher
ENGINEERED BY:
Tom Fletcher assisted by Kevin Dickey & Zang Angelfire
RECORDED AT:
Live tracks recorded at the Fremont Theatre in San Luis Obispo, California on 4, 5 & 6 March 1996; studio tracks recorded at Yesworld Studio in San Luis Obispo during the American Fall and Spring 1995/96
MIXED BY:
Live tracks by Tom Fletcher, Kevin Dickey & Bill Smith; studio tracks by Billy Sherwood
RELEASED:
October 1996
TRACKS:
Siberian Khatru/The Revealing Science Of God/America/Onward/Awaken/Roundabout/Starship Trooper/Be The One*/That That Is* (* studio recording)

Keys To Ascension 2

YES:
Jon Anderson/Chris Squire/Steve Howe/Rick Wakeman/Alan White
PRODUCED BY:
Yes & Billy Sherwood
ENGINEERED & MIXED BY:
Billy Sherwood
RECORDED AT:
Live tracks recorded at the Fremont Theatre in San Luis Obispo on 4, 5 & 6 March 1996; studio tracks recorded at Yesworld Studio in San Luis Obispo
RELEASED:
October 1997
TRACKS:
I've Seen All Good People/Going For The One/Time And A Word/Close To The Edge/Turn Of The Century/And You And I/Mind Drive*/Foot Prints*/Bring Me To The Power*/Children Of Light*/Sign Language* (* studio recording)

The period after the *Talk* tour saw the departure of Trevor Rabin and Tony Kaye to be replaced by none other than Steve Howe and Rick Wakeman to reform the classic Yes lineup. It was a move that met with the overwhelming approval of the majority of the Yes fan base. Chris Squire explained that Trevor Rabin had started work on creating film scores and given his interest in that area, they'd agreed on a parting of ways. A proposal had been received to record the *Keys To Ascension* albums using the classic Yes lineup and Chris indicated that it was "just a business decision that was guided by the offers that were out there".[243]

Jon Anderson confirmed that the reactions of the fans had been an important factor in the return to the classic Yes lineup. Although most of the band members had needed some time to initially warm to the prospect of working together again, it eventually became just a matter of timing. Jon spoke of the aim for Yes to become more musical again and to "re-invent the classic style of the band", with one idea being to "work with some orchestras around the world".[244]

The reformed classic Yes lineup gathered in the Californian coastal town of San Luis Obispo in October 1995 to begin rehearsals for the *Keys to Ascension* project. The band had agreed to a record deal with Castle Communications and a new manager was appointed in Jon Brewer of Impact. The original idea was for the albums to contain only live recordings but according to Chris Squire, Castle also suggested the addition of new studio tracks. It saw a flurry of writing activity that resulted in a wealth of material being created. Jon Anderson viewed the live recordings as being "like an encyclopedia" of Yes in drawing on the rich musical past of the band and the opportunity of recording new music as "a very good indication that Yes music still has ideas."[245]

Working as a four piece, the band put together the basis of a new epic "That That Is" as well as "Be The One". At that point, Rick Wakeman had finished his prior commitments and came in at the end in February 1996 to make his contribution on keyboards. These were the two studio tracks that were ultimately added to the *Keys To Ascension* 2 CD set. The live material was recorded in three shows performed at the beautifully restored art deco Fremont Theater in San Luis Obispo on 4, 5 and 6 March, 1996. Tickets were at a premium with only 650 seats available for each performance and excited fans from near and far converged on the town for the shows. The first show was originally intended to have just been a rehearsal but tickets were put on sale at the eleventh hour and fans lined up outside the local ticket agency Boo Boo Records in an all night vigil in an effort to see the performance. Steve Howe was so impressed with the enthusiasm of the fans that he surreptitiously made his way to the waiting group at around midnight and suddenly produced a guitar to thrill the crowd with an impromptu twenty minute acoustic set on the sidewalk.

The concerts proved to be a highly memorable event and the band played a host of material that hadn't been performed for years. Steve Howe said: "The shows went off exceptionally well. We pulled out a lot of tunes that we haven't played very often on stage. We're thinking that our fans are tired of hearing 'Heart Of The Sunrise' and the predictable numbers. We wanted to show that we can still do our music from the seventies with the same commitment to it that we had then. Collectively, we wanted to play all the songs. I suggested 'Onward' (from *Tormato*). We did a slightly different arrangement of it and I played Spanish guitar on it. We played 'Turn Of The Century', 'Going For The One' (both from *Going For The One*) and other stuff from that period. We also did side one of *Tales From Topographic Oceans*, 'The Revealing Science Of God', which is a rare thing for Yes to play. We rose to the occasion."[246]

A review of one of the shows by Adam St James in *The San Luis Obispo County Telegram-Tribune* stated: "Nearly every song was received with a standing ovation…Throughout the performance the musicians showed no sign of having lost the virtuosity that made them so popular two decades ago".[247] After playing "Close To The Edge" on the third night, Jon Anderson commented: "I still get so excited singing that song. When we first released 'Close To The Edge', the local music papers in London said it was close to the edge of disaster. And here we are twenty something years later, still close to the edge! But in our hearts, it was always close to the edge of realization. They just didn't get it…"

There is no doubt that the shows had a very special energy but given the unique nature of the event and the fact that there were only three performances, the recordings inevitably contained imperfections that later required correction in the studio. Steve Howe ended up by default with the task of overseeing the production of the live material for *Keys To Ascension* (*Keys 1*). He originally intended to spend four days checking over the recordings but ultimately spent five weeks to ensure that the sound was right with evidently little support from the other band members.

A decision was subsequently made to compile a follow up album using the balance of the live recordings that didn't make it onto *Keys 1*. It was to have the obvious title of *Keys To Ascension 2* (*Keys 2*) and would be another 2 CD set including additional new studio tracks. The recording sessions for the *Keys 2* studio material commenced in November 1996 and the result was forty-five minutes of new music completed in the fast time of only five weeks. Billy Sherwood stepped up to the role in co-producing the recordings with Yes and also handled the mixing.

Problems began to surface when Castle Communications apparently didn't have the resources to promote the release of *Keys 1* on a large scale. Yes instead did some unusual promotions in late 1996 including performing "America" and "Roundabout on the street in New York for the *Fox After Breakfast* television show, a fifty minute live performance in Tower Records in Hollywood and a meet the press promotion on the Eurostar train between London and Paris. Yes were accompanied to Paris by Roger Dean who created the outstanding cover art for the *Keys* project.

Unfortunately the scheduling of a full concert tour proved to be elusive. A further change of band management occurred with Left Bank Management taking over from Jon Brewer and an attempt at setting up a tour in 1997 went awry in total confusion when the proposed dates conflicted with Rick Wakeman's solo commitments. It all ended up going wrong to the extent that Rick again decided to depart the band. The cancellation of plans to tour had a flow on effect to the *Keys 2* album with Castle Communications deciding to postpone its release.

It seemed to be a questionable strategy to combine the live recordings with new studio tracks on the *Keys* albums. The lack of media coverage translated into mediocre album sales and the new songs were consequently virtually lost from public view. It was a situation that was very disappointing for Yes because the new material on both *Keys* albums was some of the best new music from Yes in years, particularly the epics "Mind Drive" and "That, That Is". Both of these pieces took the Yes's progressive approach from the seventies and dynamically updated it for the nineties complete with thought provoking lyrics. The studio material on *Keys 2* was at one stage going to be released as a separate new studio album titled *Know* but the idea was eventually scrapped. Jon Anderson described the new *Keys 2* music as containing "great soloing, great keyboards, great guitars—just powerful all around."[248]

For anyone interested in obtaining all of the recordings from the *Keys* project, I'd recommend purchasing the *Keys To Ascension* DVD/video that includes all of the live performances and the *Keystudio* compilation album that contains all of the studio material from *Keys 1* and *Keys 2*. The original VHS video release of *Keys* had to be immediately recalled due to problems with the sound track but it was eventually corrected after months of delay. Some Yes fans have expressed disappointment with the visual effects added to the DVD/video combined with the fact that the live sound recordings received some enhancement in the studio. Nevertheless, the DVD/video gives a good clear view of the band in an intimate setting and although the selection of camera angles is sometimes limited, the sound quality comfortably exceeds that of earlier Yes live albums.

"Mind Drive" (Anderson/Squire/White/Howe/Wakeman)

"Mind Drive" is an epic in the classic Yes style that was based around music written by Chris Squire when he worked with Alan White and Jimmy Page in the early eighties on the aborted XYZ project. Interestingly enough, Robert Plant was also in the studio with XYZ but according to Alan White, he thought that the material was too complicated and declined to become involved.

In putting "Mind Drive" together for *Keys 2*, Chris explained that he initially worked with Jon Anderson and Alan White in constructing the music by progressively planning and then playing each section. To go with the music written by Chris, Alan revealed that he wrote the "initial beat at the beginning of it and the chord sequence" while Jon also had a song that became part of the overall structure.[249] Steve Howe then returned from England to make his contributions, adopting a distinctive guitar approach incorporating influences from jazz guitarist Roland Kirk. Finally, Rick Wakeman devoted three days to recording the keyboards and put down some sizzling solos. "Mind Drive" is consequently another example of the collaborative writing style of Yes where all the members of the band had ideas that were added to the music.

Parts of "Mind Drive" are as intense as any music ever created by Yes. The introductory prelude led by Steve Howe's acoustic guitar over moody keyboard textures soon gives way to powerfully insistent bass and drums followed by searing electric guitar and Jon Anderson's vocals flying high over the top. The Yes trademark use of dynamics is evident throughout, making the maximum use of light and shade before entering the final movement which is played out with awesome instrumental energy until the last gentle fade. Only classic Yes could produce music of this type and somehow manage to avoid all of the normal clichés of rock.

Steve Howe saw Yes as pleasingly taking chances on "Mind Drive" where the band "kind of pulled out a few surprises, and that meant that it had to be well produced to get those ideas across".[250] Jon Anderson was also enthusiastic and described "Mind Drive" as "an incredible powerful moment".[251] It was lyrically based on the idea of the human mind directly driving a computer and Jon recently explained to me that "there are already computers that can recognize thirty different words just by placing your finger on a sensor pad and using your mind."

◆ ◆ ◆

Yes was starting to explore some very promising musical territory with this lineup in 1996/97 before it prematurely fell apart. The epics "Mind Drive" and "That, That Is" have both been vastly undervalued and it is material that is definitely worthy of being played live on a regular basis. The reunited classic Yes lineup performed "Mind Drive" in concert for the first time during the *35th Anniversary* tour in 2004 and even though it was played in condensed form in two parts sandwiched around other songs, it was even more powerful than on record and received a great reception from audiences. Rumors suggest "That, That Is" was also rehearsed for the 2004 tour, so it too might be premiered live in the near future.

Open Your Eyes

YES:
Jon Anderson—lead vocals/Chris Squire—bass guitars, harmonica, vocals/ Steve Howe—guitars, steel, mandolin, banjo, vocals/Billy Sherwood—guitars, keyboards, vocals/Alan White—drums, percussion, vocals
Additional keyboards by Igor Khoroshev* and Steve Porcaro**
PRODUCED BY:
Yes
ENGINEERED BY:
Billy Sherwood
MIXED BY:
Billy Sherwood & Randy Nicklaus at The Office in Van Nuys, California
RELEASED:
November 1997
TRACKS:
New State Of Mind*/Open Your Eyes**/Universal Garden/No Way We Can Lose*/Fortune Seller*/Man In the Moon/Wonderlove/From The Balcony/ Love Shine/Somehow Someday/The Solution plus unlisted ambient track

Yes confirmed their intention to carry on despite the departure of Rick Wakeman and in light of the band's return to a more progressive style of music on *Keys To Ascension*, most fans expected a continuation in that direction. It therefore came as a surprise when multi-instrumentalist and producer Billy Sherwood was announced as a new member of Yes, especially when he was perceived to have a musical leaning similar to that of Trevor Rabin. The other new face was the unknown but very talented Russian Igor Khoroshev who became the new keyboard player in Yes, although not actually as a full member of the band. He was reputed to have a style somewhere between the jazz of Keith Tippet and the classically influenced wizardry of Rick Wakeman. With Rick leaving Yes for the fourth time, it seemed to catch the rest of the band off guard and it saw them revert to a more commercial approach on *Open Your Eyes*.

Chris Squire explained that he'd been working with Billy Sherwood for the previous ten years in writing songs and that Billy was a talented vocalist, guitarist, keyboardist, bassist, drummer and producer. Billy revealed that he gradually became involved with Yes through his relationship with Chris: "I had the *World Trade* album and Chris (Squire) heard some songs off there in its demo stages and dug what he was hearing. We became friends through a mutual friend of ours and we started writing songs. He introduced me to Alan (White) and at the time it was Trevor (Rabin) and Tony Kaye and Jon (Anderson). And that's how I got introduced to Yes. And along the way, Chris and Alan and myself put together this thing that we called the Chris Squire Experiment that had Steve Porcaro the keyboard player for Toto as well. And we did a tour of California, if you will. And it went very well, it was a good experience and we enjoyed doing it. And I think that that spirit is kind of what brought me into the fold at the end of the day."[252]

The new management team from Left Bank had started to make its mark and they brought order to Yes's immediate future with a comprehensive touring program to get the band back in the public eye after the longer than anticipated gap of some three years since the previous full scale tour. A recording deal was agreed with the Beyond Music label and Left Bank suggested to Yes that there would be time to quickly do a new album before the scheduled start of the tour in October 1997. The expedient solution for the album was to build upon material that had been put together by the song writing partnership of Billy Sherwood and Chris Squire. Chris said: "Billy and I started writing songs and then Jon became involved and we realized that it could become a Yes album. Later on we overdubbed Alan White and eventually put Steve Howe on there".[253]

Jon Anderson explained that between January and March 1997 he'd been exchanging some musical ideas with Chris by sending tapes back and forth. Jon clarified that there wasn't initially a firm intent to make an album but rather it was "like a collection of ideas that started working through Billy Sherwood and Chris working in Billy's studio in L.A."[254] It wasn't until the northern summer in 1997 that Steve Howe finally entered the project. Steve admitted that *Open Your Eyes* might have raised eyebrows with its quite commercial approach but putting a positive spin on the situation, suggested that the album "kind of reflects both the seventies and the eighties period" of Yes and attempted to "make sense of them again, to reappraise what Yes is".[255]

To illustrate how the songs on the *Open Your Eyes* album were developed, Billy Sherwood explained the background to the title track: "It was actually called 'Wish I Knew' at the time (when it was first played by the Chris Squire Experiment). It was a bit different in its arrangement and the ideas that were going on in the top layer. It was one of those things that we were working on...and the record company (Beyond) heard some of the demos from the Squire Experiment and said, 'Maybe you could take this and make it Yes and change it around and let the others get in on it and that's what we did. And I think it turned into a really good Yes song at the end of the day."[256] *Open Your Eyes* was released as a single and gained some radio airplay without leaping up the charts. The original less complex version of the song was included as a bonus track on the *Conspiracy* album released by Chris Squire and Billy Sherwood and it makes for an interesting comparison with the busier Yes arrangement.

In common with earlier Yes records such as *Tormato* and *Big Generator*, the *Open Your Eyes* album contained music with substantial potential that wasn't fully unlocked. The vocal harmonies led by Jon Anderson were particularly strong and the songs were generally good but perhaps at times a little too reminiscent of Billy Sherwood's *World Trade* album. Whatever *Open Your Eyes* lacked as an album might be primarily attributable to the fact that it was rushed and that the band didn't come together as a whole to participate in the writing and arrangement of the material from the outset. Nevertheless, tracks such as "Fortune Seller" and "The Solution" were an impressive and succinct blend of both the older and newer musical styles of Yes and showed the true potential of this lineup with superb guitar from Steve Howe and excellent work from Chris Squire and Alan White.

By contrast, "Man In The Moon" was lightweight and sounded as though it wasn't the kind of song that should have been on the album while "Wonderlove" started with a promising commercial melody but seemed to bog down and get lost somewhere in the middle. "Love Shine" on the other hand appeared to have all of the right ingredients to attract radio airplay but was never released as a single. The "hidden" ambient track at the end of the album featured a montage of various elements from the other tracks and was later used as pre-concert background music during the *Open Your Eyes* tour.

Steve Howe confessed that he wasn't totally comfortable with the *Open Your Eyes* album: "I like all the second half of the album, not that I don't like the first half, but it isn't quite as I thought it was going to be. I think my favorite track at the moment is the duet that Jon and I did, "From The Balcony," just because it's the most personal statement on the record. It's not intricate or noisy, but I suppose that's the kind of music I'm closer to in Yes, the music without flashing lights, without anything other than the musical imagination. A group is a misleading title. A group is an ever-changing, evolving, rebalancing thing and that's always happening. Therefore, *Open Your Eyes* is a new record in the sense that it is quite new for Yes to sound like it does on that record. From "Wonderlove" on, I'm a happy guy; I'm sold. There's more familiarity, more of a balance of what the group really did sound like when we were carving this record. The earlier tracks have more of other peoples' view, which isn't as easy to live with, but you win some and you lose some."[257]

The problem in the eyes of the Yes fans was that they were presented with a slightly underdone commercial album in *Open Your Eyes* while Castle Communications decided to finally release the progressive *Keys To Ascension 2* album at virtually the same time. The stark differences between the two albums were reflected in the respective covers with the former sporting a plain black cover with a large, orange, classic Yes logo while the latter featured a spectacular Roger Dean landscape. The fans were confused and they didn't warmly embrace *Open Your Eyes*. And of course, by this time Yes had covered so much musical ground over the years from epic works to hit singles that it would be difficult even in the best of circumstances to produce any one album that would completely satisfy everyone.

Fortunately the *Open your Eyes* world tour balanced the scales and won Yes some much needed kudos after a difficult period. It saw Yes exhibiting renewed vigor on stage and one of the pleasant surprises of the tour was the exceptional work of Igor Khoroshev on keyboards. Igor was unheralded and only arrived in time to play on three of the album tracks during the earlier recording sessions but he quickly gained a reputation for highly skilled work on stage that often challenged the legendary standards set by Rick Wakeman.

Asked whether he was intimidated by the prospect of playing with Yes, Igor said that he wasn't daunted by following in the footsteps of Rick Wakeman and Patrick Moraz but he "was intimidated by the fact that they were so well known and so well loved by you people and millions of others. My main concern was how will you take me? I'm very privileged to be here with this band. I love being here".[258] Jon Anderson commented: "Igor is the perfect foil for Steve (Howe). I think Igor will become one of the great musicians of the next twenty years. Trevor Rabin would never have a really good keyboard player in the band. He was more happy to have Tony Kaye who is a great back up keyboard player. That's why *Big Generator* and *Talk* never really materialized as classic sounding Yes albums because we didn't have the keyboard player."[259]

The set list on the *Open Your Eyes* tour largely consisted of Yes's most popular songs but the inclusion of the epic "The Revealing Science Of God" was a highlight for many in the audience. Tellingly, the only song from *Open Your Eyes* consistently played on tour was the title track although "No Way We Can Lose" was occasionally heard as was the Jon and Steve duo piece "From The Balcony". A beautiful version of the latter was performed on 4 March 1998 in London accompanied by a guest cello player while the set list for the earlier American leg of the tour had included "Children Of Light" from the *Keys 2* album. Shows in Hungary and Argentina were filmed for television while others in Poland and Los Angeles were recorded for radio broadcast. The stage set was reminiscent of a large circus tent with colorful lighting effects being projected onto the canvas. Chris Squire said: "The whole point of that tour was to re-establish Yes as a performing unit. Also, because Steve (Howe) had only been involved in the tail end of that album, he felt there wasn't much of his soul in the project so we down-played it."[260]

Some of the critics weren't very kind to the *Open Your Eyes* album but Chris Squire had faith in the product. Chris said: "The thing about *Open Your Eyes*…my personal belief is that it reminds me a bit of *The Yes Album.* And *The Yes Album* was never actually in the (American) Billboard Top 200 except at the very bottom. But it just sold over the years. I think you'll probably find with this album that it'll end up selling a lot, even though it didn't run up the charts."[261]

"Universal Garden" (Anderson/Howe/Sherwood/Squire/White)

"Universal Garden" was one of the songs on *Open Your Eyes* that Billy Sherwood had a hand in initiating. Billy explained that he had begun to feel accustomed to working with Yes after being involved with the production of the *Keys* project and he sent tapes to Chris Squire, Jon Anderson and Steve Howe of some of the early ideas for "Universal Garden", "New State Of Mind", "Wonderlove" and "Love Shine". The exchange of tapes was used as the basis for developing the arrangements for each song rather than Yes being together in the rehearsal room to work on the structure.

"Universal Garden" commences with the simple, tasteful beauty of an acoustic guitar introduction. The melodies in the song are instantly memorable and are deftly taken to the plateau as the piece develops with strong lead vocals and harmonies. The electric guitar work is very incisive with rich supporting keyboard textures while the production is distinct, clear and clean in common with the rest of the album. The lyrics of many of the songs on the *Open Your Eyes* album contain the positive messages we've come to expect from Yes and "Universal Garden" with its references to space, time and universal love lends itself to a spiritual interpretation but ultimately leaves it to the listener to decide:

Beyond the sun…Beyond the sky
Are where the real questions lie
Wanting to know where it begins
The puzzle piece we are missing
Beyond the sun…Beyond the sky

Are where the real questions lie
Universal Garden above

—(brief extract from "Universal Garden" written by Anderson/Howe/Squire/Sherwood/White; published by Opio Publishing BMI, Carlin Music PRS, Basedown Ltd PRS, Backyard Levitation Inc ASCAP, Warner/Tamerlane Inc BMI)

While "Universal Garden" is a relatively brief Yes song at just over six minutes in length, it is a piece that contains many of the strengths of Yes in writing, arrangement, instrumentation and vocals.

◆ ◆ ◆

Some of the music on *Open Your Eyes* is a little underdeveloped but the best tracks are strong and anyone who previously dismissed the album might find it worthwhile to reconsider the material. "Universal Garden" is a very under-rated song and both "Fortune Seller" and "The Solution" also have the hallmarks of great Yes music, not in the sense of being epic works but rather as concise expressions of interesting ideas and some impressive playing.

It is relevant when comparing Yes albums to bear in mind that the vinyl records of the seventies were typically about forty minutes in length while modern CDs typically contain sixty minutes of music or more. Even in the highly creative early seventies, double albums frequently weren't that well received regardless of who recorded them because they tended to stretch the creative resources of musicians to the limit and some allowances therefore need to be made when assessing the latest CDs. For instance, *Open Your Eyes* weighs in with a total of seventy-four minutes of music and is therefore roughly equivalent to a vinyl record double album.

This is not to imply that *Open Your Eyes* stands amongst the greatest albums of Yes but rather to suggest that the achievements of the band in the mid to late nineties tend to be too readily disregarded because the best music from *Open Your Eyes* and the two *Keys* albums does stand up to scrutiny. The cream of that work joins a growing list of fine Yes songs that have seldom or never been performed live such as "Sweet Dreams", "To Be Over", "Turn Of The Century", "Release Release", "Tempus Fugit", "Brother Of Mine" (ABWH), "The More We Live—Let Go" and a song from the next album that will be discussed—"Homeworld" from *The Ladder*.

THE LADDER

YES:
Jon Anderson—lead vocals/Chris Squire—bass guitars, vocals/Steve Howe—lead & acoustic guitars, steel, mandolin, vocals/Billy Sherwood—guitars, vocals/Alan White—drums, percussion, vocals
Note: World instruments by Randy Raine-Reusch; horns on Lightning Strikes by The Marguerita Horns
PRODUCED BY:
Bruce Fairburn
ENGINEERED BY:
Mike Plotnikoff assisted by Paul Silveira
RECORDED AT:
Armoury Studios, Vancouver, Canada from February to May 1999
MIXED BY:
Mike Plotnikoff
RELEASED:
October 1999
TRACKS:
Homeworld (The Ladder)/It Will Be A Good Day (The River)/Lightning Strikes/Can I?/Face To Face/If Only You Knew/To Be Alive (Hep Yadda)/Finally/The Messenger/New Language/Nine Voices (Longwalker)

The Ladder took the potential exhibited by this Yes lineup on *Open Your Eyes* and developed it to a considerably greater degree. It saw Yes still attempting to make music that was quite accessible and commercial but it contrasted significantly with the commercial approach taken by the band in the eighties. The Yes music of the late nineties sought to retain the essential elements of the Yes sound that had been established in the seventies and used that as the basis for exploring new sounds and new directions.

Billy Sherwood viewed his role in Yes as attempting to bridge the gap between the progressive and commercial eras of the band. Billy said: "The history of the band makes it complex and the politics are incredibly deep…I've tried to bridge the two worlds…Among the fan base there's a definite line in the sand between the Steve Howe era and the Trevor Rabin era. I've always thought that that's silly because it's all under one banner and all sounds like fantastic music."[262]

Yes decided to record *The Ladder* at Armoury Studios in Vancouver, Canada with acclaimed producer Bruce Fairburn who had been recommended to the band by their management Left Bank. Bruce had previously worked with acts such as The Cranberries, Bon Jovi and Motley Crue. In preparation for the album, Yes set up camp in Canada and spent some three months together at a place called The Sanctuary where they wrote a wealth of material. Bruce Fairburn then came in and selected what he believed to be the best of the music for recording the album.

In light of the shortcomings of some previous albums, Yes recognized the importance of collectively involving all of the band in the creation of the new music right from the start. Alan White commented: "This time we are all actually going to sit in a room again and start writing...Bruce Fairburn (is) an incredible producer and musician and you might see some really good stuff this time."[263] Jon Anderson said: "This album was like, let's rehearse together, perform together, record together and then we'll finally make the album that I've been waiting to make for twenty years".[264]

As to the direction for the music, Chris Squire said that the management of Yes had been pressing for *Fragile 2* but he saw it as a case of "we'll see what happens when we get together."[265] Someone suggested to Alan White that the new album should be made to sound like *Going For The One* and his response gave a good insight into the thinking of a member of the band: "For me, every different aspect of the life of the band, every year was different going through all the Yes years, and all the albums are different because we're all living different lives and kind of basically living my life with Jon Anderson and Chris Squire and Rick (Wakeman) for many years because you really become part of a family you live with the whole time. So it's kind of like in the end *Going For The One* becomes just a part of it because all the other parts are memorable to me too."[266]

Chris Squire declared that the driving force behind Yes's music remained unaltered for *The Ladder*: "We're still trying to conquer the next hillock, the next challenge, the next musical adventure—that's what keeps us going really. To try and better ourselves and that's always been our philosophy and we're doing it again now."[267] Bruce Fairburn in his role as producer had the goal of re-capturing the elements that had contributed to the success of great Yes albums such as *Fragile* and felt that Yes could entice many new listeners if they achieved a hit song on radio. The opportunity to attract new fans appears to have been the main reason why Yes pursued a commercial direction with *The Ladder* despite the earlier rejection of that strategy before the *Keys To Ascension* project.

Yes saw it as invaluable to have an impressively credentialed producer in Bruce Fairburn to manage the recording process. Chris Squire said: "It pays to have that overview opinion from a third party". Jon Anderson agreed and commented that Bruce was "a good referee. He'd say if he didn't like the song and kick it out. He was into making us the best Yes album possible. He was like another guy in the band but when you walked into his lounge he had multi-platinum albums all over the walls. So who's going to tell him he's wrong?!"[268]

It was hoped by Yes to create some magical music on *The Ladder* but as Steve Howe pointed out, there is never a guarantee of success: "The more you look for it, the less it's there. You've got to let it just happen…it isn't so much magic as energy when we get together. It's hard if we don't go about things in the right way and we don't keep a nice balance, so the more we get things right then the better the music is…if there is magic, that's what makes it come back."[269]

The approach taken in making *The Ladder* was for it to be an album that was recorded live in the studio. Yes played together during the recording sessions and many of the original backing tracks from the keyboards, guitars, bass and drums were retained for the final mixes. The music consequently sounded very fresh and benefited from the clean and uncluttered production techniques of Bruce Fairburn. However, it was tragic that Bruce passed away from natural causes prior to the mixes being completed and it will always remain open to speculation as to whether he could have brought any extra magic to the finished album. Steve Howe commented: "Bruce Fairburn finally enabled us to record an album that was really made like a Yes album, as opposed to the previous albums which were more like a collection of solo ideas…For me the strength of any Yes product is in the collaboration."[270]

Although *The Ladder* was largely quite commercial in style, Yes were still musically adventurous as shown by their adoption of World Music influences. Jon Anderson and Alan White had spent some time in the Caribbean and brought a Jamaican feel to "Lightning Strikes", a song that was about developing a more spiritual approach to life and recognizing that there was more to existence than just making money in the material world. "Face To Face" was about becoming aware of the beauty of children and how unfortunately they can sometimes be easily destroyed or broken and it contained a different musical influence that came from Senegal and central Africa. Jon had been listening to Ethiopian and Arabic music for several years prior to *The Ladder* and pointed out that World Music had been absorbed into Yes music going as far back as *The Yes Album* and *Fragile* where Gamelan music from Indonesia had influenced rhythms and vocal treatments, the Monkey Chants from Bali being a particular source of inspiration.

The general consensus seemed to be that *The Ladder* was a good album although many fans might have preferred more material in the progressive style of the very accomplished "Homeworld" that opened the album. Perhaps the first half of "Finally" was just a little too close to straight ahead rock and "If Only You

Knew" may have been slightly too middle of the road. On the other hand, "The Messenger", "Nine Voices" and "It Will Be A Good Day (The River)" were strong but concise Yes songs. "Face To Face" came across as possessing a quintessential Yesness combined with obvious commercial potential and it was difficult to fathom why it wasn't released as a single because it seemed to have all the makings of a hit. Nick Shilton in *Classic Rock* magazine proclaimed that after the problematic *Union* and *Talk* albums, *The Ladder* demonstrated that "Yes have recaptured their form" and that "the music has plenty of freshness and vitality".[271]

The Ladder was released in a variety of different editions and the European edition, for instance, came in a state of the art enhanced CD format including a demo of the "Homeworld" PC game, a screensaver and a video interview with the band. The album looked impressive with a typically imaginative Roger Dean painting on the cover which incorporated the square, oriental style Yes logo that had first been unveiled on the *Yesyears* boxed set compilation in 1991. Roger described the cover as being a cityscape with a deliberate ambiguity between it being either a city or a fantastic giant cathedral with flying buttresses. He depicted it as a structure built out of green luminescent glass and it was intended to be a building that was fun to explore.

The signs were that *The Ladder* should have been an enormous commercial success but it never happened because it was badly promoted and radio stations just didn't give the album enough exposure. Yes became frustrated with the vagaries of radio station airplay policies, changing on air formats and narrow perceptions of what music should be given widespread exposure. Jon Anderson likened it to going to a restaurant and not being able to find what you wanted on the menu: "You wanted something special but you have to eat what they've got because that's what they've got and you're hungry and it's the same with music. If you don't get the opportunity to hear any other music, you're going to pick what there is."[272] Jon viewed *The Ladder* as "not classic Yes music in the sense, but in the same vicinity" and it was a bitter pill for him "that we don't have a forum to play it because people don't want to play our music on normal radio".[273]

After the disappointment of the album not receiving the commercial exposure it deserved, Yes did something of a radical re-think after completing the European leg of *The Ladder* tour in March 2000. It led to Billy Sherwood departing to pursue other musical interests while Yes went back on the road as a five piece unit in America in June 2000 for the two month *Masterworks* tour that saw the band concentrate on their epic progressive works. Igor Khoroshev retained his position on keyboards and continued to demonstrate a real ability to cope with Yes's most demanding music, even though he wasn't a fully-fledged member of the band.

"Homeworld (The Ladder)" (Anderson/Howe/Sherwood/Squire/White/Khoroshev)

"Homeworld" is one of the best songs recorded by Yes in the nineties and it successfully achieves an accessible but progressive musical style. Clocking in at nine and a half minutes, it covers a vast amount of musical ground from spacey sound effects at the start through verses with hints of World Music to choruses that soar in the best Yes tradition with strong melodies. "Homeworld" is a dynamic piece ranging from quiet piano and acoustic guitar to a full throttle middle section in which the band has never flown higher with stunning instrumentation before returning to a quiet but satisfying ending.

The inspiration for "Homeworld" came out of developing a piece of music for use with a computer game. The initial idea had been to create an entire album as a video game but Yes soon realized that the lead time required for technical development was too lengthy. It turned out that Alex Garden who invented the Sierra *Homeworld* computer game lived in Vancouver where Yes were recording *The Ladder* and it led to a meeting to discuss the possibilities. Jon Anderson said that the game "sort of reflected a lot of Yes's history in some ways" and "it was kind of easy to sketch out a lyric that would work with it".[274] The lyrics went with the last piece of music that Yes had recorded for the album and it was originally titled "The Ladder" before it became "Homeworld". Jon clarified that "Homeworld" was about "the power of truth and peace and how we're all trying to find our way home…we're all trying to find our homeworld."[275]

According to Steve Howe, Yes had minidisc demo recordings of some fifteen songs before Bruce Fairburn culled the material for continued work in the studio. Ironically, "Homeworld" had been one of the songs initially rejected by Bruce but after some additional work by the band, it was reconsidered and ultimately became the strongest track on the album. Billy Sherwood had a keen interest in computer games and the band as a whole saw the potential of the medium, so Steve explained that it was an opportunity for "cross-marketing" because "games as such are too important to be ignored" and it created new possibilities for both Yes and Sierra who manufactured the game.[276]

Yes played "Homeworld" on *The Ladder* tour but unfortunately it hasn't been included in subsequent set lists. Hopefully a spot will be found for "Homeworld" in the future because it has all the characteristics of classic Yes music. An impressive Dolby Digital 5.1 surround sound mix of the album version of "Homeworld" is included as a bonus feature on the *House Of Yes* DVD. An edited version of "Homeworld" was released as a single but in common with the rest of the album, it received little exposure.

◆ ◆ ◆

The Ladder had a sense of brightness about it and the collective approach taken by Yes in its creation came through as a real positive. While the album would have benefited if Yes had cut loose instrumentally a little more as they did in "Homeworld", *The Ladder* was nevertheless at this point the best Yes release since the seventies and it indicated that the band still had plenty of strong musical ideas to offer.

House Of Yes—Live From House Of Blues

YES:
Jon Anderson/Chris Squire/Steve Howe/Billy Sherwood/Alan White/Igor Khoroshev
ENGINEERED BY:
Biff Dawes; recorded by Westwood One
RECORDED AT:
Live at the House Of Blues, Las Vegas, Nevada on 31 October 1999
MIXED BY:
Mike Plotnikoff
RELEASED:
September 2000
TRACKS:
Yours Is No Disgrace/Time And A Word (excerpt)/Homeworld (The Ladder)/Perpetual Change/Lightning Strikes/The Messenger/Ritual—Nous Sommes Du Soleil (excerpt)/And You And I/It Will Be A Good Day (The River)/Face To Face/Awaken/I've Seen All Good People/Cinema/Owner Of A Lonely Heart/Roundabout

The *Open Your Eyes* tour had confirmed that Yes was still a potent force on stage but with *The Ladder* tour they seemed to take their performances a notch even higher. The band started *The Ladder* tour in South America in September 1999 before heading to North America in October through to December 1999 followed by the U.K. and Europe in early 2000. The set list was varied to some extent during the first two stages of the tour but throughout it included several new songs from *The Ladder* as well as a selection of Yes favorites from over the years.

It became fashionable in America in the late nineties for leading bands to play in more intimate venues. As part of that trend, Yes performed in a number of smaller venues during *The Ladder* tour including the very popular House Of Blues clubs that were scattered across the United States. The most notable show was at the House Of Blues located in the magnificent Mandalay Bay casino complex in Las Vegas, Nevada on 31 October, 1999. It was filmed and recorded for release on television, the internet, CD, DVD and video under the title of *House Of Yes—Live From House Of Blues*.

I recommend the DVD as being the ideal format for *House Of Yes* because it includes a 5.1 Dolby Digital sound track as well as worthwhile bonus features such as interviews and a 5.1 mix of the studio version of "Homeworld". Some people have found the sound to be a little light on bass and Steve Howe commented that he wasn't totally happy with the mix and shot editing. Nevertheless, I suggest that the overall product is impressive and most importantly it successfully captures the excitement of a Yes concert. In particular, the 5.1 surround sound mix leaves little to be desired when played on quality equipment. Many fans seem to agree that *House Of Yes* is one of the best representations of Yes live in concert.

All formats of *House Of Yes* include the entire show in the correct order of performance except for "Close To The Edge" and "Hearts" which were played on the night but left on the cutting room floor. I recommend that the best way to appreciate *House Of Yes* is to set aside the time to watch it (or listen to it) from start to finish in one sitting. It is then possible to appreciate the fascinating organic development of the show from the opening excerpt of the Firebird Suite and the initial excitement of "Yours Is No Disgrace" through the various feelings and moods of the songs until the awesome epic adventure of "Awaken". Yes build up the energy of the show until it eventually becomes white hot. Steve Howe once said that he feels he is in top form when he starts moving his head back and forth while playing and so his body language speaks for itself towards the end of "Roundabout".

It is truly extraordinary how Yes is still able to perform a piece such as "Perpetual Change" with such obvious conviction and expertise twenty eight years after it was first released. As far as the new songs from *The Ladder* are concerned, "It Will Be A Good Day (The River)" benefits considerably from the inclusion of an extended guitar solo while "Face To Face" is a memorable showstopper. Given that the concert was held in an intimate venue with a relatively small stage, the lighting and stage video effects are not clearly apparent but the high level of communication between Yes and the audience emphasizes the benefit of the small venue.

During *The Ladder* tour, Yes appeared on the *Jim Ladd's Living Room* radio program of KLOS FM in Los Angeles and Jon Anderson was asked about the central message that he and the band have attempted to convey throughout their career. Jon characterized Yes as being a group of wandering minstrels touring the world to "make people happy every night" and commented that taking music to people was "a sort of healing power" and "a sacred thing". He further explained: "We were touched by the Beatles, all of us. And 'All You Need Is Love' was like an anthem for the sixties for a lot of musicians...The Beatles had this incredible feeling coming through millions of people all over the world, that all you really need is love. And the idea to carry that on was like a musical challenge or lyrical challenge for me when I started working with Chris (Squire) and then Steve

(Howe) on lyrical content because we wanted to continue waving that flag…The idea is that we're still hopefully carrying on that flag of there is love, there is peace, there is light, and that comes through a lot in our realization of who we are."[277]

Our journey into the music of Yes started thirty long years ago in 1969 with a discussion about a Yes cover version of a Beatles song and it can be seen that the link of inspiration still exists between the two bands. Both Yes and the Beatles have achieved enormous artistic success as well as being innovators of the highest order and yet each had a sound and approach that was unique. An appropriate summary might be that the Beatles excelled at producing the hit single with immediate appeal while Yes mastered the long form of composition with epics that highlighted instrumental brilliance. It is interesting to contemplate what it was in post second world war England that fostered such incredibly rare talent.

◆ ◆ ◆

It is difficult to choose the definitive Yes live recording that strikes the ideal balance between featuring the best lineup of the band, great performance and excellent production. *Yessongs* contains great performances on CD and DVD but the technical quality of the recordings pale against what is now possible with modern equipment. *Yesshows* draws on diverse material from different tours and as a result, it doesn't convey the special feeling of actually being at a Yes show although the performances are of the high standard one expects from Yes. The *9012 Live* video features a very good performance but some of the effects are dated and it isn't the classic Yes lineup.

The high quality *Yessymphonic Live* DVD must be excluded from the contest because it doesn't qualify as a typical Yes show with the inclusion of the orchestra. *Keys To Ascension* is similarly not a typical Yes show because it didn't capture the band in mid-tour, at their peak, in the heat of battle. *House Of Yes* is consequently the best compromise at present but it notably doesn't include Rick Wakeman. Performances from the 2003 and 2004 tours have been recorded and it could be that a well produced release drawn from the cream of that material will stand the best chance of becoming the definitive Yes live recording.

MAGNIFICATION

YES:
Jon Anderson—lead vocals, midi & acoustic guitar/Chris Squire—bass guitars, vocals/Steve Howe—acoustic & electric guitars, steel, mandolin, vocals/Alan White—drums, percussion, vocals, piano
Note: Orchestral music composed, arranged and conducted by Larry Groupe
PRODUCED BY:
Yes & Tim Weidner; Executive producer Jordan Berliant
ENGINEERED BY:
Tim Weidner; additional engineering by Nick Sevilla, John Elder, Charlie Bouis
RECORDED AT:
Sound Design Studios, Santa Barbara, California; orchestra recorded by Le Mobile
MIXED BY:
Tim Weidner & Steve MacMillan
RELEASED:
September 2001
TRACKS:
Magnification/Spirit Of Survival/Don't Go/Give Love Each Day/Can You Imagine/We Agree/Soft As A Dove/Dreamtime/In The Presence Of—a) Deeper b) Death Of Ego c) Turn Around And Remember/Time Is Time

Yes recorded the *Magnification* album as a four piece band after Igor Khoroshev departed under somewhat of a cloud following the highly successful Masterworks tour. The idea of Yes working with an orchestra had been under consideration for quite some time and the absence of a keyboard player made it the appropriate time to go ahead. It was a concept that had obvious appeal to Yes, particularly in light of the much earlier flirtation with a small orchestra on the *Time And A Word* album. The music was to be recorded based around guitars, bass, drums and vocals with the orchestra to be added to take the place of what normally would have been created using keyboard instruments.

Jon Anderson explained: "Our initial idea was to work with an orchestra instead of a keyboard player. The four of us in the band felt it was worth doing another project together at this time in our evolvement. So we found a good orchestrator called Larry Groupe who helped us to do that. I think it was Steve (Howe) who made the suggestion because he was so tired of chasing the idea of becoming a commercial band. We'd been pushed in that direction on *Open Your*

Eyes and *The Ladder* and neither of those worked. So we had a meeting about what Yes really means—and it's our larger pieces of music."[278]

Magnification was recorded at Sound Design Studios in Santa Barbara, California, with production by Yes and Tim Weidner who also handled the engineering and co-mixed it. Tim had ten years earlier been involved in engineering Steve Howe's solo album *Turbulence*. Yes recognized it was critical to have the right arranger for the orchestra and they appointed Emmy award winner Larry Groupe who was a long time Yes fan and best known for his work on *The Contender*.

The band went into the studio in early February 2001 and set to work on making demo recordings as a basis for the album. Meetings were held with Larry as the work progressed and he was initially given the task of orchestrating four songs that helped to set the course for the project. The band subsequently continued to work with Larry and together they created the music with the orchestral requirements in mind. Rather than adopt the simple approach and add orchestral flourishes to otherwise completed songs, Yes took the route of more fully integrating the orchestra with the band. By May 2001, the vocals, backing tracks, guitars and overdubs for the album had been completed.

Yes notably followed on from their experience with *The Ladder* and worked together in the studio in the writing and recording of all of the music for *Magnification*. Alan White commented: "Everything was written jointly. We were all in one room everyday from lunchtime. We worked for six to eight hours together. The creativity came from everybody."[279]

Larry Groupe explained that "the songs were written to be, as much as possible, different from each other" and his role with the orchestra was "to approach the arrangements and orchestral parts also as different as possible". While the orchestra was added separately to the recording, the orchestrations were very much "part of the fabric of the original song writing" because Larry had been involved in the project at an early point and had collaborated with Yes throughout the creative process.[280] The orchestra used on *Magnification* was the San Diego Symphony Orchestra with whom Larry had previously worked.

Jon Anderson had an earlier experience of working with an orchestra when making his solo album *Change We Must* that was released in 1994 and he knew what was required. Jon commented: "We just had to make sure we had a good arranger. If you listen to the (*Magnification*) album it has this sort of ebb and flow—one moment it's sort of pretty heavy, then beautiful music, then poignant song, then a very simple sort of seventeenth century kind of feel about some songs. I like the album very much."[281]

Magnification liberated Steve Howe in that at last he could again record a new Yes album without having to work around another guitarist as he'd been required to do on the two previous albums. However, Steve admitted to having to exercise some restraint in working with the orchestra because of the large number of instruments involved but he still managed to tastefully incorporate a substantial fabric of excellent acoustic and electric guitar work. Chris Squire commented that *Magnification* contained his favorite format for Yes music with a number of songs in the range of ten minutes long together with some shorter tracks. He also pointed out that while the album essentially consisted of separate songs, the mixing deliberately created a sense of continuity with the tracks being judiciously faded into each other.

When any rock band works with an orchestra it is always bound to be controversial to some extent. In the case of Yes, it might be seen as an unnecessary move given that the band has always achieved an orchestral sound in its own right. On the other hand, it might equally be said that the use of an orchestra was a logical avenue for Yes to explore given the orchestral nature of Yes music. Despite some initial apprehension prior to release, the verdict from many fans was that *Magnification* was in fact the best Yes album since *Going For The One* in 1977. It had a refined and sophisticated sound that was different to any previous album by the band and yet it was still very distinctively the sound of Yes. The highlights of *Magnification* included the title track along with "Give Love Each Day", "Can You Imagine", "Dreamtime", "In The Presence Of" and "Time Is Time". "Can You Imagine" featured lead vocals by Chris Squire and the song originated from the XYZ sessions in the early eighties. In some ways the band seemed to be deliberately less aggressive than usual in order to blend with the orchestra and yet the overall result was still undeniably powerful. The album was extremely well packaged with artwork by Bob Cesca but strangely, it was only the all-important front cover that was a let down—unfortunately the dark, star filled sky with the tiny classic Yes logo just didn't have sufficient visual impact.

In a move that can only be viewed as courageous to say the least, the *Yessymphonic* world tour that commenced in July 2001 saw Yes perform every show with a forty-four to sixty piece orchestra, augmented by young American keyboard player Tom Brislin from the band Spiraling. The doubters said it couldn't be done and pointed to Emerson Lake and Palmer who many years before in 1977 had gone out on the road with a hand picked orchestra that soon had to be ditched for all but a handful of dates when the costs quickly escalated out of control. Yes instead opted to perform with different groupings of local musicians during the American leg of the tour and then in Europe used two dedicated orchestras to cover all of the dates. It was a triumph of massive proportions for Yes, especially considering the enormity of the task and the huge effort required in achieving the right sound at every show.

It was slightly disappointing that the only tracks from *Magnification* to make the *Yessymphonic* tour set list in America were "In The Presence Of" and "Don't Go"—the title track "Magnification" was only added for the shows in Europe. However, the cavalcade of Yes epics and other favorites performed with orchestral accompaniment made any complaints seem lame. In introducing "Magnification" on stage, Jon Anderson said: "It's a song about the idea that if you magnify everything that is good within you, everything good that is outside you shall also magnify and life will be pretty cool." The tour was brilliantly captured on *Yessymphonic Live* that is generally regarded as the best DVD/video so far released by Yes and which I highly recommend.

The timing for the release of the *Magnification* album proved to be most unfortunate. The final finishing touches were still being added to the album during the first weeks of the *Yessymphonic* tour and it wasn't released until after the American leg of the tour had ended, meaning that the fans were hearing the new material for the first time at the concerts. *Magnification* was ultimately released on the fateful day of 11 September 2001 when the terrorist attacks took place in America. Amazingly enough, Yes had played the last show of the American tour only three nights earlier in New York at Radio City Music Hall—in the same city where the World Trade Centre would tragically be destroyed. It was quite chilling how the lyrical content of the songs on *Magnification* had relevance to the terrible events of 9/11, especially the various lines from the track "Spirit Of Survival": *In this world the gods have lost their way…The spirit of survival, Who's teaching the hatred…We don't understand at all…In this world I truly do believe there is a safer place…The spirit of survival, To magnify the soul* (brief extracts from "Spirit Of Survival" by Anderson/Howe/Squire/White; published by Opio Publishing BMI, Bug Music BMI, Carbert Music PRS, Warner/Tamerlane Publishing BMI).

The album seemed to become buried in the overwhelming drama of the time and despite some very positive critical acclaim, it received shamefully little exposure and didn't sell anything like the number of copies that the music deserved. Steve Howe commented: "*Magnification* is definitely not throwaway material. It's classic Yes in the sense that the music is strong in the writing, performing and orchestration." [282] A review by Dan Aquilante in the New York Post described *Magnification* as "uplifting, optimistic music that's lush without the mush" and suggested that anyone who had previously not had an interest in Yes may well have a change of mind after hearing the album.[283]

A DVD—Audio edition of *Magnification* was subsequently released, a format that permits 5.1 Dolby Digital surround sound reproduction on most DVD players and even higher quality sound on specialized DVD-Audio capable machines. The sound quality of the original CD was excellent but it is a sumptuous experience to listen to the surround mix with its supreme clarity and I give it my highest recommendation. Co-producer Tim Weidner said: "The surround mix is quite exciting. We delegated the orchestra to the rear speakers in a lot of instances just to give the band more breathing space and that worked out really well...(The) band members were up for doing something quite drastic. They didn't want to just put ambiences there, they really wanted to use all of the speakers."[284]

"In The Presence Of" (Anderson/Howe/Squire/White)

"In The Presence Of" is one of the finest songs on *Magnification* and it has the feel of classic Yes music with beautiful melodies and a dramatic build up of celestial power. Jon Anderson said: "The idea of the song is that we are surrounded by the Divine all the time, this wonderful energy. Now and again we sort of lock into it and feel really good. It's there all the time just waiting for us to lock in there."

"In The Presence Of" is approximately seven minutes long and consists of three interlinked parts, the final part truly taking the music to a higher place. The piece starts quietly with a piano introduction played by Alan White who also wrote the initial melody. The extremely adept production permits the contributions of both the band and orchestra to come through exceptionally clearly, especially Steve Howe's soaring steel guitar and Jon Anderson's superb vocals.

In the cover notes for the DVD-Audio edition of *Magnification*, Larry Groupe said: "Possibly the most constructed song is 'In the Presence Of'. Here I had the most amount of comment from the band on the final approach with the orchestra. This is a beautiful ballad that very carefully builds it way to ever-climbing heights. For me, the final landing into the lyric 'Standing on sacred ground' is absolute Yes perfection. This is what the band is all about: their ability to wind music over a long period into an eventual higher plane. Even here we build to a dynamic conclusion, an effect similar to a powerful mantra."[285]

During the *Yessymphonic* tour, Chris Squire described "In the Presence Of" as "possibly the jewel in the crown" of *Magnification* and added that for a new song it was remarkably well received when played live.[286]

◆ ◆ ◆

It was particularly interesting to observe the reactions of the fans on the various Yes internet chat lists after they'd first listened to *Magnification*. Quite a few would post an opinion after listening to it once or twice and would not sound very enthusiastic. And then several days later the same people would say that after a few listens they really enjoyed it and therein is the key to appreciating most of the music of Yes.

It is sometimes difficult not to have a preconceived idea of what a Yes album should sound like but I reiterate the recommendation not to reach any conclusions until after listening to new Yes music at least six times. I've often found my own opinions completely changing upon hearing a particular track a few times because the complexity of most Yes music demands a certain level of familiarity in order to fully appreciate it. The temptation is often to view Yes in terms of a personal favorite album or the era in which you "discovered" the band—in my case *The Yes Album*/*Fragile*/*Close To The Edge* era—but Yes is more than that. With some pieces of Yes music, it might take a few days, weeks, months or even longer until the penny drops and suddenly the musical intent or lyrical meaning becomes clear. What it does say is that Yes music possesses a rare depth and it needs to be approached accordingly because it will be a most rewarding experience if given the time and opportunity to grow.

For my part, I had the preconceived notion that *Magnification* would sound like the studio material from *Keys To Ascension* with the addition of an orchestra and of course, it didn't and it was also nothing like *Time And A Word* which was the previous Yes album to feature an orchestra. Yes always seems to find a new direction forward with its music, always some kind of new slant or variation, and that is part of the great art of progressive music. Steve Howe once said in an interview in 1976 that even a song like the old rock classic "Long Tall Sally" can be viewed as progressive music and can be played in a totally new way—it's certainly a principle to keep in mind. At the end of the day I take the view that whether the format is an epic or a single, what really matters is that the music has the quintessential, magical quality of Yes.

It may help to think of *Magnification* as being modelled on an album like *Abbey Road* by the Beatles, both albums covering a wide range of music but still being a cohesive whole. The Beatles had the lightness of "Octopus's Garden" and Yes had the fun of "Don't Go" while the brilliance of the Beatles with the suite-like "Golden Slumbers/Carry That Weight/The End" was met with the majestic

Yes classic "In The Presence Of". *Magnification* is an album that could only be created by master musicians and for those who own a compatible surround sound system, the DVD-Audio edition is the ideal way to listen to this album.

Classic Yes Solos

The contributions of Peter Banks and Tony Kaye in the first Yes lineup in 1968 shouldn't be forgotten because they were there to start the ball rolling and to help chart the musical course for the band. Let's also give the multi-talented Trevor Rabin the kudos he deserves in being enormously influential in the eighties in taking Yes to their biggest commercial success with *90125*. People like Patrick Moraz and Igor Khoroshev also had tremendous ability and Bill Bruford was so vitally important to early Yes that he will always be thought of as a quintessential member of the band.

However, without detracting from the contributions of any of the excellent musicians who have been part of Yes, it is the evolution of the classic Yes lineup that is central to the history of the band. Indeed, the core members of the classic lineup have been responsible for the vast majority of the albums, videos and DVDs made by Yes. In comparison the *90125* lineup only recorded three studio albums, one live video and part of *Union*.

Let's now have a closer look at the solo talents of the members of the classic Yes lineup—Anderson, Squire, Howe, Wakeman and White—to provide some additional insights into what they bring to the band. It is the perfect balance of their musical abilities and contrasting personalities that has created so much magical Yes music.

Jon Anderson

Jon Anderson's beautiful vocals are the most instantly recognizable characteristic of the Yes sound. His distinctive voice has, if anything, improved with age with greater depth and no apparent loss of the higher register. Jon says of his voice: "Well, I have an alto-tenor. Because the band is so loud or so big, I have to ride on the top like the top of a pyramid. My voice has to be clear. If I try to get in the middle of it, I just get lost. So I have to hit those high notes and sail over the top."[287]. Jon also commented: "I sing every day. I love singing. I've been very careful not to strain my voice over the years and as time has gone along, I feel more comfortable with my voice."[288]

Rick Wakeman explained that Yes have never had a problem in the recording studio in achieving a sound to complement Jon's voice: "To the best of my knowledge, we have never had a situation where the sounds we put down have interfered with Jon's singing…You could put down the musical spectrum, so that there isn't a gap in sight, and still his voice will cut through it all. You can also put down something extraordinarily delicate, like a piano or a solo acoustic guitar—he'll sing in the same mode and somehow it'll match perfectly."[289]

Apart from vocals, Jon adds other elements to the Yes sound and he plays an array of percussion instruments and implements as well as harp, keyboards and acoustic and electric guitars. It's not that he is a virtuoso exponent of these instruments but he has the ability to add just the right touches and his use of a tambourine to add an extra percussive dimension to a live performance is remarkable. Of course, Jon also fills the role of the band's musical coordinator as it were. Jon said: "We all have our roles, I'm the master conductor of Yes. I'll remind Steve of a bridge he played five minutes ago or suggest to Chris that we add a new chorus. I'm stuck in the middle of these wonderful musical brains and I help them to piece together what we do. And it usually turns out great in the end."[290] One of the key statements about Jon Anderson's career with Yes comes from Jon himself: "I always questioned why it was me who became the lead singer in a rock band—the answer was to know God".

Jon's solo career has been highly productive and sometimes very commercially successful. His definitive solo statement is arguably his first solo album *Olias Of Sunhillow* (1976) and it is music that he rightfully remains extremely proud of because he not only wrote and sang all of the material but also played all of the instruments. It's a concept album on which the often exotic sounds bring to life what at face value is a cosmic fairy tale about four tribes who come together to leave a planet that is about to explode and they are led by three "riders" who deliver them from peril by way of a wondrous flying ship called the Moorglade Mover. The idea was inspired by Roger Dean's painting for the cover of Yes's *Fragile* album.

However, there was much more behind the *Olias* story than just a fairy tale as Jon pointed out: "It's based on ancient knowledge…I put a lot of mystery into the writing of *Olias*, the actual story. And if you know anything about ancient knowledge, it was once said that there were four tribes only on this planet (Earth)—Negro, Asian, Oriental and Nordic—from which we all come from, we all have a little bit of everything in us…we were all tribal people…And in the story for the album…I didn't want to just spell it out. I thought if anyone wants to know about what I've learned about, they can find it out. It was a couple of books by Vera Stanley-Adler. One is called *The Initiation Of Life* and (the other) *The Finding Of The Third Eye*"[291]

The *Olias* album cover featured an intriguing symbol and Jon explained how it came about: "The idea is you have a circle, triangle and square. They're the basic fundamental shapes we work everything from…and I decided to stick them together. And that was the design. There are many things you can read into it. The world (circle)—oneness; triangle—the three (riders, Holy Trinity)…Father, Son and Holy Ghost; the square really was the four tribes (humanity)."[292] The *Olias* symbol has subsequently been displayed on stage during Yes shows, for instance during the *Tormatour* in the late seventies and the *Union* tour in the early nineties.

For anyone unfamiliar with Jon's solo recordings, the *Affirmative: Yes Family Solos Album* compilation gives a brief snapshot of some of his work. The three pieces Ocean Song/Meeting (Garden Of Geda)/Sound Out The Galleon are the opening tracks from *Olias Of Sunhillow* while "I Hear You Now" comes from Jon's very popular collaboration with Vangelis and is the superbly melodic single from their first album *Short Stories* (1979). "All In A Matter Of Time" is a track from Jon's solo album *Animation* (1982) and it again demonstrates that one of the principal creators of the great Yes epics is more than capable of producing a short song with obvious commercial potential.

Chris Squire

Chris Squire's superlative work on bass guitar is one of the real foundation stones of the Yes sound. American radio host Jim Ladd described Chris as "one of the most gifted bassists in rock" and explained that his playing is so distinctive that it is readily identifiable by listening to only four bars of music.[293] The Who had been Chris's favorite band when he was growing up and the influence was so strong that in a nutshell, he modelled his musical career on emulating the musical excellence of bass guitarist John Entwistle and being a showman in the mold of guitarist Pete Townsend.

Chris plays a range of bass guitars but his main instrument and the one most associated with his distinctive sound is the Rickenbacker 4001 bass with Rotosound strings. He bought his original Rickenbacker in 1965 while working at the Boosey and Hawkes music store in London after leaving school and he still plays the same instrument today although he now owns similar but more modern copies after Rickenbacker released the Chris Squire Limited Edition 4001CS reproduction in 1991. Amongst Chris's other instruments are two particularly eye catching ones in a custom built triple neck bass normally used for live performances of "Awaken" and a flamboyant green Meridian bass with the stylized initials "CS" emblazoned on the body—green being Chris's favorite color.

Explaining one of the key facets of his bass technique in achieving such a distinctive sound, Chris said: "I usually play with a pick but I do some things with my fingers sometimes. I used to go and watch people play and especially John

(Entwistle) used to play with a pick and I used to really like his sound then. Through time I actually developed a style where I actually play with the pick and also with my thumb at the same time."[294] The use of a pick produces a harsher sound while the thumb gives a softer sound. The key to the Squire sound is that Chris firstly hits the string with the pick followed by the thumb immediately after, producing a combination of the sounds with a more soulful feel and a harmonic thrown in as well.

Another of Chris's considerable talents is in providing strong backing vocals as might be expected from someone who had been in one of the finest church choirs in England. It was the experience of being involved in church music that gave Chris an appreciation of the spiritual feelings that can be created through music. Surprisingly, he has so far released only one solo album in *Fish Out Of Water* (1975). However, Chris has made two albums in an ongoing collaboration with Billy Sherwood, the first *Conspiracy* (2000) and the second titled *The Unknown* released in mid 2003.

A seminal example of Chris's solo work on bass guitar is the live version of "The Fish (Schindleria Praematurus)" on the *Yessongs* album. "The Fish" originally appeared on the *Fragile* album as Chris's solo feature and it was an innovative landmark but the live version is considerably longer with a good deal of improvisation and is nothing less than a sparkling virtuoso performance of bass guitar. The sub-title "Schindleria Praematurus" came about when Yes's lighting manager Mike Tait was asked to assist by finding the name of a prehistoric fish in eight syllables to suit the background vocal for the studio track when it was being recorded and he located it in the *Guinness Book Of Records* where it was listed as being the smallest fish in the world.

Another worthwhile sample of Chris in a solo context is "Hold Out Your Hand" which is the opening song on *Fish Out Of Water* and it also appears on the *Affirmative: Yes Family Solos Album* compilation. It features Chris adopting his characteristic "lead bass" approach to the instrument while also capably handling the lead vocals with accompaniment from Bill Bruford on drums and Patrick Moraz on keyboards.

Steve Howe

It is impossible to imagine a guitarist who could bring to Yes a more unique and exciting approach than Steve Howe. Jon Anderson said of Steve: "When Steve first came to the band it kind of freaked me out because he could play so many different kinds of music. And I first saw him one time before he joined the band, I saw him in this club called The Speakeasy and I walked past and watched this guy with this amazingly beautiful Gibson guitar just freaking out. Really amazing to see someone just going for it and as most of you know who follow the band, every night he's out there taking no prisoners and that's beautiful."

It is no surprise that Steve won the prestigious readership poll of *Guitar Player* magazine five times in succession as Best Overall Guitarist from 1977 to 1981, thereafter being elevated into the Gallery Of Greats. Steve's innovative approach to the guitar is defined by his statement that he knew all of the musical clichés but refused to play them. In 1999 Steve reflected on his richly diverse musical influences and said: "I keep looking at the great musicianship of this century, not just this year. This year is just incidental compared to the other ninety eight."[295]

Steve has an outstanding ability to dexterously weave a wide variety of different guitar sounds, tones and textures into the tapestry of the music, often using more than one instrument within the course of any song. Although he uses the full spectrum of various effects at different times, the Howe electric guitar sound is primarily clean and usually heard through a Fender amplifier. However, according to Steve the essence of his sound is created by the way in which he plays rather than the particular equipment he uses.

Steve's favorite guitar is his beloved Gibson ES175D that he bought in London in 1964. Steve said of his 175D: "It's my favorite guitar, the guitar I know best. That's why I can play directly from the heart with it—I know it inside and out. Its sound is very big and not too thin and trebly. It's got a shape that I was drawn to just a couple of years after I started playing guitar back in '59."[296] The 175D has become so personal to Steve that he is the only one permitted to touch it and it can be heard in full cry on songs such as "Yours Is No Disgrace", "Starship Trooper" and "Heart Of The Sunrise".

Steve is an avid guitar collector and his extensive collection of exquisite instruments is covered in his book *The Steve Howe Guitar Collection* (Balafon Books, 1994). On the famous Yes albums made in the early to mid seventies, Steve adopted the approach of featuring a particular guitar on each record although other guitars were also used. On *The Yes Album* it was predominantly the Gibson 175D, on *Fragile* the Gibson ES5 Switchmaster, on *Close To The Edge* the Gibson ES345TD, on *Tales From Topographic Oceans* the Gibson Les Paul Junior and on *Relaye*r the Fender Telecaster. To supplement those guitars he used instruments such as the Martin 00-18 acoustic guitar, the Portuguese 12 String guitar, the Coral Sitar and the Fender Dual 6 steel guitar.

Steve has made several solo albums over the years and he has been particularly active as a solo artist in the past decade. The scope of his guitar work is very broad but his two most famous solo pieces "Clap" and "Mood For A Day" provide prima facie evidence of his status as one of the greatest guitarists to emerge from rock music. "Clap" is Steve's crowd pleasing signature solo acoustic guitar piece that first appeared as a live recording on *The Yes Album* and is also included on the *In A Word: Yes* compilation. Steve said: "It (Clap) was very much influenced by Chet Atkins and I think it's the main guitar tour de force that I've written. That type of tune is very important to me and has a lot to do with Chet, Merle Travis, Big Bill Broonzy and even some jazz guitarists. I wrote it all in the one sitting because I was determined to finish because my first son Dylan was being born that night. This was in 1969 before I joined Yes."[297] "Clap" was musically based around the idea of maintaining a particular syncopated rhythm. Bill Bruford suggested the title "Clap" because it made you want to clap along but to Steve's annoyance it has often been incorrectly referred to as "The Clap", a most inappropriate connotation.

"Mood For A Day" is Steve's outstanding solo acoustic guitar feature on the *Fragile* album and a live version is included on *Yessongs*. It was played in a style suggestive of flamenco guitar and was influenced by Sabecas and Carlos Montoya. Steve wrote "Mood For A Day" for his wife Jan and he remarked: "At the time I had settled down and just started new roots in my life and 'Mood For A Day' was supposed to represent a happy mood for a day. I was about twenty eight when I realized that there should be something more in my life than just the guitar."[298]

Rick Wakeman

Rick Wakeman provided some of the most spectacular and enduring memories of Yes performing live in the early seventies. He personified the image of the Caped Crusader with the glittering cape and long blonde hair while brilliantly mastering the latest in keyboard technology that surrounded him. In 1973 well known Australian music identity and critic Ian "Molly" Meldrum wrote: "The real highlight for me was seeing Rick Wakeman in action…the sound effects and music that he had at his finger tips I would have imagined would have substituted for a 150 piece orchestra. His solo spot was truly unbelievable…it had me sitting on the edge of my seat gripping it and at any moment I thought I was going to scream for joy."[299]

No other keyboard player in rock music has captured the imagination of the audience as vividly as Rick. He has had a long and prolific solo career and in the mid-seventies enjoyed commercial success at the highest level. Rick has continued to release a string of solo albums in various musical styles over the years and still displays the Wakeman charisma and supreme technical ability. His return to Yes in 2002 was an extremely pleasing event for many longtime fans. Rick commented: "I'm very happy at the moment. It's really good. It really is lovely to be back with these guys. I have to be honest, I do miss it when I'm away. It's a strange thing. It's hard to equate but I've always been a fan of the band, even when I'm not in it...As a professional musician, you don't always get the chance to play what you'd like to play. I've done all sorts of musical things throughout the years that, if given the choice, I wouldn't have done. Now I'm back doing what I really like doing. That doesn't happen very often, so you grab it while you can."[300]

When Rick first joined Yes in 1971 he went straight to the leading edge of keyboard technology but the capabilities of the early monophonic analog synthesizers and tape-based mellotrons from those days were a mere fraction of what is now possible with modern digital technology. Upon taking to the road with Yes in 2002, Rick demonstrated that he remained at the technological forefront with a huge sophisticated modern keyboard set up consisting of nine digital keyboards including a Korg Prophecy, a Korg 01WProX, a Korg Karma, a Korg Triton, a Korg Trinity, a Korg CX-3, a Generalmusic ProMega 3, a Roland XV-88 and a Roland RD-700, plus one of the legendary Minimoogs to recreate some of those earlier classic sounds.

Rick's most successful and popular solo work continues to be his early solo albums *The Six Wives Of Henry VIII* (1973), *Journey To The Centre Of The Earth* (1974) and *The Myths And Legends Of King Arthur And The Knights Of The Round Table* (1975). A taste of the material from the *Henry* album can be found on the *Yessongs* live album as "Excerpts From 'The Six Wives Of Henry VIII'" with Rick playing solo using the full potential of his battery of keyboards. It sounds quite different to the studio recordings of the same material and more prominently highlights the unmistakable vintage sounds of Minimoogs and mellotrons.

A book titled *The Private Life Of Henry VIII* was Rick's initial inspiration for the *Henry* concept and it led him to reading some fifty books in order to form his own opinions about each of the six wives. He then spent eleven months in creating the album itself. Rick commented: "The first track I wrote about was Catherine Of Aragon, relating her feelings for Henry. That's more of a Henry theme than anything else...Anne Boleyn thought a lot of Henry too. In fact they corresponded when she was in the Tower waiting to be executed. The Henry theme appears again at the end of Anne Boleyn's track but with incredibly distorted minor chords indicating her beheading. Jane Seymour was a tragic character, the only wife who gave Henry a male heir. And she knew she would die afterward because she was so frail. I recorded that track on a church organ to show the horror of her situation, adding a weird moog for the childbirth...I thought Anne Of Cleves was stark raving bonkers...so the different instruments are written in different time signatures. Catherine Howard seemed to be the court groupie and Catherine Parr liked enjoying herself, so I wrote her a jolly piece."[301]

Another prime example of Rick's solo work is "Merlin The Magician" that originally appeared on the *Arthur* album but is also included on the *Affirmative: Yes Family Solos Album.* Rick described it as a honk tonk piece of music "to show the light hearted madness of a magician in a king's court" and the parts played by the Minimoogs were designed to conjure up the vision of potions being crazily created in cauldrons.[302]

Alan White

Alan White entered Yes with a reputation as a powerful drummer but he has become an adept technician over the years to cope with the consistently testing requirements of the band's adventurous music. Right from the start, Alan demonstrated a rare capacity to come to grips with demanding musical situations and in 1973 after his first year with Yes he said: "It's taken a long time but now I think it's starting to work well. Yes are not the easiest band to fit into straight away—especially as I only had three days rehearsal (after joining the band) before I had to go on stage with them. But that's been the story of my life really as far as joining groups goes—the Plastic Ono Band (with John Lennon), nobody had played with anyone else before on that live *Toronto* album, and I never did much rehearsing with Joe Cocker either. We'd go to rehearsals but everybody would just jam for three hours and then Chris Stainton would disappear, and all of a sudden we were on stage doing a tour."[303]

On the subject of performing with Yes, Alan explains that "the challenge of going on stage and playing all those notes" is the driving force in his musical career, a demanding task given the myriad of notes required.[304] Alan has always played Ludwig drums throughout his time with Yes and his equipment in 2003 was based around a Ludwig Super Classic series kit with Remo drum heads, Gibraltar hardware and Zildjian cymbals, augmented by electronics from Roland. A striking Yes logo adorning Alan's bass drum has often been a feature.

In addition to drums and percussion, Alan contributes to writing the music for Yes and has occasionally provided backing vocals but he has so far released only one solo album *Ramshackled* (1976). He has a large stockpile of musical ideas that may be used for future Yes recordings or will possibly become a second solo album at some stage. Alan's musical life outside of Yes has included working with MerKaBa in his home city of Seattle, a group he describes as "more an ethnic type of band with percussions" and the music as "kind of like crazy stuff but it's actually what I like to do (apart from Yes)."[305]

Alan recorded *Ramshackled* with friends from northern England who had played with him in the band Griffin and it was the kind of music he'd been involved in before joining Yes. Alan commented: "I tried to get a lot of different kinds of music on the album because I like playing lots of different kinds of music. It's really a drummer in a band's album rather than a Yes solo album."[306]

A song from *Ramshackled* that is also on the *Affirmative: Yes Family Solos Album* is "Spring Song Of Innocence" which is based on a poem by William Blake. Alan commented: "I'm not as clued in on Blake as some people but I do like him very much. I've read his biography and a couple of things about him. His pictures drive me around the bend (grins enthusiastically), they're fantastic, the colors, the themes…"[307] Although not very demanding of Alan's great expertise on drums, "Spring Song Of Innocence" is very melodic and is likely to appeal to most Yes fans with guest appearances from Jon Anderson on vocals and Steve Howe on guitar. It sees Alan using his noted ability to tastefully play whatever is required to suit a particular piece of music.

WHAT MAKES A GREAT YES ALBUM?

There could never be a formula for the creation of great music and art. Whichever way you look at it, however, a band as talented as Yes certainly has a flying start and there always seems to have been an abundance of inspiration. Each Yes album has contained strong musical ideas and the band has never suffered from a paucity of creativity. The central question becomes what is it that separates the greatest Yes albums from the others? The answer requires a degree of generalization and an array of factors obviously comes into play but there are key factors that become apparent when reviewing the recording history of Yes.

The particular musicians in Yes at any time have had a fundamental influence on the music being produced. The greatest Yes music has come about by having the right musicians together to establish a very special chemistry. If one defines Yes in terms of the complex and adventurous music that it is best known for, then the core members of the classic Yes lineup are essential ingredients in creating that music. It is those musicians who have truly expressed the essence of the panoramic music of Yes with its inherent spiritual power and life affirming qualities. However, the *90125* lineup has proven that a simpler and more commercial Yes can also be very successful.

Most of the greatest Yes albums have been created when the band collaborated as a unit in writing and recording the music rather than independently contributing to a project. This is not to say that good music hasn't been created by the more independent approach but in those cases where certain band members dominated the creative process or the band wasn't cohesive in recording the album, the results generally speaking weren't as successful. Almost by definition, great Yes music demands a collective approach from the band.

Additionally, the creation of great Yes music requires the right technical support in terms of production, engineering and mixing. Yes albums that didn't reach their full potential have been deficient in these areas to some extent. The characteristic complexity of Yes music clearly provides a testing challenge in finely balancing the creative input of the musicians in the band to achieve a definitive Yes soundscape. Eddie Offord appears to be the person who consistently had the best understanding of what was required to help the band produce a great Yes record and his legacy is rich when listening to the glorious sounds of albums like *Close To The Edge.*

The history of Yes suggests that when all of these key factors properly come together, the chances are that great Yes music is likely to be created.

References

1 Interview by T.H.W., *RAM*, May 1975
2 Interview by Dave Miller, *Soundblast*, May 1973
3 Interview by Darel Nugent, *Go Set*, April 1973
4 Chris Welch, *Close To The Edge*, Omnibus Press, 1999, p.59
5 Radio interview by David Watt, 2SM Sydney, March 1973
6 Dan Hedges, *Yes The Authorised Biography*, Sidgwick & Jackson, 1981, p.35
7 Peter Banks, August 1997 from CD booklet notes for *Something's Coming* 2CD set, New Millennium Communications, 1997
8 Dan Hedges, *Yes The Authorised Biography*, Sidgwick & Jackson, 1981, p.37
9 Interview by Chris Welch, *Melody Maker*, October 1969
10 Interview by Chris Welch, *Melody Maker*, December 1969
11 Interview by Gustavo Lutteral, *En Concierto*, I Sat TV, Argentina, 1999
12 Review by Ed Nimmervoll, *Go Set*, 1971
13 Interview by Steve Clarke, *NME*, 1973
14 Interview by Tiz Hay, *Yes Music Circle* fanzine, issue 5, August 1993
15 Interview by Darel Nugent, *Go Set*, April 1973
16 Interview by Penny Valentine, *Sounds*, 1972

19 Interview by Penny Valentine, *Sounds*, 1972
20 Interview by Darel Nugent, *Go Set*, April 1973
21 Interview by Penny Valentine, *Sounds*, 1972
22 Review by Wayne Thomas, *Go Set*, October 1971
23 Interview by Penny Valentine, *Sounds*, 1972
24 Interview by Steve Clarke, *NME*, 1973
25 Interview by Dan Hedges, *Guitar Player*, May 1978
26 Interview by Darel Nugent, *Go Set*, April 1973
27 Interview by Steve Clarke, *NME*, 1973
28 Interview by Penny Valentine, *Sounds*, 1972
29 *Steve Howe Interactive CD-ROM*, Beyond Sound, 1999
30 Interview by Darel Nugent, *Go Set*, April 1973
31 Interview by Steve Clarke, *NME*, 1973
32 Interview by Steve Clarke, *NME*, 1973
33 Interview by Douglas Noble, *The Guitar Magazine*, September 1992
34 Radio interview by Joe Benson, *Off The Record*, Arrow 93.1 FM, January 2004
35 Interview by John Gabbard, *Audio Vision*, US TV (Warner Cable), 1997
36 Interview, *An Evening With Jon Anderson*, Atlantic Records, 1977
37 *Yesyears* video, Atco Video, 1991
38 Interview by Steve Clarke, *NME*, 1973
39 Radio interview, 2SM Sydney, June 1977
40 Interview by Darel Nugent, *Go Set*, April 1973
41 Interview by Bob Doerschuk, *Keyboard*, July 1984
42 Dan Wooding, *The Caped Crusader Rick Wakeman*, Granada Publishing, 1979, p.77
43 *Yesyears* video, Atco Video, 1991
44 *The History of Rock*, vol.8, issue 85, article by Peter Clark, Orbis Publishing, 1983
45 Dan Hedges, *Yes The Authorised Biography*, Sidgwick & Jackson, 1981, p.67
46 Interview by Douglas Gottlieb, *Yes Magazine*, vol.4 no.2, 1992
47 Dan Hedges, *Yes The Authorised Biography*, Sidgwick & Jackson, 1981, p.63
48 Interview by Richard Wilkins, Nine Network, Australian TV, December 2002
49 Interview by Penny Valentine, *Sounds*, 1972
50 Radio interview, 2SM Sydney, June 1977
51 Radio interview, *Rock Stars*, Westwood One, 1988
52 *Chris Squire, Starlicks Master Series* video, 1991
53 Radio interview, *Rock Stars*, Westwood One, 1988
54 Interview, *Words and Music with Lich*, CPTV US TV 1997
55 Ibid
56 Interview by Douglas Noble, *The Guitar Magazine*, September 1992
57 Radio interview, 2SM Sydney, June 1977

58 Interview by Darel Nugent, *Go Set*, April 1973
59 Interview at *Yestival*, Glendale, California 1994
60 Interview by Jerry Gilbert, *Sounds*, 1972
61 Ibid
62 Interview by Ken Achard, *The Guitar Magazine*, February 1973
63 Mike Channell, *The Sun*, Sydney, 1973
64 Review by Ian McDonald, *NME*, 1972
65 Interview, *Soundblast*, December 1972
66 Interview by Ray Hammond, *Sounds*, December 1972
67 *Bruford & The Beat* video, Axis Video, Warner Bros, 1982
68 Interview by Darel Nugent, *Go Set*, April 1973
69 Interview at *Yestival*, Glendale, California, 1994
70 Interview by Darel Nugent, *Go Set*, April 1973
71 Interview at *Yestival*, Glendale, California, 1994
72 Interview by Ken Achard, *The Guitar Magazine*, February 1973
73 Interview by Penny Valentine, *Sounds*, 1972
74 Ibid
75 Interview by Douglas Noble, *The Guitar Magazine*, September 1992
76 *Steve Howe Interactive CD-ROM*, Beyond Sound, 1999
77 Interview, *Words and Music with Lich*, CPTV U.S. TV, 1997
78 Radio interview by David Watt, 2SM, Sydney, March 1973
79 Radio interview, 2SM Sydney, June 1977
80 *Steve Howe Interactive CD-ROM*, Beyond Sound, 1999
81 Interview by Darel Nugent, *Go Set*, 1973
82 Radio interview by David Watt, 2SM, Sydney, March 1973
83 Interview by Dan Hedges, *Guitar Player*, May 1978
84 Interview by Doug and Glenn Gottlieb, *Yes Magazine*, vol. 5 no. 3, 1995
85 Interview by Darel Nugent, *Go Set*, April 1973
86 Interview by Richard Green, *Music Scene*, 1973
87 Roger Dean, *Views* DVD, Classic Rock Productions, 2002
88 Interview by John Bagnall, *NME*, 1972
89 Mike Channell, *The Sun*, Sydney, March 1973
90 Anthony O'Grady, *RAM*, December 1976
91 Interview by Chris Welch, *Melody Maker*, 1973
92 Ibid
93 Interview by Ray Hammond, *Sounds*,1973
94 Interview by Gordon Fletcher, *Modern Hi Fi & Stereo Guide*, June/July 1974
95 Interview by Dan Hedges, *Guitar Player*, May 1978
96 Review by David Pepperell, *Go Set*, April 1973
97 Interview by Dan Hedges, *Guitar Player*, May 1978
98 Interview at *Yestival*, Glendale, California, 1994
99 Interview by Ray Telford, *Sounds*, 1973
100 Interview by Gordon Fletcher, *Modern Hi Fi & Stereo Guide*, June/July 1974

101 Interview by Alan Di Perna, *Guitar World*, January 2000
102 Ibid
103 Interview by Chris Welch, *Melody Maker*, 1973
104 Interview by Dave Ling, *Classic Rock*, December 2001
105 Interview, *Rock Family Trees*, UK TV 1998
106 Interview by Dave Ling, *Classic Rock*, December 2001
107 Interview by Karl Dallas, Melody Maker, 1973
108 Ibid
109 Interview by Ray Telford, *Sounds*, 1973
110 Interviews by Nick Shilton, *Classic Rock*, Nov/Dec 1999
111 Rick Wakeman, *Say Yes—An Autobiography*, Hodder and Stoughton, 1995
112 Chris Welch, *Melody Maker*, November 1973
113 Mike Channell, *The Sun*, Sydney, 1974
114 *Yesyears* video, Atco Video, 1991
115 Interview by Ray Telford, *Sounds*, August 1973
116 Interview by Gordon Fletcher, *Modern Hi Fi & Stereo Guide*, June/July 1974
117 Interview by Douglas Noble, The *Guitar Magazine*, September 1992
118 Interview, UK music press, source and date unknown
119 Interview by Dominic Milano, *Keyboard*, November 1981
120 *Yesyears* video, Atco Video, 1991
121 Bernie Tier, *The Sun*, Sydney, 1974
122 Dan Hedges, *Yes The Authorised Biography*, Sidgwick & Jackson, 1981, p.104
123 Radio interview, 2SM Sydney, June 1977
124 Interview by Mike Tiano, *Notes From The Edge #238*, 21 September 2000
125 Interview by Dominic Milano, *Keyboard*, November 1981
126 Interview by Allan Jones, *Melody Maker*, September 1980
127 Interview by John Orme, *Melody Maker*, July 1977
128 Ibid
129 Radio interview, 2SM Sydney, June 1977
130 *Yesyears* video, Atco Video, 1991
131 Review by Chris Welch, *Melody Maker*, July 1977
132 Radio interview, 2SM Sydney, June 1977
133 Review by Wayne Elmer, *The Sun*, Sydney, July 1977
134 Interview by Bob Hart, *Daily Telegraph*, Sydney, November 1977
135 Interview by John Orme, *Melody Maker, July* 1977
136 Review by Phil Manzie, *RAM*, August 1977
137 Interview by Douglas Noble, *The Guitar Magazine*, September 1992
138 Interview with John Orme, *Melody Maker*, July 1977
139 Interviews from the *Yesyears* video, Atco Video, 1991 and *Words and Music With Lich*, CPTV US TV, 1997
140 Thomas Mosbo, *Yes But What Does It Mean*, Wyndstar, 1994, p.148
141 *Yestival*, Glendale, California, 1994

142 Review by Chris Welch, *Melody Maker*, July 1977
143 Radio interview by George Taylor-Morris, *Deep Tracks*, XM radio, August 2002
144 Interview by Dan Hedges, *Guitar Player*, May 1978
145 Radio interview, 2SM Sydney, June 1977
146 *Yesyears* video, Atco Video, 1991
147 Interview by Chris Welch, *Melody Maker*, June 1978
148 Interview with Douglas Noble, *The Guitar Magazine*, September 1972
149 Interview by Chris Welch, *Melody Maker*, June 1978
150 Interview by Chris Welch, *Melody Maker*, September, 1978
151 Interview by Allan Jones, *Melody Maker*, September 1980
152 Interview by Cathy Gray, *Sonics*, Oct/Nov 1983
153 Review by Karl Dallas, *Melody Maker*, November 1978
154 Interview by Chris Welch, *Melody Maker*, September 1978
155 Ibid
156 Interview by Douglas Noble, *The Guitar Magazine*, September 1992
157 Interview by Chris Welch, *Melody Maker*, June 1978
158 *Yesyears* video, Atco Video, 1991
159 Review by Chris Welch, *Melody Maker*, September 1978
160 Interview by Karl Dallas, *Melody Maker*, July 1980
161 *Yesyears* video, Atco Video, 1991
162 Ibid
163 Interview by John Gill, *Juke*, July 1980
164 Roger Dean & Martin Dean, *Magnetic Storm*, Dragon's World, 1984, p.77
165 Interview by John Gill, *Juke*, July 1980
166 Interview by Russell Wiener, *Pop Rock*, January 1981
167 Review by John Gill, *Juke*, September 1980
168 Review by John Hall, *Melbourne Herald*, September 1980
169 Review by Michael Smith, *RAM*, October 1980
170 Radio interview, *Rock Stars*, Westwood One, 1988
171 Review by John Gill, *Sounds*, September, 1980
172 *Rock Family Trees*, BBC TV, 1998
173 Interview by Dave Ling, *Classic Rock*, December 2001
174 Interview by Christie Eliezer, *Juke*, June 1982
175 Review by John Gill, *Juke*, September 1980
176 Review by Michael Smith, *RAM*, October 1980
177 Interview by Douglas Noble, *The Guitar Magazine*, September 1992
178 Interview by Bud Scoppa and Billy Cioffi, *Guitar World*, September 1987
179 Interview by Philip Bell, *Juke*, December 1983
180 Ibid
181 Interview by Ron Bienstock, *Electronic Soundmaker*, May 1984
182 Interview by Philip Bell, *Juke*, December 1983
183 Interview by Bob Doerschuk, *Keyboard*, July 1984
184 Ibid

185 Interview by Philip Bell, *Juke*, December 1983
186 Ibid
187 Ibid
188 Review by Geoff Barton, *Juke*, December 1983
189 Interview by Ray Telford, *Juke*, June 1984
190 Interview by Philip Bell, *Juke*, December 1983
191 Interview by Ray Telford, *Juke*, June 1984
192 *Chris Squire, Starlicks Master Series* Video, 1991
193 Interview, *Le Mag*, MCM French TV, 1998
194 Review by Geoff Barton, *Juke*, December 1983
195 Interview by Bud Scoppa, *Guitar World*, September 1987
196 Interview by Hugh Fielder, *Juke*, July 1984
197 Interview by Bud Scoffa and Billy Cioffi, *Guitar World*, September 1987
198 Interview by Bud Scoffa, *Guitar World*, September 1987
199 Ibid
200 Interview by Simon Barrow, *Progressive Forum* fanzine, Issue 1, January 1993
201 Interview by Anil Prasad, *Innerviews*, January 1998
202 British cable TV, 1991 (from Yes Music Circle)
203 Interview by Nick Shilton, *Classic Rock*, Nov/Dec 1999
204 Radio interview, *Rock Stars*, Westwood One, 1988
205 British cable TV, 1991 (from Yes Music Circle)
206 Radio interview, source unknown, Montreal, August 1989
207 Interview by Robert Doerschuk, *Keyboard*, September 1989
208 Ibid
209 Interview by Eddie Allen, *Guitarist*, December 1989
210 Interview by *The Revealing* fanzine, Issue 7, July 1990
211 Radio interview, source unknown, Montreal, August 1989
212 Interview by Bill Milkowski, *Guitar World*, October 1989
213 Radio interview, source unknown, Montreal, August 1989
214 *Rock Family Trees*, BBC TV 1998
215 Review by John Mackie, *The Vancouver Sun*, March 1990
216 Interview by Tiz Hay, *Progressive Forum* fanzine, Issue 1, January 1993
217 Article by Julian Colbeck, *The Revealing* fanzine, July 1990
218 Interview by Martin Townsend, *Vox*, July 1991
219 Ibid
220 Interview by Robert Doerschuk & Mark Vail, *Keyboard*, July 1991
221 Interview by Martin Townsend, *Vox*, July 1991
222 Ibid
223 Interview by Mike Mettler, *Guitar World*, July 1991
224 Interview by Douglas Noble, *The Guitar Magazine*, September 1992
225 Interview by Nick Shilton, *Classic Rock*, Nov/Dec 1999
226 Interview by Robert Doerschuk & Mark Vail, *Keyboard*, August 1991
227 Article by Martin Townsend, *Vox*, July 1991
228 Interview by Dave Ling, *Classic Rock*, December 2001

229 Interview by Mike Mettler, *Guitar World*, July 1991
230 Ibid
231 Interview by Robert Doerschuk & Mark Vail, *Keyboard*, August 1991
232 Interview by Chris Jisi, *Bass Player Online*, 1994
233 Radio interview by Bob Coburn, KLOS FM 95.5, March 1994
234 Article by Tiz Hay, *Progress* fanzine, Issue 1, March 1994
235 Ibid
236 Interview by Anil Prasad, *Innerviews*, January 1998
237 Interview by Nick Shilton, *Classic Rock*, Nov/Dec 1999
238 Interview by Anthony Vita, *Retro Rewind*, July 2000
239 Editorial, *Yes Magazine*, vol.5 no.2, 1994
240 Interview by *Music News Network*, 1994
241 Radio interview by Bob Coburn, KLOS FM 95.5, March 1994
242 Interview by Chris Jisi, *Bass Player Online*, 1994
243 Interview by Anil Prasad, *Innerviews*, January 1998
244 Interview by Doug and Glenn Gottlieb, *Yes Magazine*, vol.5 no.4, 1995
245 Interview, *Le Mag*, MCM French TV 1998
246 Interview by Chris Gill, *Guitar World*, June 1996
247 Review by Adam St James, *San Luis Obispo County Telegram-Tribune*, 5 March 1996
248 Interview by Glenn Gottlieb, *Yes Magazine*, vol.7 no.1, 1997
249 Interview by *Music Street Journal*, 1998
250 Interview by Mike Tiano, *Notes From The Edge #196*, February 1998
251 Interview by Glenn Gottlieb, *Yes Magazine*, vol.7 no.1, 1997
252 Interview, *Yestival*, Cherry Hill NJ, June 1998
253 Interview by Nick Shilton, *Classic Rock*, Nov/Dec 1999
254 Interview, *Words & Music With Lich*, US TV 1997
255 Ibid
256 Interview, *Yestival*, Cherry Hills NJ, June 1998
257 Interview by Lisa Sharken, *The Guitar Magazine*, July 1998
258 Radio interview, *Jim Ladd's Living Room*, KLOS FM 95.5, November 1999
259 Interview by Nick Shilton, *Classic Rock*, Nov/Dec 1999
260 Ibid
261 Interview, *Yestival*, Cherry Hills NJ, June 1998
262 Interview by Nick Shilton, Classic Rock, Nov/Dec 1999
263 Interview, *Yestival*, Cherry Hill NJ, 1998
264 Interview by Nick Shilton, *Classic Rock*, Nov/Dec 1999
265 Interview, *Yestival*, Cherry Hill NJ, 1998
266 Ibid
267 *House Of Yes DVD*, Beyond Music, 1999
268 Interview by Nick Shilton, *Classic Rock*, Nov/Dec 1999
269 Interview by Gustavo Lutteral, *En Concierto*, I SAT TV Argentina, 1999
270 Interview by John 'Bo Bo' Bollenberg, *Prog-Nose*, May 2001
271 Review by Nick Shilton, *Classic Rock*, Nov/Dec 1999

272 Interview by Tim Morse, *Notes From The Edge #243*, 28 April 2001
273 Interview by Gary Hill, *Crud Magazine*, October 2001
274 Radio interview, *Jim Ladd's Living Room*, KLOS FM 95.5 November 1999
275 Interview by *Gaming Pro World*, November 1999
276 Interview by John 'Bo Bo' Bollenberg, *Prog-Nose*, May 2001
277 Radio interview, *Jim Ladd's Living Room*, KLOS FM 95.5 November 1999
278 Interview by Dave Ling, *Classic Rock*, December 2001
279 Interview by Sven Kardelke, *Kuno Online,* November 2001
280 Interview, *Yessymphonic* DVD, Eagle Vision, 2002
281 Interview by Gary Hill, *Crud Magazine*, October 2001
282 Interview by Will Romano, *New York Post*, 8 September 2001
283 Review by Dan Aquilante, *New York Post*, 4 December 2001
284 Interview by Jim Batcho, Digidesign (Pro Tools), 2001
285 Cover notes, *Magnification* DVD-Audio, Rhino Entertainment Company, 2002
286 *Yessymphonic* DVD, Eagle Vision, 2002
287 Interview, *Music Scene*, RTL 5, Dutch TV, April 1994
288 Radio interview by Don Cassidy, *Delicious Agony*, February 2004
289 Interview by Robert Doerschuk, *Keyboard*, September 1989
290 Interview by Dave Ling, *Classic Rock*, December 2001
291 Interview, *Yestival*, Glendale CA, 1994
292 Ibid
293 Radio interview, *Jim Ladd's Living Room*, November 1999
294 Interview by Billy Cioffi, *Guitar World*, September 1987
295 Interview by Gustavo Lutteral, *En Concierto*, I SAT TV, Argentina, 1999
296 Interview by Bill Milkowski, *Guitar World*, October 1989
297 Interview by Douglas Noble, *The Guitar Magazine*, September 1992
298 Ibid
299 Ian 'Molly' Meldrum, *Go Set*, April 1973
300 Interview by Tom Brislin, *Keyboard*, November 2002
301 Interview by Camilla Beach, *Australian Women's Weekly*, January 1975
302 Dan Wooding, *The Caped Crusader Rick Wakeman*, Granada Publishing, 1979, p.135
303 Interview by Steve Peacock, *Sounds*, 1973
304 *Yessymphonic* DVD, Eagle Vision, 2002
305 Interview by Igor Italiani, *Progressive World*, December 2001
306 Interview by Vivien Goldman, *Sounds*, March 1976
307 Ibid

4

Long Distance Runaround

YES CONCERTS

The studio recordings of Yes are superb but it is on stage where Yes reaches its absolute peak. The ultimate Yes experience is to attend a Yes concert and the band has amassed a well earned, legendary reputation for delivering the most brilliant of live performances. So what is the nature of the irresistible force that has continued to draw people from all over the world to Yes concerts for more than three decades?

Let's take a step back in time for a moment to the *Close To The Edge* tour in 1972/73 when Yes really began to assert that it was one of the greatest ever rock bands. *The Yes Album*, *Fragile* and *Close To The Edge* had demonstrated that Yes made magnificent albums but the question was could this band that had so much expertise in the studio actually cut it on stage in front of an audience? The response from Yes could not have been more emphatic. Not only did Yes successfully reproduce all of the intricate details of their music on stage but they achieved it with breathtaking flair and commitment. Yes concerts were an event that entertained, excited, generated wide-eyed wonder, evoked beauty, stimulated the mind and raised the spirit. Somehow Yes had the ability to penetrate deeply into the psyche and to leave an indelible mark on all those who opened themselves to the experience. It left thousands of people around the world "bitten by the Yes bug" with a fervent desire to revisit that very special high place that the band and its music had taken them.

It seems unbelievable in the fickle world of rock music that it is still possible to be able to attend a Yes concert in the early years of the twenty-first century. Yes with its various lineups had continued to tour throughout its long career but there were the inevitable roller coaster ups and downs. It was my perception in the late nineties that Yes had appeared to be climbing back up to the top of the musical mountain after periods of uncertainty in the wake of the *Talk* and *Keys*

To Ascension projects. It is here that the focus is on Yes concerts in the modern era covering the period 1997 to 2003 with a look at progress to date in 2004.

Yes Tours 1997 To 2003

Yes toured extensively in the period 1997 to 2003 and gave a total of some 433 concerts. It amply illustrates that the band worked hard in performing for audiences around the globe including shows in North America, South America, Europe, Asia and Australia. During this period Yes toured for an average of approximately fifteen weeks each year, performing an average of seventy-two shows per year which equates to five shows per week of between two and three hours in length. The average "typical" show was two and a half hours in length, representing a very generous level of performance. It should also be pointed out that all of the members of Yes were involved in solo work of different types along with their activities with the band. Additionally, in the same period Yes released three new studio albums, a documentary and three new live recordings together with other compilations. It paints the picture of a very diligent and committed working band.

To put these figures in perspective, the book *Perpetual Change* by David Watkinson indicates that Yes performed on 1502 occasions in the period 1968 to 1996.[1] This equates to an average of fifty-two performances per year but after allowing for the fact that Yes didn't give any shows at all in the years 1981, 1982, 1983, 1986, 1993 and 1995, the average increases to sixty-five performances per year. It should also be remembered that Yes was prevented from touring for most of the first half of 2003 as a result of a serious injury to Jon Anderson's back after he accidentally fell from a ladder at his home on the unlucky day of Friday 13 December, 2002. In summary, it can be concluded that the touring activity of Yes in the period 1997 to 2003 with an average of seventy-two shows per year is certainly in keeping with the overall history of the band and demonstrates no sign of dissipation, an impressive achievement over such a long career.

Here are the details of the Yes tours from 1997 to 2003 along with information to date for 2004:

Open Your Eyes Tour:
North America (1st leg)—17 October 1997 to 14 December 1997, 43 shows
Europe—26 February 1998 to 24 April 1998, 45 shows
South America—7 May 1998 to 28 May 1998, 14 shows
North America (2nd leg)—18 June 1998 to 8 August 1998, 41 shows

Japan—8 October 1998 to 14 October 1998, 5 shows
Typical length of show—2hrs 30m (Europe)

The Ladder Tour:
Latin America—6 September 1999 to 24 September 1999, 9 shows
North America—15 October 1999 to 13 December 1999, 42 shows
Europe—6 February 2000 to 25 March 2000, 35 shows
Typical show—2hrs 10m (North America)

Masterworks Tour:
North America—20 June 2000 to 4 August 2000, 32 shows
Typical show—2hrs plus support act Kansas

Yessymphonic Tour:
North America—22 July 2001 to 8 September 2001, 33 shows
Europe—25 October 2001 to 13 December 2001, 36 shows
Typical show—3hrs (North America)

2002 Tour:
North America (1st leg)—17 July 2002 to 25 August 2002, 26 shows
North America (2nd leg)—24 October 2002 to 8 December 2002, 29 shows
Typical show—2hrs 40m (1st leg)

Full Circle Tour:
Europe—3 June 2003 to 22 July 3003, 33 shows
Asia/Australia/USA—12 September 2003 to 3 October 2003, 10 shows
Typical show—2hrs 30m

35th Anniversary Tour:
North America (1st leg)—15 April 2004 to 15 May 2004, 18 shows
Europe—2 June 2004 to 12 July 2004, 25 shows
North America (2nd leg)—17 August 2004 to 22 September 2004, 23 shows
Note: Additional shows under consideration for late 2004
Typical show—2hrs 30m (North America 1st leg)

On The Road

One is naturally tempted to think of the life of a rock band on the road as being glamorous but from my observations, it isn't necessarily the case. In recent years I've had the opportunity to follow Yes on the road for a few shows on different tours and it has provided some valuable insights into how the band operates. It soon became apparent that the lifestyle of Yes on the road is no easy walk in the park and it has enhanced my respect for the musicians who spend so much time travelling from place to place to perform for the fans. It is often tiring enough just getting to the next destination aside from meeting the prime requirement of having to give an excellent show.

The Yes tour schedule of the last few years has generally followed the pattern of performing for two or three nights in succession before taking a day off. Similar to any tour by a major band, both the musicians and the road crew hauling the equipment have been required to adhere to a disciplined and rigorous schedule in order to arrive at each destination on time and be ready for the next performance. As an example of the significant logistical demands, the distances covered from one show to the next on the Yes *2002* American tour were as great as 1930km (1200 miles) while distances in the range of 480 to 640km (300 to 400 miles) were common.

The members of Yes in recent times have travelled by both air and road depending on the logistics involved. Unlike the heady days of the seventies where private jets were often the order of the day, Yes now generally travels on regular commercial flights or by bus, passenger van or limousine. Regardless of the mode of transport, travel clearly remains a time consuming business with relatively long lead times either at airports or on the road. After arriving at a new destination, there could be some promotional or press obligations and there could be line checks, sound checks or rehearsals at the concert venue depending on the requirements for any particular tour or show.

A typical Yes show generally commences between 7.30pm and 8pm and concludes between 10pm and 11pm. A show of that duration is obviously demanding of the band, particularly considering the complexity of the music and the fact that the performances sometimes take place in outdoor venues in less than ideal conditions with extremes of weather to be dealt with. Of course, it is natural that every audience at every venue will have the expectation that the evening's performance by Yes will be as fresh and as perfect as possible, almost as though it was the only show being given by the band on the tour. Additionally, the members of Yes might choose to meet and greet fans before or after a show while at some point finding a period for rest and relaxation. Being on the road could clearly be a test of endurance in living out of a suitcase but it could also be a stimulating lifestyle in briefly visiting many different places, glimpsing interesting sights and meeting all kinds of people around the world.

There is no doubt that it is the experience of performing in front of an audience that keeps propelling Yes forward on its relentless musical journey despite the challenges of being on the road. Chris Squire commented: "I always feel very charged (after a show)...Sometimes I think its (becoming) easier (being on the road) and that might be because we've learned all of the pot holes of travelling...Over the years you learn a few tricks about how to travel. And I think sometimes I just kind of go into a desensitized state (laughs) during the moving from A to B and put my head in a book. And try to put my blinkers on, try not to really notice what's going on and then sort of wake up an hour before the show."[2]

Steve Howe said: "Touring is all about schedules, all about meeting that schedule and it's quite demanding in that way."[3] Steve's view is that each audience and each concert are equally important and that there is always a special feeling about a Yes show. The downside as he points out is the big sacrifice in being separated from family and loved ones over a long period of time but Steve maintains he is driven to keep going because of a feeling that it all has a significant meaning in the end.

Jon Anderson often makes the comment during a Yes show that the more closely an audience listens, the better the band plays. Ultimately it is the mutual thirst for that inspiring interaction and exchange of energy between the musicians and the listener that is the key factor in continuing to bring Yes and audiences together. However, Jon knows as much as anyone in Yes that being on the road can be a trial: "It's a great feeling to be on stage. It really is a fantastic energy...(But) if I was touring all the time, I'd definitely go crazy...The first month of touring is like 'Yes! Gung ho! We're out here, we can do this!' And the second month is 'When are we getting home, when can we get back to the real world?' A day without travelling I think is very healthy."[4]

The members of Yes have each developed their own ways of coping with the demands of touring. For instance, Jon Anderson has recognized the importance of resting his voice for the shows and he often minimizes the use of his voice during the day. Steve Howe dislikes flying and he prefers where possible to be driven in one of his own vehicles to each destination by his personal assistant. As far as Steve is concerned, the day of a show is essentially about conserving energy in order to give the best possible performance that night. Alan White shares a similar view: "I think after the experience of all those years (in Yes), you try to put yourself in the right frame of mind to be able to approach the concert and go on there and perform your best. I see everybody (in the band) on stage performing at least at 110 percent the whole time...The band loves playing in front of all those smiling faces and we aim to please. Smiling faces are the best things for us to see on stage."[5]

Musicians on the road inevitably have a mixture of memorable, testing and comical moments. On the *Union* tour of America in 1991, Rick Wakeman decided to drive himself around the country in a luxury van and he amusingly highlighted the pitfalls when he told the story of having the unsettling experience of staying in a roadside motel that was run by a man who looked suspiciously like the owner of the infamous Bates establishment in the Alfred Hitchcock film "Psycho", complete with a voice suited to a horror movie! However, Rick's approach to being on the road is very down to earth and he says: "I absolutely love being on stage...it's the Jekyll and Hyde thing. I like to think I'm just a normal person when off the stage but you become who you are, Rick Wakeman or whatever, when you wander on which is just fantastic."[6]

Concert Venues

The schedule for every Yes tour always lists many intriguingly named concert venues. Here is a snapshot of the kinds of venues that Yes performed at during the period 1997 to 2003, categorized as outdoor amphitheatres, theatres, indoor arenas, intimate venues and special venues.

Outdoor Amphitheatres:

Yes has frequently toured America in the warmer months of the year and outdoor amphitheatres were the venues mainly used for those tours. Outdoor amphitheatres host many major concerts and they vary in capacity and format with some of the smaller ones holding only 3,000 people with no covered seating. However, the most typical type in the larger cities feature covered seating for approximately 7000 people with a large, open air, sloping grassed area behind increasing the total capacity to about 20,000. There are usually video screens that enable the audience at the rear to have a close up view of Yes on stage such as at the Mars Music Amphitheatre in West Palm Beach, Florida.

Theatres:

Yes has performed many shows in theatres throughout the world in recent years. The theatres have ranged from historic venues through to modern state of the art buildings. Most of the theatres have seating capacities in the range of 2,000 to 3,000 people while the theatres in some of the larger cities have capacities in the vicinity of 6,000. Amongst the larger types of theatre-style venues where Yes has played are the Radio City Music Hall in New York and the Universal Amphitheatre in Los Angeles.

Indoor Arenas:

Yes often played in multi-purpose indoor arenas in earlier eras but has done so only occasionally in the period 1997 to 2003. In 2004, however, Yes returned to performing in a range of major indoor arenas including Madison Square Garden in New York, the Philadelphia Spectrum, Wembley Arena in London and the Manchester Evening News Arena that is reputed to be the largest indoor concert venue in Europe with a seating capacity of up to 21,000 people. Indoor arenas generally have capacities in the range of 5,000 to 15,000 people, the Sydney Entertainment Centre in Australia being an example of an arena visited by Yes in 2003.

Intimate Venues:

One of the trends in the past few years has been for major bands to play in smaller venues to give the audience a more intimate music experience. These intimate venues typically have capacities in the range of 1,000 to 2,000 people, sometimes with general admission rather than reserved seating. Yes played at a number of such venues during *The Ladder* tour in 1999 including the trendy House Of Blues on the Sunset Strip in Los Angeles and more recently during the *2002* tour performed in the Showroom of the Las Vegas Hilton.

Special Venues:

In recent times Yes has performed at some venues that are so unique and famous that they fall into a special category. These special venues include the Royal Albert Hall in London, the Kremlin State Palace in Moscow and the Hollywood Bowl in Los Angeles. Special venues also include festivals and there have been a number of those on the Yes tour schedule including the Montreux Jazz Festival in Switzerland and the Glastonbury Festival in England.

Staging and Road Crew

Jon Anderson frequently remarks on stage that Yes has the best road crew in the business and a number of the people involved have been with the band for several years. In 2003 Jon said: "We've had the same crew on and off for ten, fifteen, twenty years. The lighting crew change every time. The sound people change. The crew that look after the guitars, drums and keyboards are generally the same people."[7] Amongst the stalwarts in the Yes crew have been Tour Manager Paul Silveira, guitar tech Ron "Shooz" Mathews, bass tech Richard Davis and Rick Wakeman's keyboards tech Stuart Sawney. However, some new faces were evident amongst the crew during the 2004 tour.

The considerable demands placed on the Yes road crew were obvious when watching the stage being set up for the *Yessymphonic* show in 2001 at the Sunset Casino Amphitheatre in Henderson, Nevada. The show took place in the summer heat in late July and it was an outdoor venue in a desert environment with very little shade available. The arduous task for the road crew in the oppressive conditions was to set up the tons of equipment from three large articulated trucks for Yes and the accompanying orchestra. And of course, it would only be a matter of hours later after the show that the road crew then had to dismantle and re-pack all of the equipment in order for it to be transported to the next stop on the tour. Typically the road crew sleep on the crew bus during the overnight trip to the next venue so as to be ready to do it all again the next day.

The Henderson show highlighted the great challenge that Yes had undertaken with the *Yessymphonic* concept in which the band performed with a different orchestra on each date of the American leg of the world tour. The orchestra that assembled in Henderson was a collection of various local musicians and they hadn't seen the scores or rehearsed any of the music until the day of the performance. The orchestra rehearsed for approximately two hours in the afternoon but didn't actually play with Yes until the show commenced that night. It was a methodology adopted to keep the costs under control but it must be said that at this show the orchestra noticeably took some time to eventually warm to the task. One could only admire the bravery of Yes in taking on the unpredictability of that situation for an entire American tour.

The wide variety of indoor and outdoor venues typically played by Yes in the course of each tour requires the band's sound engineers to vary the concert sound system to suit each different location. For example, the main PA system consisted of a massive nineteen large speaker bins on each side of the stage for the outdoor amphitheatre show at the Cricket Pavilion in Phoenix, Arizona in 2002 while only eight speaker bins were required each side of the stage for the indoor show two nights later at the Universal Amphitheatre in Los Angeles. The acoustics at each venue can vastly differ and similarly, the sound in an empty concert hall can alter drastically when it is filled with people. Part of the challenge for the sound engineers is to make the correct allowances to achieve the balance and clarity needed to fully appreciate the complex music of Yes and it can make or break the way in which the performance is perceived by the audience. It requires a real skill and understanding of the music to deliver the right sound through the PA and it is not unusual at Yes concerts for it to take a song or two at the beginning of each show for the mix to be fine tuned and optimized to suit the conditions in the venue on the night.

One of the significant costs of touring is in the transportation of equipment and the test for Roger Dean in designing the Yes stage set for the 2004 tour was to create a strong visual impact while keeping the equipment light and easily transportable. Roger's solution was to build a stage set using inflatable shapes made of woven nylon that enabled him to achieve large-scale design elements of some six or seven metres in height without the handicap of heavy weights. The final result was compromised to some extent by last minute budgetary constraints that resulted in the stage being incomplete for some of the early shows on the tour. The design was nevertheless still very effective in achieving the larger than life sense of theatre that goes hand in hand with Yes music.

Backstage And Beyond

I had the opportunity during the *Masterworks* tour in 2000 to get a much closer look at Yes backstage than might have normally been possible. It came about through a chance meeting with Robby Steinhardt, the electric violinist and vocalist with the well known American band Kansas who supported Yes on that tour. In fact it was the first in a series of quite incredible coincidences during the *Masterworks* tour and subsequent tours where I've come into contact with Yes in completely unexpected ways.

I flew from Australia to attend the last four shows of the *Masterworks* tour in America and it was at the airport in Charlotte, North Carolina that I first met Robby Steinhardt. We enjoyed a pleasant conversation for a few minutes while waiting for a flight to Nashville, Tennessee and he was intrigued that I'd travelled so far to see the shows. Amazingly after boarding the aircraft, it turned out I was seated next to Steve Brownlow who was the Road Manager for Kansas with Robby only two seats away across the aisle. It ultimately led to an invitation to go backstage that night for the *Masterworks* show at the Amsouth Amphitheatre in Nashville but not before I went to my hotel to check in and found myself once again standing next to Robby, Steve and the rest of Kansas who were staying at the same place!

Later that night the affable Robby took me by complete surprise when he announced to the audience during Kansas's set that I'd made the pilgrimage from Australia to see the *Masterworks* tour. After the performance he signed autographs and posed for photographs for the fans while explaining that he enjoyed contact with the people who liked his music and only found it off putting when some people occasionally came on a little too strongly. When asked about the demands of touring, he referred to it as the "waiting game" because it was necessary for musicians to wait for flights, to wait to go on stage, to wait for virtually everything while they were on the road. It was an interesting insight into the life of a touring musician.

Robby then told me that he had someone he would like me to meet and a couple of minutes later a smiling Alan White emerged from the dressing rooms. The good humored Yes drummer revealed to me that the next Yes album was going to be similar to *Tales From Topographic Oceans*, or at least that was the original concept for the *Magnification* album. Within minutes, Jon Anderson had appeared and I managed to have a brief discussion in which he explained the problems in organizing a Yes tour of Australia but reassured that the tour would indeed take place, a promise that was actually made good in 2003.

Moments later, I had a quick chat with Chris Squire who also confirmed the intent of Yes to record a new album (*Magnification*) before he moved on to quietly mingle with other visitors in the backstage area. I then noticed Alan White near the stage entrance starting to go through a series of stretching exercises in preparation for the physical demands of the show. Steve Howe hadn't yet appeared and I wasn't surprised because he was known to have a meticulous preparation for each performance, typically including a lengthy late afternoon sound check followed by a private session of meditation and exercise. Suddenly the recorded strains of "A Young Person's Guide To The Orchestra" could be heard and all of the members of Yes filed past heading towards the stage. Steve Howe had a very serene expression on his face and wore a long brown robe draped around his shoulders that was removed by one of the road crew at the last moment before he stepped on stage. It had been a fascinating backstage glimpse of Yes and it was notable how very approachable and down to earth the members of the band had been.

The following morning it was time to move on to the next show in Atlanta, Georgia and bizarrely, Robby Steinhardt was once again standing there in the airport gate lounge waiting for the same flight. After jokingly branding me as a stalker, Robby insisted that I join him backstage again that night and presented me with his personal *Masterworks* tour All Access pass. I'm not sure that it was strictly according to the rulebook but it was a wonderful and generous gesture. To add to the atmosphere of unreality, a lady I sat next to on the same flight introduced herself as a musician and television actress. After speaking to me for a few minutes, she made the intriguing and profound prediction that I would soon be writing a book. I didn't quite know what to say because I didn't have any firm plans to do so at the time but then that was before *The Extraordinary World Of Yes* became a reality.

Thanks to having Robby's All Access pass, I had the opportunity at the Lakewood Amphitheater in Atlanta to watch the energetic and skilful performance of Kansas from the side of the stage while Chris Squire and some other members of the Yes entourage lingered around me. The Yes road crew were standing by to put Yes's equipment in place and Chris took a peek at the audience from behind the concert PA system before retiring to the dressing rooms to make final preparations for the show. Kansas completed their set and the adrenalin pumping through their bodies was obvious as they left the stage with the audience still applauding. Suddenly technicians converged from everywhere and the changeover between bands was handled so efficiently that it had taken no more than fifteen minutes to finally set the stage for Yes.

An unusual consequence of my *Masterworks* sojourn was that I received a mention in a story about Yes that was written by Yes fan Rene Lester and placed in a time capsule in Luverne, Alabama. The Mayor of Luverne became aware that a group of Yes fans from the chat list YesTalk at Yahoo Groups had organized via the internet to get together to see the shows in Nashville and Atlanta and that it involved people from all over America with the addition of an Australian. The Mayor was so impressed that modern technology had brought together such a diverse group of people to celebrate a mutual interest in a band called Yes, that he asked Rene in her capacity as Luverne City Librarian to write a story about the event to demonstrate a facet of life in the year 2000. The story included the names of the Yes members, the set list for the shows, details of the Yes fans and a photo of Rene with Jon Anderson that was taken by Eddie Lee. The story about Yes and those Yes fans is now in two identical time capsules that will be unearthed in Douglass Park, Luverne, Alabama—the first on 4 July 2026 and the second on 4 July 2076. The dates represent fifty years and one hundred years respectively from the American bicentennial in 1976. It is quite astonishing to think that people will read about Yes, along with my interest in the band, so many years from now.

My visits to America to see Yes have somehow always been extraordinary in one way or another. In 2001 at a *Yessymphonic* show I met Gary Lauer and it led to us formulating the concept for the *Yesology* project over the following eighteen months that in turn resulted in this book. It was on the *Yessymphonic* tour that Yes made a return appearance at the Hollywood Bowl and I had the memorable experience of being one of only a handful of people who watched the band rehearse with the Hollywood Bowl Orchestra in the afternoon prior to the show. Yes broke from the general pattern of the *Yessymphonic* tour in actually playing with the orchestra before that show and it was like being at a grandiose private concert in hearing the new songs "Don't Go" and "In The Presence Of" from the *Magnification* album with orchestral backing in the empty expanses of such a large outdoor venue

Some more coincidences involving Yes occurred during the first leg of the *2002* tour of America. I'd flown into Los Angeles from Phoenix for the show at the Universal Amphitheatre and after a trip by shuttle van from the airport, I walked up to the hotel check-in desk to find myself rubbing shoulders with Alan White, Rick Wakeman and Paul Silveira who'd arrived minutes earlier. It proved to be a most remarkable way of learning that the Yes tour of Australia in 2003 had been confirmed, an event I'd been willing to happen for thirty years and somehow fate had deemed that I would actually hear the news first from the members of Yes.

The morning after the Los Angeles gig, I went to the airport to fly to Las Vegas to catch the next two shows before heading home to Australia. I'd been standing in the security queue outside one of the terminals waiting to enter when the Yes entourage arrived in two passenger vans. I must explain beyond any shadow of a doubt that I have no inside information whatsoever on the travel arrangements of Yes and yet incredibly our paths had crossed again and we were in the same place at the same time in an airport as large as Los Angeles International. The band congregated in the terminal foyer for a few minutes with families and luggage in tow before moving through to the gate lounges.

I stayed at the Las Vegas Hilton where the two shows took place and upon going to have breakfast the next morning at the hotel buffet, the waiter showed me to a table next to that occupied by Steve Howe and his personal assistant Lane Seiger. Again, I have no adequate explanation for such a coincidence and by this stage it seemed quite routine when I almost bumped into Rick Wakeman while walking around the casino. I also noticed Chris Squire and Alan White when I spent some time around the swimming pool. One thing it did bring home to me is that while Yes are obviously musicians extraordinaire, off stage they give every appearance of being low-key in going quietly about their business.

My next Yes inspired visit to America was in 2004 when I attended the last four shows of the first leg of the *35th Anniversary* tour. The set list for the tour included a number of songs featured in *The Extraordinary World Of Yes*, most notably a selection of strong Yes songs that had rarely or never been played on stage. The remarkable aspect was that these songs were included an early draft of the book that I personally presented to Yes and Roger Dean in September 2003 as part of a package of material associated with the *Yesology* project. It may have been purely coincidental but members of the band read the draft and it might have provided some positive reinforcement to Yes in playing largely unexpected pieces such as "Every Little Thing", "Sweet Dreams", "Turn Of The Century" and "Mind Drive".

One of the 2004 shows was at the breathtaking Mohegan Sun casino in Uncasville, Connecticut and I stayed at the hotel which was part of the complex. A few minutes after checking in I decided to go downstairs and that's when I had to shake my head in disbelief. After taking a photograph of the colorful entrance foyer I noticed a large black limousine at the front door. Chris Squire, Alan White and Paul Silveira stepped out and made their way inside to the hotel desk. I admit on this occasion to being completely stunned that I'd yet again been standing right on the spot when members of Yes arrived. I could only mutter a somewhat dazed greeting to Alan as he walked past and hoped that he didn't think I'd been waiting there in ambush like some paparazzi because it couldn't have been further from the truth. Of course, there was more to come. The next morning on the day of the show I stepped out of the elevator in the hotel foyer to head off for breakfast and a sixth sense made me suddenly spin around—no more than five paces behind was Paul Silveira walking in the same direction! Even if Paul had been James Bond he would have been hard pressed to keep his man under closer surveillance!

Perhaps the greatest coincidence of all was still to occur. The last show of the first leg of the 2004 tour was in Lowell, Massachusetts and the day after I was scheduled to start the long trip home to Australia by flying from Boston to Los Angeles. I arrived at the airport about ninety minutes early and after sitting around for most of that time, walked away for a few moments before returning to the gate lounge in readiness to board the flight. It was then that I saw Paul Silveira using a public phone and before I could move any further, I was standing next to Jon Anderson. I looked at Jon and dryly said: "Hey, are you following me around?" He just laughed and fortunately remembered my face. Paul had joined us by this time and I began to explain how astounding it was that I kept appearing in the same places at the same times as the members of Yes and how it was all completely unpremeditated. Jon simply smiled and sagely waved my concerns away.

We ended up having a very interesting forty-five minute conversation about Yes, the current tour and the deeper meaning of life before boarding the plane together. Yet strangely it was a conversation that should never have taken place because the flight had been running exactly forty-five minutes late. It fills me with a child-like sense of wonder at the seemingly impossible, perfect synchronicity of these encounters with Yes that in many ways mirrors the cosmic nature of Yes music itself. As I said to Jon, I've come to appreciate that there is a great deal of truth in what he writes in the lyrics of Yes and there is much more to life than immediately meets the eye.

There was a certain poetic sense of completion when that flight from Boston finally touched down in Los Angeles. Another Yes tour had ended and the band members and crew could return to their private lives for a few days before doing it all again in another part of the world. Jon had to move fast to make his connecting flight home while Paul and I stood around the carousel waiting for the luggage to arrive. Paul asked me whether I'd seen where Jon had gone to before we finally shook hands and parted. As I walked over to the international terminal to wait for my flight home, I contemplated what had been another fabulous Yes experience. I'd always wanted to know what it was like to be on tour with Yes and the question had been answered.

Great Yes Shows

Even though the internet has revolutionized communications and has made it possible to virtually keep up with every move that Yes makes, there is nothing like being there at a Yes concert to capture the moment, to experience the excitement, to see the faces of the happy fans, to witness the colorful spectacle and to be carried away into that extraordinary world of Yes music.

The experience of seeing several shows on particular tours has confirmed that the average standard of a Yes performance remains supremely high. However, it should also be remembered that the band is human and they do have the occasional blooper, sometimes due to technical reasons beyond their control. Yes is a band often playing close to the edge of their abilities in attempting to push the boundaries further than the last time and this perpetual drive towards the perfection of their music results in some Yes shows rising above the others to the point where they are truly magical events of the highest order. If you have the opportunity of seeing Yes more than once on any given tour, my advice is don't hesitate.

Even if the set list is identical, each Yes show tends to be an organic entity in its own right that is largely dependent on how the band and audience react together on the particular night. The arrangements for the songs provide the framework but the solos within each piece are open to interpretation by the musicians and are never exactly the same in each performance.

The *Open Your Eyes* tour in 1997/98 had steadied the ship after the uncertainties in the Yes camp in the mid nineties but it was *The Ladder* album and tour in 1999/2000 that saw Yes really regain their form. And then it was the *Masterworks* tour in America in 2000 that re-established Yes to a position on one of the highest musical peaks, arguably as high as they had ever previously climbed. The *Yessymphonic* tour in 2001 was a spectacular event but in the eyes of most fans, it was the return of Rick Wakeman to Yes in 2002 that fully consolidated the revitalization of the band and was further built upon during the *Full Circle* tour in 2003. Somehow each tour has had something new to say about the band and some truly great gigs come to mind.

In 1999 during *The Ladder* tour there was an unmistakably special atmosphere when arriving at the Sun Theatre in Anaheim with the evening light giving the venue a golden glow. The excitement began to mount when Steve Howe appeared in the forecourt for a photo shoot and it reached fever pitch by the time Yes walked on stage with the entire audience jumping to its feet to loudly proclaim the band. It was a performance in which Yes wiped away any doubts that the band could still cut it at the highest level and the concert was so memorable that it was difficult not to think back to it when attending other shows on the same tour.

The factors that came together to make the Anaheim show seem so special were that Yes was in top form, the audience was extrovertly enthusiastic, the sound mix was excellent and the well appointed intimate venue with seating for only 1200 people gave the audience a close view while enabling the band to present itself to the best advantage. The additional "X" factor was the surprise inclusion of "Close To The Edge" because it was played at only three shows on *The Ladder* tour of North America and it made for a very potent set that also included "Awaken", five new songs from *The Ladder* and a selection of Yes classics.

The rave reviews filtering through from the thrilled fans in America during the *Masterworks* tour in 2000 were most persuasive. Yes had adopted an ambitious set list based around their great epics, some of which hadn't been performed live since 1976. After a shaky moment or two in coming to grips with some of the complex compositions in the first couple of performances, Yes rapidly came to terms with the music in no uncertain fashion. Many shows on this tour were of a very high standard but the unforgettable gig at the Mars Music Amphitheatre in West Palm Beach saw Yes generating more electricity on stage than the thunder and lightning from the threatening storm in the tropical Florida air. The stage set was comprised of sail-like sections of material that were hoisted into position and they were a simple but ingenious method of creating an eye pleasing setting. The blaze of colored light that illuminated the sails on the stage delighted the senses and combined with the legendary epic music, it was an emotional experience that sent a tingling sensation down the spine.

It was a rare treat indeed to hear "The Gates Of Delirium" and Yes were flying so high going into the so-called battle sequence in West Palm Beach that it seemed as though the whole venue had taken off and had soared into space. The performances of epics such as "Close To the Edge" and "The Gates Of Delirium" were astounding enough but there was more to come with "Ritual" and its ferocious four man drum solo that seemed to be pounding out the heart beat of the whole world with a relentless intensity that reverberated through mind and body. Yes appeared to be much more comfortable having reverted to their standard format of a five piece lineup for the *Masterworks* tour and the challenge of reaching back to resurrect seldom played but inspired music saw them rise mightily to the occasion. It left one wondering whether Yes had ever performed better.

In the first few days of the *Yessymphonic* tour in 2001, Alan White told me that Yes was still adapting to playing with an orchestra but he felt that the particular shows featuring established orchestras that regularly played together would provide some real highlights. Alan's words proved to be most prophetic because at the Queen Elizabeth Theatre in Vancouver, Canada the *Yessymphonic* concept came together at its absolute best. Unlike some *Yessymphonic* gigs where the orchestras were disparate collections of musicians with little or no experience in working together, the show in Vancouver started with a significant advantage in that the orchestra was the Vancouver Symphony Orchestra which was reputed to be one of the best orchestras in Canada. The second advantage was that the show took place in the Queen Elizabeth Theatre, a venue that had excellent acoustics and there was consequently far less risk of any subtleties of the orchestral sound being lost as might have been more likely with some of the outdoor venues on the tour.

Yes had carried over their superb form from the Masterworks tour to the *Yessymphonic* tour and new keyboardist Tom Brislin had slotted in surprisingly smoothly. The Vancouver Symphony Orchestra was excellent and Yes's sound engineers consequently had the luxury of being able to give the orchestra full volume as opposed to some other shows where the contributions of the different orchestras were sometimes minimized by judicious mixing of the sound. It was in fact a work of art in itself that such a brilliant sound mix was achieved because every musician in Yes and in the orchestra could be heard to utmost advantage with perfect clarity in a venue that gave the audience a superb view of the band. The result was so impressive that it was the finest example I've ever heard of a rock band and orchestra performing together.

The classic Yes lineup that performed in America in 2002 hadn't toured extensively together as a discrete five piece band since 1979. The cover notes for the Yes DVD/video *Live In Philadelphia 1979* succinctly described the qualities of this lineup when they referred to the "fragile balance of individual personality, visionary writing, telepathic interaction and brilliant instrumentation". When seeing this lineup together again on stage in 2002, it was evident that the same description remained perfectly valid twenty-three years later. Somehow more than the other fine Yes lineups of recent years, the classic Yes lineup exhibited an extraordinary intuitive chemistry with an ability to create a sound that was both powerful and infinitely detailed.

It was true that some early shows on the *2002* tour did betray evidence of the band readjusting to being together again but that was only to be expected. However, the performance at the Cricket Pavilion in Phoenix on 21 August 2002 was classic Yes at its spellbinding best. The precision of the band was largely anticipated but it was the high level of rocking energy that exceeded all reasonable expectations, especially on a very hot summer's night. It wasn't Yes jumping around the stage pretending to be twenty-five years old again but it was the equivalent effort and energy directly injected into the music. It transported everyone with an open mind to that special high place that only Yes music can and there were constant murmurings amongst the audience of "brilliant" or "incredible" that turned into standing ovations at the end of every song.

The *Full Circle* tour in 2003 saw Yes primarily focus on concerts in the U.K., Europe, Asia and Australia. The band continued on from where it left off in 2002 with performances that drew rapturous responses from audiences everywhere and the enthusiasm was reflected at the box office with a string of sold out shows. One of the most noteworthy gigs was at the Glastonbury Festival in England, the largest music event of its type in Europe. Tickets for the festival were so sought after that they were sold out long before it was announced that Yes would be appearing. However, despite the absence of a committed Yes audience, a packed crowd of thousands congregated around the One World Stage where Yes played. Eyewitness accounts described the atmosphere as "electric" and the reaction of the audience as "ecstatic" as Yes delivered what was said to be a "triumphant" performance. It supports my firmly held belief that discerning music fans everywhere will enthusiastically embrace the musical brilliance of Yes if given the opportunity to listen to and see the band.

Towards the end of the *Full Circle* tour Yes played in Sydney, Australia for the first time since the *Close To The Edge* tour in 1973. The main test facing the band with this show was to live up to its own formidable reputation because many in the audience had been fans for years but had never seen Yes live. Remarkably Yes set the bar even higher than on the *2002* tour with a performance at the Sydney Entertainment Centre in 2003 that must rank with the best that the band has ever delivered. There were lengthy standing ovations after every song and the palpable feeling in the arena was that one was indeed fortunate to have witnessed an irresistible musical force called Yes that was incredibly still at the height of its extraordinary powers.

At the time of writing in 2004, Yes's *35th Anniversary* world tour was underway and the band's continued powerful mastery of live performance prompted Jeffrey Morgan of Creem Magazine in America to declare that Yes would win hands down in a battle of the bands against even the legendary might of Led Zeppelin and Cream. It is unlikely that any Yes show has surpassed the magical performance at Mohegan Sun in Uncasville, Connecticut on 12 May 2004. The 10,000 seat arena was packed to capacity and there was an audible gasp from the audience when the curtain dropped to the floor to reveal the fantastic Roger Dean stage set that was probably seen to best advantage when sitting several rows back from the stage.

In the slipstream of the great Yes epics, it is sometimes forgotten that Yes is also a great rock'n'roll band and they proved it at Mohegan Sun with definitive performances of "Sweet Dreams", "Rhythm of Love" and "Every Little Thing". Contrast that with the thrilling live debut of "Mind Drive", the delicacy of "Turn Of The Century", the white hot solos during "Southside Of The Sky", a steaming "Yours Is No Disgrace", a new acoustic arrangement of "Roundabout" along with the infinite cosmic power of "And You And I" and there was nothing left to be desired—except to finish with the surprise addition of "Starship Trooper" with a blistering closing guitar solo by Steve Howe that even had Chris Squire looking amazed. The peerless music combined with a surreal stage set proved to the audience that Yes in 2004 was still at the zenith of its amazing career.

Perhaps the last word on great Yes shows should go to the Yes fans and here is what some of them had to say at YesNet on the YesWorld website[8]

I would recommend people who aren't even fans of Yes to go see them live, it's something you'll never forget. (fifteen year old fan, *The Ladder* tour, Sun Theatre, Anaheim, 1999)

The feelings and emotions that I experienced last night were transcendental and brought to me a sense of awe and wonder which I thought no band on earth could provide. (*Masterworks* tour, West Palm Beach, Florida, 2000)

The band was bang on all night...just reaffirmed my belief that no other band can touch these guys. (*Yessymphonic* tour, Vancouver, Canada, 2001)

This was absolutely the best concert I have ever experienced (2002 tour, Phoenix, Arizona)

Truly a religious experience...Their musicianship is unparalleled, certainly in the realm of rock. (*2002* tour, Phoenix, Arizona)

The show in Sydney was a triumph, a blessing, a movement of souls to some higher plane, if ever so briefly. (*Full Circle* tour, Sydney, Australia, 2003)

I was absolutely blown away by the fire, power and intensity of the musicianship!...Yes gets better as time goes on and it was clearly evident last night. (*35th Anniversary* tour, Uncasville, Connecticut, 2004)

◆ ◆ ◆

There is a great deal of hype in modern society and it is no more prevalent than in rock and pop music—every new trend or fashionable new face is always the biggest, the best and so on. It sometimes has the effect of obscuring music and musicians that are truly exceptional and have something very worthwhile to say of lasting value. The main goal of *The Extraordinary World Of Yes* will have been realized if you've been prompted to look deeper beneath the surface to discover that the musical achievements of Yes are worthy of the highest accolades and that in some way your enjoyment of Yes music has been enhanced.

Indeed, there is a strong and logical argument to suggest that Yes might well be the most unique, most progressive and most talented rock band of all. Despite the often steep challenges and the sniping of the critics, Yes has prevailed. It is inviting to think that the world would somehow be a better place if "All Good People" everywhere took to heart the positive message of hope that this extraordinary band called Yes continues to deliver.

References

1 David Watkinson, *Perpetual Change*, Plexus, 2001, p.138
2 *Yesspeak* DVD, Classic Pictures, 2003
3 Ibid
4 Ibid
5 Ibid
6 Ibid
7 Ibid
8 Concert reviews from YesNet at the YesWorld web site

APPENDIX

Roundabout

SELECTIVE YES BIBLIOGRAPHY

Yes Books and Fanzines

Close To The Edge, Chris Welch, Omnibus Press 1999 (second edition 2003)
Magnetic Storm, Roger Dean & Martyn Dean, Dragon's World 1984
Music Of Yes—Structure And Vision In Progressive Rock, Bill Martin, Open Court Publishing 1996
Perpetual Change, David Watkinson, Plexus Publishing 2001 (second edition 2002)
Say Yes, Rick Wakeman, Hodder & Stoughton 1995
The Caped Crusader, Dan Wooding, Granada Publishing 1979
The Revealing (fanzine), edited by Paul Williams and Ian Hartley
The Steve Howe Guitar Collection, Steve Howe with Tony Bacon, Balafon Books 1994
Views, Roger Dean, Dragon's Dream 1975
Yes But What Does It Mean?, Thomas Mosbo, Wyndstar 1994
Yes The Authorised Biography, Dan Hedges, Sidgwick & Jackson 1981
Yes Magazine (fanzine), editors Doug & Glenn Gottlieb, regularly published from 1987 to 1999
Yes Music Circle (fanzine), editor Tiz Hay, regularly published from the eighties until the late nineties including related titles *Going For The 2, Yes Music Circle, Progress, Progressive Forum* and *Yes-Talk*
Yesstories—Yes In Their Own Words, Tim Morse, St Martin's Press 1996

Primary Yes Internet Resources

www.yesworld.com, the official Yes site
www.nfte.org, Notes From The Edge

www.jonanderson.com, the official Jon Anderson site
www.chrissquire.com, the official Chris Squire site
www.stevehowe.com, the official Steve Howe site
www.rwcc.com, the official Rick Wakeman site
www.alanwhite.net, the official Alan White site
www.billbruford.com, the official Bill Bruford site
www.yesfans.com, YesFans
www.yesservices.com, YesServices
www.bondegezou.demon.co.uk/wnyesm.htm, Yes—Where Are They Now?

General Rock Music and News Resources 1968 To 2004

Angela Catterns (ABC Radio 702, Sydney, Australia)
Australian Women's Weekly (Australian magazine)
Bass Player (US magazine)
Billboard (US magazine)
Classic Rock (UK magazine)
Daily Telegraph (Australian newspaper)
Deep Tracks, George Taylor-Morris XM satellite radio (US)
Electronic Soundmaker (UK magazine)
En Concierto with Gustavo Lutteral (I Sat TV, Argentina)
Go Set (Australian newspaper)
Guitar Player (US magazine)
Guitar World (US magazine)
Guitarist (UK magazine)
Jim Ladd's Living Room (radio KLOS FM 95.5, Los Angeles)
Juke (Australian newspaper)
Keyboard (US magazine)
Le Mag (French TV)
Melbourne Herald (Australian newspaper)
Melody Maker (UK newspaper)
Modern Hi Fi And Stereo Guide (US magazine)
Music Scene (UK magazine)
Music Scene, (RTL 5 Dutch TV)
New York Post (US newspaper)
Nine Network (Australian TV)
NME (UK newspaper)
Off the Record with Joe Benson (radio Arrow 93.1 FM Los Angeles)
Pop Rock (US magazine)

Radio 2SM (Sydney, Australia)
RAM (Australian newspaper)
Record Mirror (UK newspaper)
Rock Family Trees (BBC TV, UK)
Rock Stars (radio Westwood One, US)
Rockline, Bob Coburn (radio KLOS FM 95.5 Los Angeles)
Sonics (Australian magazine)
Soundblast (Australian newspaper)
Sounds (UK newspaper)
The Guitar Magazine (UK magazine)
The Sun (Australian newspaper)
The Vancouver Sun (Canadian newspaper)
Vox (UK magazine)
Words And Music With Lich (CPTV, Connecticut, US TV)
Yestival 1994 and 1998 (fan convention coordinated by Christine Holz and Lisa Mikita)

Other Internet Resources

http://creemmagazine.com, Creem Magazine
Kuno Online
www.2-4-7-music.com, Crud Magazine
www.bassplayer.com, Bass Player
www.deliciousagony.com, Delicious Agony progressive rock internet radio
www.digidesign.com, Digidesign (Pro Tools)
www.innerviews.org, Innerviews, Music Without Borders
www.musicnewsnetwork.net, Music News Network
www.musicstreetjournal.com, Music Street Journal
www.prog-nose.org, Prog-Nose
www.progressiveworld.net, ProgressiveWorld
www.retrorewind.com, Retro Rewind

SELECTIVE YES DISCOGRAPHY

Studio Albums

Yes
Time And A Word
The Yes Album
Fragile
Close To The Edge
Tales From Topographic Oceans (2 CD set)
Relayer
Going For The One
Tormato
Drama
90125
Big Generator
Union
Talk
Keystudio (all studio tracks from *Keys to Ascension 1 & 2*)
Open Your Eyes
The Ladder
Magnification

Live Albums

Yessongs (2 CD set)
Yesshows (2 CD set)
Keys To Ascension (2 CD set including new studio tracks)
Keys To Ascension 2 (2 CD set including new studio tracks)
House Of Yes—Live From House Of Blues (2 CD set)
Something's Coming (2 CD set, live and studio tracks from BBC)

Best Compilations

Classic Yes
Affirmative: Yes Family Solos Album (solo material)
Yes Years (4 CD set)
In A Word: Yes (5 CD set)
Ultimate Yes (2 CD set)

Best DVD/Video

Yessongs
9012 Live
Yes Greatest Video Hits
Live In Philadelphia 1979
Yesyears
The Union Tour Live
Keys To Ascension
House Of Yes—Live From House Of Blues
Yessymphonic Live
Yesspeak
Yes Acoustic

DVD—Audio

Fragile
Magnification

Anderson Bruford Wakeman Howe

Anderson Bruford Wakeman Howe (studio album)
An Evening Of Yes Music Plus (live CD/DVD/video)
In The Big Dream (DVD/video)

Best Of Classic Yes Solo Work

Jon Anderson:
Olias Of Sunhillow
Short Stories (with Vangelis)
Change We Must
Deseo
Earth Mother Earth

Chris Squire:
Fish Out Of Water
Chris Squire, Starlicks Master Series Video
Conspiracy (with Billy Sherwood)
The Unknown (with Billy Sherwood)

Steve Howe:
Beginnings
Turbulence
Not Necessarily Acoustic
Steve Howe Interactive CD-ROM
Natural Timbre

Rick Wakeman:
The Six Wives of Henry VIII
Journey To The Centre Of The Earth
The Myths And Legends Of King Arthur And The Knights Of The Round Table
Journey To The Centre Of The Earth—Live In Concert (DVD)
The Legend—Live In Concert 2000 (DVD)

Alan White:
Ramshackled

Yes Fan Clubs

(Source: www.yesservices.com)

Argentina

Club name: TBA
Contact: Patricio Mátteri, patricio_matteri@arnet.com.ar

Australia and New Zealand

YesFANZ
Web: www.yesfanz.com
Contact: Robert Forbes, yes@robert-forbes.com

Brazil

South American Khatru
Web: www.sak.com.br
Contact: Lais, lwitzel@globo.com

England

Steve Howe Appreciation Society
Contact: Pam Bay, pshasb@aol.com

France

Nous Sommes du Soleil
Web: http://noussommesdusoleil.free.fr
Contact: Yann Clochec, noussommesdusoleil@free.fr

Germany

German Khatru
Web: www.sallyskhatru.com
Contact: Sally Kunis, sally.kunis@gmx.de

Hungary

Hungarian Yes Forum
Web: www.geocities.com/yesforum/
Contact: megaterra@hu.inter.net

Italy

Tempus Fugit
Web: www.tempus-fugit.it
Contact: Giorgio Salvadego, salvadeg@tin.it

Indonesia

Indonesian Progressive Society
Contact: Kiki Caloh, id_prog@yahoo.com

Japan

Yes Family Fan Club
Web: www.nets.ne.jp/~yffc/
Contact: Shoji Yamada, yffc@nets.ne.jp

Netherlands

YesFocus
Web: www.yesfocus.org
Contact: Winston Arntz, info@yesfocus.org

Norway

NorskeYESfans
Web: www.norskeyesfans.com
Contact: Glen Paul, glenalup@c2i.net

Poland

Yesomania
Web: www.yesomania.net
Contact: Robert Drózd, yes@iq.pl

Scotland

Scottish YES Network
Web: http://hem.passagen.se/yespage/syn/main.htm
Contact: Brian Neeson, yescelt@aol.com

Sweden

SvenskaYes
Web: www.svenskayes.com
Contact: Torbjörn Häggmark & Göran Wallby, sys@svenskayes.com

Turkey

TurkiYes, The Turkish YES Network
Web: www.geocities.com/turkishyesnet
Contact: Cengiz Varlik, relayer@aktifkablo.net

USA (Delaware)

YesBrew
Contact: Mike McKinney, normnomo@aol.com

USA (New England)

YesFans Chapter #1 New England
Contact: Harry Sargent, benzback@comcast.net

USA (Oklahoma)

High The Memory
Contact: Michele Marie Moore, believers@unplugusa.com

The Story Of YesFANZ

By Robert Forbes, President of YesFANZ, the Yes fan group in Australia and New Zealand

"Love is a very very powerful thing. Love can conquer everything." These are the words of Jon Anderson. Love of Yes music is a very powerful thing—it was the motivation to start up the YesFANZ group and it conquered our frustration of waiting thirty years to see Yes performing in Australia again after the previous tour in 1973.

The internet is also a powerful thing. Various Yes fans in Australia and New Zealand had been regular readers of the Notes From The Edge web site and realized that there were, after all, many other fans of Yes in our part of the world. Some had made the long trip to America, the U.K. and other lands to see the band play. But enough was enough. It was time to make sure that Yes returned to Australia for another concert tour.

The experience of attending the 1973 Yes concerts during the Australian leg of the *Close To The Edge* tour was etched in the minds of those who were fortunate to be there and their experiences had been re-told many times since. Those experiences formed the basis of a twenty-two page full color "invitation" prepared by YesFANZ members and was delivered to Yes via their management offices in Los Angeles in August 2002.

YesFANZ started up in September 2001 when there were hints that a Yes tour of Australia could be on the agenda. The core group of Steve Black, Robert Forbes and Alan Farley in Australia and Paul Rogers in New Zealand had been in contact via email, making the connection via posts on the Notes From The Edge web site. By the middle of October 2001 there were eighteen members, some referred by Michele Marie Moore from the YesServices web site (Like Leaves We Touch) and some from Tim Lutterbie at the Yesfans web site. The YesFANZ web site opened in late October 2001 and preliminary contact was made with Yes management and local concert promoters. Toivo Pilt, the keyboard player with veteran Australian prog-rock band Sebastian Hardie, was approached about the possibility of getting that group back together again as a support act for Yes. Rumors of a possible Yes tour of Australia also started surfacing on the YesWorld web site.

By the beginning of 2002 there were twenty-seven YesFANZ members actively working towards the dream of the next Yes tour of Australia. Graphic designers such as Justin Heffernan and Lew Keilar designed the YesFANZ logo,

T shirts and promotional stickers. A YesFANZ meeting on 24 January 2002 resolved to lobby Yes management and to send posts to Notes From The Edge. Planning started for the "Yes Festivals"—private parties to be held in conjunction with the Yes concerts. Issues such as catering, entertainment, souvenirs, promotion, assistance to visitors, internet information services, pricing and other issues were talked about. At this time, local record companies in Australia had not even released the latest Yes album *Magnification* that could only be ordered from overseas. A lot of work needed to be done to bring Yes back into the public eye in Australia.

In February 2002, Issue #254 of Notes From The Edge was released containing our call to all Aussie and Kiwi Yes fans. This generated even more interest and brought the membership of YesFANZ to sixty people by the beginning of March 2002. A database of all concert promoters in Australia was prepared and each one was sent an email from YesFANZ. All of these emails were followed up but only Michael Chugg showed any real interest.

As 2002 progressed, the rumors of a Yes tour of Australia kept circulating but so far, nothing was confirmed. The invitation booklet was prepared and the idea was that Robert Forbes would travel to America to deliver it in person to Yes management. August 2002 seemed to be a good time—it was then that Yes would be performing in Los Angeles. By this stage, Rick Wakeman had re-joined Yes which considerably increased the enthusiasm of promoter Michael Chugg. Things were starting to fall into place and it was time to plan in earnest—the word was that Yes would be coming to Australia!

We then had the thought that if Yes were coming, why not have Roger Dean here as well? An invitation was sent to Roger to have an exhibition of his paintings in Australia to coincide with the Yes tour and we were blown away when one night, in the middle of a YesFANZ meeting, Roger Dean phoned and said yes, he was interested.

Early 2003 was being suggested as the likely timing for the Yes tour. Tentative bookings were made for function rooms at the proposed Yes concert venues—Vodafone Arena in Melbourne and the Sydney Entertainment Centre. And we had to find a suitable gallery for Roger Dean's exhibition. The Glass Artists Gallery in Glebe, Sydney was the one that showed the most interest—so much so, that they expanded into a vacant area next door and opened the GIG Gallery in preparation for the occasion.

With the YesFANZ need for T shirts, the printing of promotional posters and with deposits required for catering, an outside agency was appointed to handle our funds and manage payments. YesFANZ also appointed a coordinator for each of the six mainland states and territories of Australia and also for New Zealand. They would help with travel arrangements and in organizing local gatherings of Yes fans. At this stage it was becoming clear that Sydney and Melbourne would be the only cities to host Yes concerts this time around. With Roger Clark appointed as the Production Manager for the YesFANZ parties and with Brian Draper's regular YesFANZ newsletter and Alex van Starrex's web publicity, membership of YesFANZ was soaring.

The regular meetings of YesFANZ in Sydney were full of excitement and usually ended with the most recent Yes release being played. One particularly big night was held at the Toxteth Hotel in Glebe when YesFANZ rented the courtyard area and watched the *Yessymphonic Live* DVD on a huge outdoor screen.

The news we really wanted to hear became a reality when Yes concert dates were announced for 28 February 2003 in Melbourne and 1 March 2003 in Sydney. The Melbourne YesFANZ group led by Mark Hawes was now also meeting regularly in planning for the Melbourne party. Many meetings were held with promoter Michael Chugg who was very cooperative and helped with function room hire, staffing and promotional posters. YesFANZ members were now contacting radio stations, television networks and newspaper journalists, resulting in some interviews being granted and news items appearing. As 2002 came to its end, plans were well advanced for the Yes concerts and the Roger Dean exhibition. By then, 160 YesFANZ party tickets had been sold.

And then in January 2003 came the devastating news—Jon Anderson had hurt his back and the Yes tour was postponed. Happily Yes made a decision to continue with plans for the Australian tour and revised concert dates of 19 September 2003 in Melbourne and 20 September 2003 in Sydney were announced. A beautiful get well card was prepared by YesFANZ and sent to Jon Anderson—"Get Well Soon Oh Soon Jon".

As a result of the Yes tour postponement, Sebastian Hardie decided to do a concert at the Metro Theatre in Sydney and it was a well attended and exciting event. Additionally, given that many fans had purchased non-refundable air tickets, it was decided to proceed with the YesFANZ parties in Melbourne and Sydney on the original dates for the Yes concerts. Rooms were hired in hotels in Melbourne and Sydney and YesFANZ members spent the night swapping Yes stories and watching concert videos.

By June 2003 there was increasing evidence of promotional activity for the Yes concerts by both Michael Chugg, and YesFANZ, together with the newly formed GIG Gallery promoting the Roger Dean exhibition. A second run of YesFANZ T shirts was ordered with new artwork including the revised Yes concert dates.

Warner Brothers donated CDs and DVDs to YesFANZ to be given away as door prizes and a special deal was organized for the purchase of *The Ultimate Yes* compilation album that was to be given away to attendees at the Yes concert parties.

The logistics were put in place for the Roger Dean art exhibition and for the display of framed prints of Roger's work at the YesFANZ parties. Peter Waters looked after the security and insurance issues for the parties and coordinated various Yes memorabilia displays including his own Roger Dean art collection and Ian Aird's album collection. Roger Dean confirmed that he would be attending the YesFANZ parties, as did Sebastian Hardie. YesFANZ designed and printed its own promotional posters for Yes and Roger Dean, and enthusiastic YesFANZ members placed them in cafes all over Australia and New Zealand. By this stage there were now hundreds of members of YesFANZ.

Only ten of the original YesFANZ invitations to Yes had been printed and we decided to print another 500 copies to give to attendees of the YesFANZ parties. With the assistance of Jon Dee at Planet Ark, the YesFANZ calico bag was designed and printed. It promoted Yes, Roger Dean, YesFANZ and Planet Ark and each person attending the parties received one of these bags containing the reprinted invitation book and *The Ultimate Yes* CD, along with Roger Dean postcards, posters and other memorabilia.

By August 2003, YesFANZ meetings were being held weekly at its de facto office at Robert Forbes and Associates in Glebe, Sydney. The Melbourne YesFANZ group was also meeting on a more frequent basis. The well known Australian rock historian, Glenn A Baker (aka The Rock Brain of the Universe) was invited to interview Sebastian Hardie at the Sydney party. John Miller organized our own PA and projector system to assist in facilitating the interviews at the parties and to allow us to show Yes DVDs.

In early September 2003 YesFANZ emailed all members about the Yes parties with full details including times, locations and the expected program. It was stipulated that Yes had been invited to attend the parties but while the band had indicated that they were keen to do so, the logistics of the concerts meant that there could not be any guarantees.

So how did it all go? Quite unexpectedly! Yes appeared at the Melbourne pre-show party and they answered questions and spent time giving autographs and talking to fans. All members of Sebastian Hardie were also interviewed and met fans. Roger Dean showed what a gentleman he is by being more than generous with his time. In Sydney, Yes were unable to appear at the well-attended pre-show party. Sebastian Hardie were interview by the popular Glenn A Baker, Roger Dean again charmed everyone and many prizes were distributed to attendees. And the surprise? After last minute negotiations with Michael Chugg and Yes tour management, a ballroom was hired at the Four Seasons Hotel in Sydney to hold a post-concert party at which Yes promised to make an appearance! After such an exceptional concert it was a treat to be able to mix with all the Yes members. The night finished on a high!

And that was not all. The next day on a balmy Sunday 21 September 2003, we had arranged for YesFANZ to have a special function at the Roger Dean art exhibition in Glebe. We specially hired a baby grand piano for the occasion and Rick Wakeman kindly gave an impromptu forty minute free concert to a packed and rather hot gallery. Steve Howe, Chris Squire and Alan White also visited the exhibition and spent time with Roger and the members of YesFANZ.

Where to from here for YesFANZ? Three years, an incredible 13,000 emails, fifteen newsletters and numerous meetings later, it is 2004 and YesFANZ has regrouped and is planning ahead for future tours by Yes and visits from Roger Dean. YesFANZ Inc. is now an incorporated association registered under NSW state law in Australia that allows the group to operate a bank account as a non-profit entity. YesFANZ "*...is a non-profit community organization for the promotion of the music of Yes and the promotion and appreciation of progressive music*".

"Music has magic" and one aspect of the magic of Yes is the enduring relationships that have been formed between YesFANZ members both locally and internationally. A family of long lost souls reunited, people brought together by a mutual love of Yes music.

For anyone interested in joining us or learning more about our activities, please visit the YesFANZ web site at www.yesfanz.com or contact us by email via yes@robert-forbes.com.

Robert Forbes
August 2004

Yes 35th Anniversary Quiz

Test your Yes knowledge over the entire history of the band. The questions are based on *The Extraordinary World Of Yes* and the answers are listed at the end of the quiz. There is only one correct answer for each of the multiple-choice questions.

1. **1968**—The three names considered by Mabel Greer's Toyshop before it evolved to become Yes.
   a. The Nice, Fifth Dimension and Yes
   b. World, Life and Yes
   c. The Syn, the Gun and Yes
   d. La Chasse, Sweetness and Yes
2. **1969**—An important aspect of early live performances by Yes.
   a. Cover versions of songs by other artists
   b. Smashing guitars during the show
   c. Achieving a sound like the Beatles and the Fifth Dimension combined
   d. Achieving a sound like the Beatles and The Nice combined
3. **1970**—An important facet of the Yes sound that became established on *Time And A Word* as a result of the way the album was mixed using headphones.
   a. The prominent bass of Chris Squire
   b. Steve Howe's guitar
   c. The orchestral sound of Yes
   d. None of the above
4. **1971**—A notable aspect of *The Yes Album* that set it apart from the two previous Yes albums.
   a. A cover by Roger Dean
   b. The first Yes songs longer than five minutes

c. The entire album was recorded live in the studio

d. All songs were original Yes compositions

5. **1972**—A key thing to remember in interpreting the lyrics of Yes in songs like "Close To The Edge", according to Jon Anderson.

   a. It is all psychedelic gibberish

   b. It is all metaphors

   c. Meditate before listening

   d. The words are only used for their sonic value

6. **1973**—An important characteristic of a live album like *Yessongs,* according to Chris Squire.

   a. The special energy that originates from the audience

   b. Fans could buy a triple album cheaply

   c. It made available recorded versions of all songs with Alan White

   d. None of the above

7. **1974**—The affirmation of Yes in *The Gates Of Delirium*

   a. War is a terrible thing

   b. Light can come out of adversity

   c. War is a devilish business

   d. It was lightweight rock theatre

8. **1975**—The pair of solo albums by Steve Howe and Chris Squire released in late 1975.

   a. *The Steve Howe Album* and *Fish Out Of Water*

   b. *Beginnings* and *Conspiracy*

   c. *Ramshackled* and *Fish Out Of Water*

   d. None of the above

9. **1976**—The meaning of the symbol on the cover of Jon Anderson's *Olias Of Sunhillow* solo album.

   a. The world, Holy Trinity and humanity

b. It was just an intriguing combination of shapes

c. The initiation of life, the third eye and the sixth sense

d. Ancient knowledge and the Moorglade Mover

10. **1977**—The type of approach taken by Yes in creating "Awaken" and many other classic Yes songs.

a. A collective effort by the band

b. Independent musical contributions by the band members

c. Spaced out and spontaneous creation of music

d. None of the above

11. **1978—**A problem with the *Tormato* album according to Jon Anderson, Steve Howe and Rick Wakeman.

a. An inappropriate cover

b. Lack of epic songs

c. Lack of good production

d. None of the above

12. **1979**—How the stage revolved during the in the round Yes tours in 1978/79.

a. Clockwise

b. Anticlockwise

c. Both clockwise and anticlockwise

d. It was fixed and didn't revolve

13. **1980**—The meaning of the title of "Tempus Fugit" on the *Drama* album.

a. Fast tempo

b. Fierce storm

c. Angry tempest

d. Time flies

14. **1981**—The short-lived band formed by Chris Squire, Alan White and Jimmy Page.

    a. SWP

    b. XYZ

    c. YEZ

    d. Page Squire White

15. **1982**—The former Yes member who joined Chris Squire and Alan White in Cinema.

    a. Peter Banks

    b. Patrick Moraz

    c. Geoff Downes

    d. Tony Kaye

16. **1983**—Two words to describe the musical style of Yes on the *90125* album.

    a. Epic and grand

    b. Simplified and commercial

    c. Progressive and metallic

    d. None of the above

17. **1984**—The cause of the delayed start to the *90125* world tour.

    a. Jon Anderson wasn't available

    b. Eddie Jobson decided not to tour

    c. Tony Kaye broke his leg

    d. None of the above

18. **1985**—The crowd that Yes performed for at Rock In Rio in South America.

    a. 150,000

    b. 200,000

    c. 250,000

d. None of the above

19. **1986**—The Beatles album used by Yes as a model for recording *Big Generator.*

a. *Revolver*

b. *I Am The Walrus*

c. *Sgt Pepper*

d. *Abbey Road*

20. **1987**—Chris Squire's perspective on the *Big Generator* album.

a. The preceding success of *90125* was almost a curse

b. It was one of the best Yes albums ever recorded

c. The recording technology made it a very progressive album

d. It was one of the most enjoyable Yes albums to record

21. **1988**—The event in New York where Yes performed live in April 1988

a. Ahmet Ertegun's 40th birthday party celebrations

b. Atlantic Records 40th anniversary celebrations

c. Melody Maker rock poll awards

d. The premiere of the *9012 Live* video

22. **1989**—Steve Howe's dream that helped inspire "Brother Of Mine".

a. Waking up to find the world had changed, not physically but mentally

b. A surrealistic vision of the Arizona desert

c. A dream of the mystical beauty of Devon during the full moon

d. A dream of reuniting with Anderson, Bruford and Wakeman

23. **1990**—The epic song Yes recorded with Bill Bruford that Bill didn't play live until the ABWH tour

a. "Heart Of The Sunrise"

b. "Close To The Edge"

c. "Roundabout"

d. "Yours Is No Disgrace"

24. **1991**—The strange thing producer Jonathan Elias did during the recording of the *Union* album

a. He rarely attended the recording sessions

b. He begged to be allowed to complete the project

c. He brought in session musicians to replace Yes members

d. He brought scenery into the recording studio

25. **1992**—The thing that made the *Union* project worthwhile, according to Jon Anderson.

a. Playing as an eight piece Yes lineup on the revolving stage

b. Writing new music again with Steve Howe

c. Playing "Awaken" as an eight piece Yes lineup

d. Working again with Chris Squire

26. **1993**—The long time Yes associate who formed the Victory Music label and signed the *90125* Yes lineup.

a. Mike Tait

b. Ahmet Ertegun

c. Brian Lane

d. Phil Carson

27. **1994**—A key problem with the *Talk* album as identified by Yes Magazine.

a. It was overly dominated by one band member in Trevor Rabin

b. It didn't have a cover by Roger Dean

c. The computer recording technology made it sound impersonal

d. None of the above

28. **1995**—The Californian town where Yes gathered to record *Keys To Ascension.*

    a. San Clemente

    b. San Luis Obispo

    c. Santa Barbara

    d. Santa Maria

29. **1996**—The action by Steve Howe to reward loyal fans at Boo Boo Records before the *Keys To Ascension* live performances.

    a. Gave an impromptu acoustic performance on the sidewalk around midnight

    b. Gave fans food and drinks around midday

    c. Gave away autographed photos

    d. Invited them to an impromptu acoustic performance at the Fremont Theatre

30. **1997**—The two Yes members who composed most of the *Open Your Eyes* album.

    a. Jon Anderson and Steve Howe

    b. Jon Anderson and Chris Squire

    c. Chris Squire and Billy Sherwood

    d. Chris Squire and Alan White

31. **1998**—The Yes epic played during the *Open Your Eyes* tour that was a highlight for many fans.

    a. "Awaken"

    b. "The Revealing Science Of God"

    c. "Ritual"

    d. "The Gates Of Delirium"

32. **1999**—The central message in Yes music, according to Jon Anderson.

    a. There is love, peace and light.

   b. Be positive
   c. Make the most of your life
   d. None of the above

33. **2000**—An apt description of the stage set for the *Masterworks* tour.
   a. Surrealistic
   b. Complex
   c. Sail-like
   d. Organic

34. **2001**—A vital factor in successfully recording *Magnification* with an orchestra, according to Jon Anderson
   a. Writing suitable music
   b. Having a good arranger
   c. Showing restraint so the orchestra could be heard
   d. Choosing a good orchestra

35. **2002**—A description of what Yes music is all about, according to Jon Anderson.
   a. A positive statement about life and all that surrounds us
   b. A psychedelic experiment in music
   c. A cosmic opportunity to communicate with many people
   d. A profound religious experience

36. **2003**—The Yes album that made the Top 10 in the UK charts.
   a. *In A Word: Yes*
   b. *Magnification*
   c. *Classic Yes*
   d. *Ultimate Yes*

37. **2004**—The two famous groups that Yes would beat hands down in a battle of the bands, according to Creem Magazine.

    a. The Beatles and The Who

    b. ELP and Cream

    c. Pink Floyd and Led Zeppelin

    d. Led Zeppelin and Cream

Answers

1 b, 2 a, 3 a, 4 d, 5 b, 6 a, 7 b, 8 d, 9 a, 10 a, 11 c, 12 c, 13 d, 14 b, 15 d, 16 b, 17 d, 18 c, 19 d, 20 a, 21 b, 22 a, 23 b, 24 c, 25 c, 26 d, 27 a, 28 b, 29 a, 30 c, 31 b, 32 a, 33 c, 34 b, 35 a, 36 d, 37 d.

Rate Your Score

30 to 37 UltimateYes!
20 to 29 Yes!
10 to 19 Almost Yes!
0 to 9 No!

About The Author

The Extraordinary World Of Yes evolved out of my extensive research and writing for *Yesology*, an innovative project about Yes that I played a leading role in developing and which was available on the internet in 2003/2004. The intent of *Yesology* was to highlight the excellence of the musical contribution of Yes and it succeeded in gaining the band some additional exposure on television and radio in America, as well as receiving mention around the globe in publications such as *Classic Rock* magazine and at websites such as *Billboard* and the official Yes internet site YesWorld.

I live in Australia and have been a Yes music enthusiast since hearing "Your Move" in 1971 when I was fifteen years old. My formal education in music began at the age of eight and from the start it gave me an appreciation of what it was like to be part of a group of people in a musical environment, regularly performing in public with the school band. I swapped participation in music for a career in professional soccer from the age of fourteen while continuing to study at school and then university. It coincided with the start of a life-long interest in creative rock music although one thing I never anticipated was the important role that a rock band could play in my life, but then Yes is no ordinary group. In fact Yes music directly provided the spark of inspiration I needed in literature and poetry at school to deliver the marks required to enter my chosen field of Town Planning at university. It led to a long career as a senior executive with one of Australia's leading companies in property development and management.

My interest in Yes music has been a both a source of joy in symbolizing the good times in life and also a comfort in occasional times of duress, always being exciting, entertaining and beautifully artistic while having something relevant and uplifting to say about human existence. My desire to attend Yes concerts has taken me on several trips half way around the world and I've met incredible people and travelled to fabulous places. I've discovered over time that many other people have similarly been positively affected by Yes music and it has become the soundtrack to the lives of a generation of music fans.

Alan Farley
August 2004

AUTHOR CONTACT DETAILS

Alan Farley
Email: alfar01@yahoo.com.au
Web: www.farley.ozefamily.com
Please visit my web site to view exclusive photographs of Yes and for details of how to obtain copies of *The Extraordinary World Of Yes.*

0-595-33133-5

Lightning Source UK Ltd.
Milton Keynes UK
29 March 2010

152057UK00002B/90/A